NOTES

NOTES

_____

_____

_____

_____

_____

_____

_____

_____

_____

NOTES

NOTES

_____

_____

_____

_____

_____

_____

_____

_____

NOTES

NOTES

NOTES

_____

_____

_____

_____

_____

_____

_____

_____

Information about NOAA Weather Radio

NOAA Weather Radio broadcasts National Weather Service (NWS) warnings, watches, forecasts, and other non-weather related hazard information 24 hours a day. During an emergency, NWS sends a special tone that activates weather radios in the listening area. Weather radios equipped with a special alarm tone feature can sound an alert and give you immediate information about a life-threatening situation.

NOAA Weather Radios are found in many electronics stores and cost about $25-$100. Some features to consider are alarm tone, battery backup, and "Specific Area Message Encoding" (SAME) programming.

NOAA Weather Radio (NWR) broadcasts warnings and post-event information for all types of hazards - **weather** *(blizzards, thunderstorms, etc.)*, **natural** *(floods, hurricanes, tornadoes and earthquakes)*, **technological** *(chemical or oil spills, nuclear power plant emergencies, etc.)*, and **national emergencies**.

NOAA collaborates with other Federal agencies and the FCC's Emergency Alert System (EAS) to issue non-weather related emergency messages including the issuance of "AmberAlerts".

Programming Your NOAA Weather Radio

If you purchase a Weather Radio receiver with "Specific Area Message Encoding", you should program it with coding for your area. By doing so, you can limit the alerts which will trigger your weather radio to only those affecting your warning area.

Follow the manufacturer's directions to program your receiver using the six-digit SAME code(s) for the warning areas of interest to you.

For more about **NOAA Weather Radios** visit www.weather.gov/nwr *(Click on "SAME Coding" to find state, county, territory & marine codes)*

ST County/City	SAME #	NWR TRANSMITTER	FREQ.	CALL	WATTS

IT'S A DISASTER!

...and what are <u>you</u> gonna do about it?

5th Edition

A Disaster Preparedness, Prevention
& Basic First Aid Manual

by Bill & Janet Liebsch

www.itsadisaster.net or call 1-888-999-4325

Published by Fedhealth • www.fedhealth.net • www.itsadisaster.net
Prepress by Jeremy Wesanen
Printed by CDS Publications • www.cdspubs.com

5th Edition: August 2009 (Revised April 2013)
    paperback ISBN 978-1-930131-25-5
    ebook ISBN 978-1-930131-26-2

Library of Congress Catalog Card Number: 2006938576

To order additional copies and to learn about fundraising
programs and free customization, please visit
www.itsadisaster.net

ABOUT THE AUTHORS

Bill and Janet Liebsch are the founders of FedHealth, a publishing and marketing company formed to help the public focus on preparedness and health-related issues. They are dedicated to developing and marketing programs that primarily benefit First Responders, schools, and volunteers. FedHealth books and ebooks are continually updated on preparedness and safety-related topics.

DISCLAIMER

The authors of this Manual are not licensed physicians, and the enclosed suggestions should not replace the advice of trained medical staff and officials. This information is not intended as a substitute for a first aid course, but reviews basic first aid measures that could be used when professional medical assistance is delayed or temporarily unavailable due to a major disaster or crisis. All data compiled here is for informational purposes only and neither the authors nor FedHealth can accept responsibility for any injury, loss or damage arising from the use of this information. During a time of crisis, citizens should heed the advice of local officials over the data contained in this book.

DEDICATION

*This manual is dedicated to Volunteers all around the
world who give their heart, soul, energy, and time
unselfishly for the betterment of our society.
Thank you.*

ACKNOWLEDGEMENTS

We would like to personally thank the following individuals for their support and belief in us and in this venture:

Stephen R. (Dex) Dexter, William H. (Bill) Holt of Sammamish, WA, and Genevieve, Richard and Ann Worley.

We also would like to thank several individuals who contributed materials, expertise and time to help us during the compilation and enhancement of this manual:

Doug Abromeit (USFS National Avalanche Center), Peter Baker (American Red Cross), Ken Arnold (Arnold Business Enterprises, LLC), Jeff Brown (American Avalanche Association), Dan Hosford (President, The Cure Inc.), Max London (OCIPEP), Craig Marks, CEM (President, Blue Horizons Consulting, and Adjunct, UNC-Pembroke), Gary O'Keefe (Retired, Latah County Disaster Services), Rick Tobin (President and CEO, TAO Emergency Management Consulting), Chris Tucker (OCIPEP), Donna Warner, Patrice White (HSEMA), and various personnel from the Canadian Red Cross.

And MOST important of all ... thank you to our family and friends who believed in us and supported us spiritually and emotionally!

INTRODUCTION

If you have never been involved in any type of major disaster, count your-self among the lucky ones and realize that emergencies and disasters can happen anywhere and anytime.

The confusion immediately following a disaster is <u>scary</u> - especially if you have not prepared yourself in advance and discussed these ideas with your family members.

Hopefully every time you see or hear about a disaster it makes you stop and think... "What if that was me or my family?" But what have <u>YOU</u> done to get yourself and your family ready? The best thing you can do to deal with any type of emergency situation is...

<u>BE AWARE</u>... <u>BE PREPARED</u>... and... <u>HAVE A PLAN</u>!

If you do these 3 things, the life you save could be your own... because what you <u>don't</u> know <u>CAN</u> hurt you!

The more the public is prepared for a disaster, the less strain we place on our local emergency services. Any major disaster will temporarily swamp First Responders, therefore, both the Red Cross and the Federal Emergency Management Agency recommend persons to try to be self-sufficient for at least 72 hours following a disaster. And if you are prepared for a longer period (like 2 to 4 weeks or more)... that's even better!

A majority of this information was compiled from various publications provided by the U.S. Department of Homeland Security, FEMA, the Red Cross, Public Safety Canada, the CDC and the Public Health Agency of Canada to help assist you in preparing for various types of disasters and basic first aid. It also offers suggestions on personal checklists and important telephone numbers for your family members and emergency groups that can be written in the spaces provided or attached inside this manual. Most importantly, there are many web sites throughout the book to help you find more information.

We realize you may not experience every type of disaster in your part of the world, but if you ever travel you could potentially be placed in a disaster situation so please educate yourself and your family.

Please stop your hectic lives for just a few hours and sit down with your entire family (from children to seniors) to read this Manual and discuss how each of you would handle these types of situations.

It will be quality time with your loved ones and could save your lives!

CONTENTS

DISASTER FACTS & FIGURES

Both natural and man-made disasters are becoming more common all around the world. El Niño and La Niña events impact billions of people since these climate extremes disrupt jet streams and regions of high and low pressure. These disruptions can potentially increase or decrease weather-related disasters such as extreme heat and cold, floods, hurricanes and thunderstorms.

According to the National Oceanic and Atmospheric Administration's Pacific Marine Environmental Laboratory Tropical Atmosphere Ocean project, El Niño happens when tropical Pacific Ocean trade winds die out and ocean temperatures become unusually warm. La Niña occurs when the trade winds blow unusually hard and sea temperatures become colder than normal. These warm and cold phases are referred to as El Niño/Southern Oscillation, or ENSO, which has a period of roughly 3-7 years. Although ENSO originates in the tropical Pacific system, it has effects on patterns of weather all over the world.[1]

El Niño (warm episodes) occur about every 4-5 years and can last up to 12 to 18 months.[2] La Niña (cold episodes) conditions recur every few years and typically last 9 to 12 months but can persist for as long as 2 years.[3] There are also periods where the system is neither warm nor cold (called neutral conditions).

Even though there is still much to learn about these systems and their impacts on the global community, ENSO forecasts can help individuals, businesses, and governments prepare for these events.

To learn more about NOAA's Pacific Marine Environmental Laboratory Tropical Atmosphere Ocean project visit www.pmel.noaa.gov/tao/

In addition to the climate extremes mentioned above, some key elements in the increasing numbers of worldwide disasters include:

- Global warming / cooling, volcanic activity, sunspots, etc.
- Larger cities are sprawling into high-risk zones
- World population is over 6 billion and growing causing global water consumption to increase
- Humans damaging our natural resources (e.g. pollution, destroying rain forests, coral reefs, wetlands, etc.)

As the warming and cooling debate rages on, keep in mind there's a lot of scientific data supporting and refuting both sides and many unknowns. But one thing is for certain ~ disasters happen daily no matter what.

GENERAL FACTS & FIGURES ON DISASTERS

As our violent planet's surface continues to shift and move it will continue to alter sea levels, food and water supplies and climate conditions around the world.

The costs of weather-related disasters in just the United States alone average $1 billion per week.

Year after year it appears the most frequent natural disasters are windstorms and floods, which combined usually account for 80%-90% of the worldwide economic losses.

Every year hundreds of millions of people worldwide are evacuated or driven from their homes due to natural disasters.

According to Munich Re, the following summarizes <u>major</u> catastrophes:

Year	Worldwide Economic Losses	# of Major Disasters	# of deaths by Major Disasters
2012	$160 billion (in US $)	900	9,500
2011	$400 billion (in US $)	820	27,000
2010	$130 billion (in US $)	950	295,000
2009	$50 billion (in US $)	850	10,000
2008	$200 billion (in US $)	750	220,000
2007	$82 billion (in US $)	960	11,000
2006	$45 billion (in US $)	850	18,000
2005	$220 billion (in US $)	670	101,000
2004	$150 billion (in US $)	650	245,473
2003	$65 billion (in US $)	700	89,000
2002	$60 billion (in US $)	700	11,000

Please note the above figures do not include economic losses and deaths caused by smaller natural disasters that occur daily around the world. Also note that the years with a small number of deaths are usually due to the fact that few severe catastrophes occurred in developing countries, where disasters tend to have more human losses due to poor infrastructure, etc.

Now let's look at some facts and figures on specific types of disasters to get a better understanding of how they impact our world.

FACTS & FIGURES BY TYPE OF DISASTER

Avalanches, Landslides & Mudflows

There are about 1 million snow avalanches worldwide each year.

Flooding in Venezuela triggered landslides and mudflows that washed away entire villages and mountain slopes claiming over 30,000 lives in 1999.

Earthquakes

The U.S. Geological Survey estimates that several million earthquakes occur each year but most go undetected. About 500,000 are detected each year - only 100,000 are felt and 100 cause damage.

The world's deadliest earthquake on record hit central China in 1557 killing an estimated 830,000 people.

Scientists believe the Cascadia Subduction zone along the Northwest coastline could produce mega-quakes similar to the 9.0 that rocked Indonesia.

Some of the strongest earthquakes in U.S. history occurred on the New Madrid fault (area between St. Louis and Memphis) in 1811-1812. This area still experiences about 200 earthquakes a year.

Aftershocks may be felt for several days, weeks, months or even years depending on the force of a major earthquake.

Extreme Heat

According to NOAA's National Climatic Data Center, 80% of the contiguous United States was in moderate-to-extreme drought back in July 1934.

Today less than half a billion people live in water-stressed countries but projections indicate by 2025 that number could increase to 3 billion.

Fire

Fire kills more Americans every year than all natural disasters combined.

At least 80% of all fire deaths occur in residences -- and careless smoking is the leading cause of fire deaths. And cooking fires (leaving food unattended or human error) is the leading cause of home fires.

Floods

According to FEMA, everyone lives in a flood zone - it's just a question of whether you live in a low, moderate or high risk area.

More than 90% of declared disasters include flooding.

Flash floods can cause walls of water reaching heights of 20 feet (6 m).

Hailstorms
On May 22, 1986 an unusual killer hailstorm in China's Sichuan Province left 9,000 people injured and 100 dead.

The largest known hailstone ever measured in the U.S. was found in Vivian, South Dakota in July 2010 with a record 8-inch (20.32 cm) diameter and a circumference of 18.625 inches (over 47 cm).

Hazardous Materials
As many as 500,000 products pose physical or health hazards and can be defined as "hazardous materials" and over 1,000 new synthetic chemicals are introduced each year.

Each year about 400 million metric tons of hazardous wastes are generated worldwide.

According to FEMA, varying quantities of hazardous materials are manufactured, used, or stored at an estimated 4.5 million facilities in the U.S.

Hurricanes, Cyclones & Typhoons
The 2005 U.S. season broke records with 27 named storms (previous record was 21 in 1933) and 15 hurricanes (previous record was 12 in 1969). The National Hurricane Center states this cycle could last 10-20 more years similar to the above-average activity from the 1940s through the 1960s.

Nine out of 10 hurricane deaths are due to storm surge (a rise in the sea level caused by strong winds). Storm surges can get up to 20 feet (6 m) high and 50 miles (80 km) wide!

One of the worst cyclone disasters in recorded history struck Bangladesh and India killing between 500,000 and 1 million people back in 1970.

Nuclear Power Plants
Japan's Fukushima core meltdowns caused by earthquakes, tsunami and design flaws demonstrate how critical multi-disaster planning is for plants.

The April 1986 explosion at Ukraine's Chernobyl nuclear power plant burned for 10 days releasing about 5% of the radioactive reactor core into the atmosphere exposing millions of people to varying doses of radiation.

Terrorism

Between 1993 and 2006 there were 1,080 confirmed incidents of illicit trafficking in nuclear materials -- with 18 of these cases involving weapons-grade materials and another 124 involving material capable of making a so-called dirty bomb that would use conventional explosives to spread nuclear material.[4]

If a nuclear device is detonated in the air high above North America, it would create a high-density electrical field called an electromagnetic pulse. According to FEMA, most electronic devices within 1,000 miles of a high-altitude nuke could be damaged by an EMP.

Experts at the 2009 World Economic Forum at Davos estimated the global damage from data loss / cybercrimes now exceeds $1 trillion a year.

Thunderstorms & Lightning

At any given moment, about 2,000 thunderstorms can be in progress over the face of the earth.

There are 8 million lightning strikes per day!

It is a myth that lightning never strikes the same place twice -- it often strikes the same site several times in the course of one storm.

Tornadoes

The U.S. has more tornadoes than any other place in the world and averages 1,200 tornado sightings each year.

According to NOAA, 2004 had a record 1,817 tornado reports in the U.S.

Tornadoes can last for several seconds or more than an hour, but most last less than 10 minutes.

The force of a tornado can strip asphalt chunks off roads, rip clothes off people and pluck feathers off chickens.

Tsunamis

A tsunami [soo-nah´-mee] is a series of huge, destructive waves usually caused by an earthquake, volcanic eruption, landslide or meteorite.

The 2004 seaquake-generated tsunami that slammed 12 countries in the Indian Ocean is the deadliest on record with almost 187,000 people killed and 42,883 still missing. *(Per UN OSE's web site as of October 2006)*

A tsunami is NOT a tidal wave — it has nothing to do with the tides.

Volcanoes

More than 65 active or potentially active volcanoes exist in the U.S. and over 40 of them are in Alaska.

According to the Smithsonian Institution's Global Volcanism Program, about 1,300 volcanoes have erupted in the last 10,000 years and should be considered "historically active". This does not include the large number of eruptions from an estimated 1 million young volcanoes on the ocean's floor which pump out roughly 3/4 of the lava reaching the earth's surface.

The "Ring of Fire" that encircles the Pacific Ocean has about 450 historically active volcanoes.

Volcanic eruptions can hurl hot rocks easily 20 miles (32 km) or more.

Yellowstone National Park actually sits on top of a supervolcano which erupted 3 times in the past 2 million years forming 3 massive calderas (or huge craters). The largest one (Yellowstone Caldera) is more than 60 miles (100 km) across.

Some other large calderas formed by supervolcanoes are in Alaska, eastern California, Indonesia, Japan, New Zealand and South America.

Winter Storms / Extreme Cold

The leading cause of death during winter storms is from automobile or other transportation accidents.

Cold weather puts an added strain on the heart. Exhaustion or heart attacks caused by overexertion (like shoveling snow or pushing a car) are the second most likely cause of winter storm-related deaths.

The risk of hypothermia is greatest among elderly persons who literally "freeze to death" in their own homes.

Section 1

Family Emergency Plan, Kits & Shelter

FAMILY EMERGENCY PLAN CHECKLIST

The next time disaster strikes, you may not have much time to act and local first responders may not be able to reach you right away. PREPARE NOW for a sudden emergency and discuss these ideas with your entire family to create a **Family Emergency Plan**.

Even though this checklist looks long and scary, it is easy to do and can help you make a plan. We suggest you and your family review this list, then read through the Manual since there are many tips mentioned in various topics and Sections that could help develop your plan.

PLEASE make some time in your busy lives to prepare for a disaster... a few minutes now could possibly save a life when a disaster hits. Remember - **be aware... be prepared... and have a plan**!

LEARN ABOUT RISKS & EXISTING PLANS:

(See Section 4 for phone numbers of State & Provincial Emergency Management offices and Red Cross - or check city/county white pages)

[ ] Find out which disasters could occur in your area and ask officials how to prepare for each disaster... but read this Manual first.

[ ] Ask how you will be warned of an emergency.

[ ] Learn your community's evacuation routes and map them out using a free service like Google Maps or Mapquest or order Depiction.

[ ] Ask about special assistance for elderly or disabled persons.

[ ] Ask your workplace about emergency plans and learn about plans at your children's school(s) or day care center(s).

TIPS ON MAKING YOUR FAMILY PLAN:

*(Review all and complete **Family Emergency Plan** on pages 12-13)*:

[ ] Meet with household members to talk about the dangers of fire, severe weather, earthquakes and other emergencies. Explain how to respond to each using the tips in this Manual.

[ ] Find safe spots in your home for each type of disaster that affects your community. *(see Section 2 for explanations of each disaster)*

[ ] Talk about what to do when there are power outages and injuries.

[ ] Take a basic first aid and CPR class (or join a CERT - see page 224).

[ ] Draw a floor plan of your home showing doors, windows and stairways. Mark locations of first aid and disaster kits, fire extinguishers, smoke detectors, ladders, and utility shut-off points. Next, use a colored pen to draw a broken line charting at least 2 escape routes from <u>each</u> room. And practice drills!

[ ] Show family members how to turn off water, gas and electricity at the main switches when necessary.

[ ] Post emergency telephone numbers near telephones and teach children how and when to call 9-1-1. *(see Section 3)*

[ ] Make sure household members understand they should turn on the radio for emergency information.

[ ] Pick one out-of-state and a local friend or relative for family members to call if separated during a disaster. (It is often easier to call out-of-state than within the affected area.)

[ ] Pick two emergency meeting places in case you can't go home: 1) A place near your home. 2) A place outside the neighborhood.

[ ] Teach children meeting places and emergency phone numbers in case you get separated during a crisis.

[ ] Put **ICE** before a name and number in cell phone address books so First Responders would know who to call "**In Case of Emergency**".

[ ] Make sure family members know how to send and receive photos and text messages (if you have those capabilities on your cells). Also consider joining a network like Twitter or a local text message alert system to receive emergency broadcast warnings, updates, etc.

[ ] Get some FRS walkie-talkies and teach family how to use them.

[ ] Practice emergency evacuation drills with all household members at least <u>two</u> times each year.

[ ] Consider doing a Living Will and/or a Healthcare Power of Attorney.

[ ] Keep family records in a water- and fire-proof container. Consider keeping another set of records in a safety deposit box offsite.

[ ] Check if you have enough insurance coverage. *(see Section 2 for more information on <u>flood</u> insurance.)*

TIPS FOR ELDERLY & DISABLED FAMILY MEMBERS:

[ ] Ask about special aid that may be available in an emergency for elderly and disabled family members. Find out if assistance is available for evacuation and in public shelters. FEMA suggests people with a disability register with local fire department so help can be provided quickly in an emergency (if available in your area).

[ ] Ask your children's teachers and caregivers about emergency plans for schools, day care centers or nursing homes.

[ ] If you currently have a personal care attendant from an agency, check to see if the agency will be providing services at another location if there is an evacuation -- and tell family members.

[ ] Learn what to do and where to go for each type of emergency. For example, basements are not wheelchair-accessible so you should have alternate safe places for different types of disasters for disabled or elderly persons.

[ ] Learn what to do in case of power outages and injuries. Know how to start a back-up power supply for essential medical equipment!

[ ] If someone in the home uses a wheelchair, make sure 2 exits are wheelchair-accessible in case one exit is blocked.

[ ] Consider getting a medical alert system that will allow you to call for help if you have trouble getting around.

[ ] Both elderly and disabled persons should wear a medical alert bracelet or necklace at all times if they have special needs.

[ ] Talk to your doctor to ask if you can keep a 60-90 day supply of medications and special medical parts and supplies on-hand in case of emergency.

[ ] Consider setting up a "Buddy" system with a roommate, trusted friend or neighbor. Give buddy a copy of your **Family Emergency Plan** and an extra house key or tell them where one is available.

[ ] Consider putting a few personal items in a lightweight draw string bag (e.g. a whistle, some medications, a small flashlight, extra hearing aid batteries, etc.) and tie it to your wheelchair or walker for emergencies. Make sure to rotate items so current and working.

[ ] Visit the **National Organization on Disability** web site to learn more about Emergency Preparedness issues at www.nod.org .

TIPS FOR PETS OR LIVESTOCK / LARGE ANIMALS:

TIPS FOR PETS

[ ] If you have to evacuate your home, DO NOT leave pets behind! Make sure you take a secure pet carrier, leash or harness with you.

[ ] Emergency shelters may not accept pets (unless it is a service animal). Find out which motels and hotels in your area allow pets in advance of needing them. Ask your veterinarian or animal shelter if they board animals during a disaster or emergency.

[ ] Make sure identification tags are current and securely fastened to pet's collar or get a microchip implanted in your pet. Keep a current photo in your wallet or cell phone for identification purposes.

[ ] Make sure a roommate, trusted neighbor or friend has an extra house key to evacuate your pets in the event you are unavailable.

TIPS FOR LIVESTOCK / LARGE ANIMALS

[ ] Evacuate livestock whenever possible. Make arrangements for evacuation, including routes and host sites, in advance. At least two alternate evacuation routes should be mapped out as a backup.

[ ] The evacuation site should have food, water, veterinary care, handlers, equipment and proper facilities. Also consider getting a copy of SAVE YOUR HORSE! A Horse Owner's Guide to Large Animal Rescue by Michelle Staples at www.redjeansink.com

[ ] Trucks, trailers, and vehicles for transporting animals should be available with experienced handlers and drivers to transport them.

[ ] If evacuation is not possible, a decision must be made whether to move large animals to available shelter or turn them outside. This decision should be based on the type of disaster and the soundness and location of the shelter or structure.

[ ] If you board animals, ask if facility has an evacuation plan in place.

Next, we suggest you sit with your family and write down your **Family Emergency Plan** using the next 2 pages as a guide. Then review how to put together a **Disaster Supplies Kit** since you may not have much time if you are told to evacuate quickly.

Again, we suggest you and family members read this manual together - especially your kids - since there are many tips here that could help you make a plan and learn what to do if the unexpected happens. You may just want to review the book first and then come back to this Section later.

FAMILY EMERGENCY PLAN

EMERGENCY CONTACT NUMBERS

(Post a copy of this information near each phone for easy access!)

Emergency Numbers

In a life-threatening emergency, **call 9-1-1** or local emergency number:

Police Department: _____

Fire Department: _____

Ambulance: _____

Hospital: _____

Poison Control: 1-800-222-1222 (U.S. only) _____

Out-of-State Contact

Name _____

Address _____

Telephone (Day) _____ (Evening) _____

Local Contact

Name _____

Telephone (Day) _____ (Evening) _____

Family & Friends Work / Cell Numbers

Name: _____ Phone#: _____

Name: _____ Phone#: _____

Name: _____ Phone#: _____

Neighbors

Name: _____ Phone#: _____

Name: _____ Phone#: _____

Name: _____ Phone#: _____

School Information (if you have children)

Child / School Name: _____ / _____ Ph#: _____

Child / School Name: _____ / _____ Ph#: _____

EMERGENCY PLAN, continued

Family Doctors

Name: _____ Phone#: _____

Name: _____ Phone#: _____

Other

Veterinarian: _____

Animal Shelter or Humane Society: _____

Electric company: _____

Gas company: _____

Water company: _____

EMERGENCY MEETING PLACES (OR AREAS)

In case you get separated during an emergency or disaster, decide on <u>two</u> Meeting Places or Areas where you can join each other. Include children in this decision so they understand why they should meet here.

1. Right outside your home _____

_____

 (Example: meet by the curb or by the mailbox in front of home or apartment building)

2. Away from the neighborhood, in case you cannot return home

_____

 (maybe choose the home of a relative or family friend)

Address _____

Telephone # _____

Directions to this place _____

_____

Note: If these meeting places cannot be reached, text or send pictures of a new location or a landmark you are near so others can find you.

DISASTER SUPPLIES KIT

Disasters happen anytime and anywhere -- and, when disaster strikes, you may not have much time to respond. And sometimes services may be cut off or first responders can't reach people right away. Would you and your family be prepared to cope until help arrives?

Both FEMA and the Red Cross recommend keeping enough supplies in your home to meet your family's needs for at *least* three days (we suggest 2 to 4 weeks or more in home.) Once disaster threatens or hits, you may not have time to shop or search for supplies ... but, if you've gathered supplies in advance in your **Disaster Supplies Kit**, your family could handle an evacuation or shelter living easier. And since everything is all together in one place... all you gotta do is **GRAB & GO**!

Put items you'd most likely need (water, food, first aid, emergency items, etc.) in a container that is easy-to-carry and that will fit in your vehicle. For example, a large trash can or storage container with a lid that snaps shut tightly (some even come with wheels), or a waterproof backpack or large duffel bag (waterproof, if possible) would be useful.

We're also including suggestions for a CAR KIT and a CLASSROOM / LOCKER / OFFICE KIT since these are usually the most common places you would be if and when a disaster strikes.

There are seven basic categories of supplies you should stock in your home kit: **water**, **food**, **first aid supplies**, **tools and emergency supplies**, **sanitation**, **clothing and bedding**, and **special items**.

Take advantage of sales and stock up as you can -- also put dates on food cans or labels to show when they were purchased. Supplies should <u>ALL</u> be checked every 6 months to make sure they are still good and working! We suggest you mark dates on your calendar and have the entire family help check all the items together. It'll be good quality time with the family and give you all a chance to update any phone numbers or information that has changed.

WATER

A normally active person needs to drink at least 2 quarts (2 litres) of water each day and possibly as much as a gallon (4 litres) a day.

[ ] Store one gallon of water per person per day (two quarts/litres for drinking and two quarts/litres for food preparation and sanitation).

[ ] Keep at <u>least</u> a three-day supply of water for each person in home and store extra water for pets. <u>Rotate</u> new cases / bottles every 6 months. Consider getting large 55-gallon drums or containers for long-term water storage from a reputable dealer and treat the water.

[ ] Consider purchasing a certified portable water purification filter.

[ ] Review TIPS ON WATER PURIFICATION at end of Section 2.

FOOD

Choose foods that require no refrigeration, preparation or cooking and little or no water. If you must heat food, pack a can of sterno or a small propane camping stove. Select foods that are compact and lightweight and <u>rotate</u> food out every 6 months. (Keep items like this handy in pantry too.)

[ ] Ready-to-eat canned meats, fish, fruits, and vegetables (and put in a <u>manual can opener</u>!!) Make sure cans don't have dents in them.

[ ] Canned juices, milk, soups (if powder or cubes, store extra water)

[ ] Staples - sugar, salt, pepper

[ ] High energy foods - peanut butter, jelly, crackers, granola bars, trail mix, nuts, jerky, dried fruits, Emergency Food bars, etc.

[ ] Vitamins & herbs (e.g. a good multiple, Vitamins C & E, garlic pills [boosts immune], L-Tyrosine [an amino acid for stress], etc.)

[ ] Foods for infants, elderly persons or persons on special diets

[ ] Foods for your pet (if necessary)

[ ] Comfort / stress foods - cookies, hard candy, suckers, sweetened cereal, instant coffee, tea bags, powdered drink mixes, etc.

[ ] Some companies offer survival and long-term storage foods that are freeze dried and sold in months, 1-year, and 2-year supplies

FIRST AID KITS

You should always be prepared and keep a First Aid Kit in your home <u>and</u> in every car and make sure everyone knows where kits are and how to use them. And if you like the outdoors (hiking, biking, etc.) you should carry a small Kit in your fanny pack or backpack as a precaution.

There are many different sizes of First Aid Kits on the market that vary in price. You can also make your own kits using things that may already be in your home. Consider including the following items in a **waterproof** container or bag so you can be prepared for almost any type of emergency.

We realize there are a <u>lot</u> of items suggested here, but the more you prepare … the better off you and your family will be during a disaster situation.

ITEMS TO INCLUDE IN FIRST AID KIT

- Ace bandage(s)
- Adhesive bandages in assorted sizes
- Adhesive tape
- Antibiotic ointment or gel
- Antiseptic towelettes
- Assorted sizes of safety pins & needles
- Box of Baking soda
- Cleansing agent (isopropyl alcohol, hydrogen peroxide and/or soap)
- Cold & Heat packs
- Contact lens solution and Eyewash solution
- Cotton and Cotton swabs
- Copy of *IT'S A DISASTER!* manual
- Dental repair kit (usually near toothpaste section)
- Disposable Face shield for Rescue Breathing
- Disposable gloves
- Face masks (with N95 rated particulate filter and/or Nanomasks)
- Flashlight & batteries - check often to make sure it works & batteries are good (Tip: remove batteries while stored or get hand crank units)
- Gauze pads
- Hand sanitizer (with at least 60% alcohol)
- Hydrogen peroxide
- Lip balm (one with SPF is best)
- Liquid bandage (to seal cuts or scrapes)
- Moleskin (for blisters on feet)
- Petroleum jelly or other lubricant
- Plastic bags
- Roller gauze
- Scissors
- Small bottle of hand lotion
- Snake bite kit with extractor
- Sunscreen (one with SPF 30 or higher and 3 or 4 star UVA protection)
- Thermometer
- Tweezers

NON-PRESCRIPTION DRUGS TO INCLUDE IN FIRST AID KIT

- Activated charcoal (use if advised by the Poison Control Center)

- Antacid (for upset stomach)
- Anti-diarrhea medication
- Antihistamine and decongestant (for allergic reactions or allergies and sinus problems)
- Aspirin, acetaminophen, ibuprofen and naproxen sodium
- Laxative
- Potassium Iodide *(see NUCLEAR POWER PLANT EMERGENCY)*
- Vitamins & herbs (e.g. a good multiple, Vitamins C & E, garlic pills or zinc [boosts immune sys], L-Tyrosine [amino acid for stress], etc.)

PRESCRIPTION DRUGS TO INCLUDE IN FIRST AID KIT

Since it may be hard to get prescriptions filled during a disaster, talk to your physician or pharmacist about storing these types of medications. Keep a 3-month supply of medications and supplies on-hand if at all possible. And make sure to check labels for special instructions and expiration dates.

TIPS ON SOME INEXPENSIVE FIRST AID ITEMS

Activated charcoal - absorbs poisons and drugs in the stomach and intestines and helps prevent toxins from being absorbed into the bloodstream by coating intestinal walls. (Check with the Poison Control Center before taking since it doesn't work on all toxic substances.) It's found at natural foods stores and pharmacies in powder, liquid, and capsule forms. Capsules can be broken open to use powder for making a paste on insect bites and stings.

Baking soda - aid for heartburn or indigestion; use as substitute for toothpaste; sprinkle in bath water for sore muscles or bites & stings; or make a paste (3 parts baking soda to 1 part water) to use on stings or insect bites, poison ivy, canker sores, sunburn, and rashes (but too strong for infants!)

Hydrogen peroxide - can help clean and disinfect wounds, treat canker sores, gingivitis, and minor earaches. Also can be used for cleaning hands or for brushing teeth. (The reason it foams up on skin or item is because of the oxygen at work - means it's killing germs!)

Meat tenderizer - (check ingredient list on bottle for "papain") make a paste to use on insect bites and stings. Papain is a natural enzyme derived from papaya that can help break down insect venom.

Vinegar - helps relieve jellyfish stings, sunburn, and swimmer's ear.

TOOLS AND EMERGENCY SUPPLIES

The following items may come in handy if you have to evacuate or if stuck at home short or long-term.

[ ] Aluminum foil and resealable plastic bags

[ ] Battery-operated radio and extra batteries (remember to check batteries every 6 months). Also consider radios like the NOAA Weather Radio and Environment Canada's Weatheradio with one-alert feature that automatically alerts you when a Watch or Warning has been issued. Or get a hand crank radio with flashlight.

[ ] Battery-operated travel alarm clock

[ ] Cash or traveler's check and some change

[ ] CD (could be used as a reflector to signal planes if stranded)

[ ] Compass

[ ] Extra copy of *IT'S A DISASTER!* manual

[ ] Flashlight & headlamp plus extra batteries & bulbs (check every 6 months) and/or get solar, hand crank or shake flashlights / lanterns

[ ] Fire extinguisher: small canister, ABC type

[ ] Generator (learn how to use and store it in advance)

[ ] Manual can opener and a utility knife

[ ] Map of the area (to help locate shelters, alternate routes, etc.)

[ ] Matches, lighters, flint and candles in a waterproof container

[ ] Medicine dropper (e.g. measure bleach to purify water, etc.)

[ ] Needles & thread

[ ] Paper, pencil (store in baggies to keep dry)

[ ] Paper or plastic cups, plates, utensils, a few pots & pans

[ ] Plastic sheeting (for shelter, lean-to, or sealing room during chemical / hazardous material threat - *see HAZARDOUS MATERIALS*)

[ ] Power inverter

[ ] Radiation detection devices (like a dosimeter, etc - see page 112)

[ ] Tape (plastic & duct), rope, twine, paracord and bungee cords

[ ] Signal flares

[ ] Small hand tools (pliers, screwdrivers, shovel or trowel, etc.)

[ ] Solar (or handcrank) charger for cell phone, PDA, etc.

[ ] Sterno or small camp stove and mini propane bottle

[ ] Walkie-talkies (low cost set of FRS radios and store extra batteries)

[ ] Whistle (can be used to call for help in an emergency)

[ ] Wrench (to turn off household gas and water)

SANITATION

Make sure all these items are in a waterproof containers or plastic bags.

[ ] Disinfectant *(see TIPS ON SANITATION OF HUMAN WASTE)*

[ ] Feminine supplies (tampons, pads, etc.)

[ ] Household chlorine bleach (regular scent), disinfectant spray/wipes

[ ] Personal hygiene items (toothbrushes, toothpaste or baking soda, brush, comb, deodorant, shaving cream, razors, etc.)

[ ] Plastic garbage bags with twist ties and small plastic grocery bags

[ ] Plastic bucket with tight lid (for human waste) or waste kits, WAG Bags, Poo powder, etc

[ ] Soap, liquid detergent, hand sanitizer (with at least 60% alcohol), moist towelettes or sanitizing wipes, hydrogen peroxide, etc.

[ ] Toilet paper, baby wipes and paper towels

[ ] Wash cloths, hand and bath towels, dish rags & towels, etc.

CLOTHING AND BEDDING

[ ] At least one complete change of clothing and footwear per person

[ ] Sturdy shoes or work boots and extra socks

[ ] Hats, work and regular gloves, and thermal underwear

[ ] Blankets or sleeping bags (small emergency ones are cheap and about the size of a wallet ... or pack extra garbage bags)

[ ] Rain gear or poncho (or use plastic garbage bags)

[ ] Safety glasses and/or Sunglasses

[ ] Small stuffed animal, toy or book for each child at bedtime

SPECIAL ITEMS

[ ] Entertainment - games, books and playing cards

[ ] Important Family Documents (keep in waterproof, portable safe container and update as needed. Keep copies of papers off-site in safety deposit box or with a family member [or scan all to a CD].)
   - Extra set of car keys, cash, traveler's checks and credit card
   - Will, insurance policies, contracts, deeds, stocks and bonds
   - Passports, social security #s/cards, immunization records
   - Bank account numbers
   - Credit card numbers, card companies + phone numbers
   - Inventory of valuable household goods
   - Family records (birth, marriage, death certificates, photo IDs)
   - Recent pictures of all family members and pets for i.d. needs

[ ] RED and GREEN construction paper or RED and GREEN crayons or markers (can signal rescue workers to stop or move on)

Remember to pack things for family members with special needs:

For Infants

[ ] Bottles, Formula, powdered milk, cereals and juices

[ ] Diapers, baby wipes and diaper rash ointment

[ ] Medications

[ ] Small soft toys

For Elderly and Disabled (Children & Adults)

[ ] Bladder control garments and pads

[ ] Denture needs

[ ] Extra eye glasses or contact lenses and supplies

[ ] Extra hearing aid batteries

[ ] Extra wheelchair batteries, oxygen, catheters or special equipment

[ ] A list of style and serial numbers of medical devices such as pacemaker, defibrillator, etc. and copy of Medicare card

[ ] List of prescription medications and dosages or allergies (if any)

[ ] Special medicines for heart, high blood pressure, diabetes, etc.

[ ] Store backup equipment (such as a manual wheelchair, cane or walker) at a neighbor's home or at another location

For Pets

[ ] Cage or carrier, bedding, leash, muzzle, litter & box, trash bags, etc.

[ ] Food, manual can opener, bowls, chew toys or treats, etc.

[ ] Medications and copies of medical / immunization records

CAR KIT

Keep most or all of these items in a waterproof pack so <u>everything is together</u> and easy to grab. Make one for <u>each vehicle</u> too!

[ ] Battery or crank radio, flashlight/headlamp, extra batteries & bulbs

[ ] Blanket (small emergency ones are cheap and the size of a wallet)

[ ] Bottled water and non-perishable foods (Tip: store food in empty coffee cans to keep it from getting squashed)

[ ] CD (could be used as a reflector to signal planes if stranded)

[ ] Copy of *IT'S A DISASTER!* manual

[ ] Extra clothes (jeans and sweater), sturdy shoes and socks

[ ] First Aid Kit (with disposable gloves and N95 rated face masks)

[ ] Local maps with evacuation routes pre-marked

[ ] Personal hygiene items (hand sanitizer, toilet paper, tissues, tampons, etc)

[ ] Plastic bags that seal

[ ] Shovel (small collapsible ones are available)

[ ] Short rubber hose (for siphoning)

[ ] Small fire extinguisher (5 lb., ABC type)

[ ] Tools - Tire repair kit, booster cables, flares, screw drivers, pliers, knife, wire or rope, etc.

[ ] Work gloves

CLASSROOM / LOCKER / OFFICE KIT

Keep items in a small pack, drawstring bag or duffel so everything is together and easy to grab!

[ ] Battery-operated radio and extra batteries (or a hand crank radio)

[ ] Copy of *IT'S A DISASTER!* manual

[ ] Emergency blanket (small, cheap, & light - the size of a wallet)

[ ] A few plastic trash bags with twist ties

[ ] Mini flashlight, bulbs and batteries, or headlamp or hand crank unit

[ ] Non-perishable foods like crackers, cookies, trail mix, granola bars, etc. (Ask children to help choosing food and make sure they understand this is for Emergencies!)

[ ] Personal hygiene items (packet of tissues, moist towelettes, hand sanitizer, comb, toothbrush, tampons, etc)

[ ] Small First Aid kit (with disposable gloves and N95 face masks)

[ ] Small stuffed animal, book, or toy (for children)

[ ] Sweatshirt or sweater (or a full change of clothes if enough room)

[ ] Walkie-talkies (low cost set of FRS radios and store extra batteries)

[ ] Water ... as much as you can fit! Small juice boxes are good too.

[ ] Work gloves to protect your hands (especially from broken glass)

SUGGESTIONS & REMINDERS ABOUT KITS

Remember, both the Red Cross and FEMA recommend keeping enough supplies to meet your family's needs for at *least* three days, but consider a longer period like 96 hours or 2 weeks or more.

You may not have time to shop or search for items once a disaster threatens or hits so make your kits now so you're prepared for the unexpected.

Some things to keep in mind include ...

- Store your **Disaster Supplies Kit** in convenient place known to <u>ALL</u> family members. Keep a smaller version in the trunk or back of every vehicle (see CAR KIT).

- Keep items in airtight plastic bags to keep them dry in kit.

- Take advantage of end-of-season clearance sales and grocery sales (esp. can goods) and stock up as you can. Look around your home since you may be able to put a lot of these things together from what is already on shelves or in drawers or medicine cabinets.

- Replace your stored food and water supply every 6 months. It's best to test or replace batteries at this time too. Make a game of it by keeping track on a calendar or on a poster drawn by children so they can help. Also, everyone should meet every 6 months anyway to go over the **Family Emergency Plan** and update any data (phone numbers, address changes, etc.) *Suggestion: Do this every Daylight Savings time - it's twice a year on a weekend so easy to remember.*

- Ask your physician or pharmacist about storing prescription medicines.

- Visit the U.S. Department of Homeland Security web site for more tips about Kits at <u>www.ready.gov</u>

THINK ABOUT SHELTER

Sheltering may take many forms since it depends on the type of disaster or situation. There may be times where you and your family may need to "shelter-in-place" meaning you stay put wherever you are (home, school, work or car) until wicked weather passes or local authorities say it's okay to come out. Or, in some cases, your family may have to leave your home and go to a shelter or mass care facility determined by local officials (like a high school gym or convention center.)

For example, during a tornado warning you should seek shelter in a basement or an inside room away from windows. However, during a hazardous spill or chemical attack you should take shelter in a room above ground and possibly seal off room to keep gas or fumes from coming in. Or if there's a wildfire nearby or a hurricane brewing along the Coast your family may need to evacuate your home.

Some things you should talk about in advance with family include:

Make a plan - Develop a **Family Emergency Plan** and **Disaster Supplies Kits** for home, car and office / locker (covered on previous pages). Make sure you include important paperwork, money, etc.

Pick safe rooms - Talk about which room would be best for each type of disaster that may occur where you live.

Where would we go? - Decide in advance where you would go in case you can't return home for weeks or months .. or ever. If your home is damaged or destroyed or you're forced to leave your home due to on-going threats (like mudslides or flooding), you will need to find temporary or permanent living quarters. This could mean staying in a public shelter or hotel, living with friends or relatives, or renting a home or apartment in the middle of all the chaos, so discuss several options now. Then, write down those options and share them with relatives and friends.

Away from home - Learn "shelter-in-place" procedures at work and school so everyone knows what to expect for each type of disaster or incident.

Also review specific disasters in Section 2 for additional things to think about and do as it relates to sheltering. For example, fallout and pole-covered trench shelters are covered in the TERRORISM topic. And see TIPS ON RECOVERING FROM A DISASTER and TIPS ON SHELTER LIVING DURING OR AFTER AN EMERGENCY at the end of Section 2.

By planning ahead, your family will know where to go and what to do which can help reduce some fear and anxiety that surrounds a disaster.

Section 2

Disaster Preparedness, Prevention & Recovery

What to Do **BEFORE** a Disaster Strikes (Mitigation Tips)...

There are many things you can do to protect yourself, your home and your property BEFORE any type of natural hazard or disaster strikes. One of the most important things citizens can do is learn about hazards and risks in your area and take personal responsibility to prepare for the unexpected.

Please realize that natural disasters have common elements that overlap (like wind and floods) and we are only summarizing some key topics here to help get you started.

There are many mitigation tips and programs available from government agencies, public and private businesses, nonprofits and NGOs listed here and in Section 4 of this book that can help you and your family learn more.

What is Mitigation?

Mitigation simply means an effort to lessen the impact disasters have on people, property, communities and the economy. It is also about reducing or eliminating risks before disasters strike and involves planning, commitment, preparation and communication between local, state and federal government officials, businesses and the general public.

Some examples of mitigation include installing hurricane straps to secure a structure's roof to its walls and foundation, building outside of flood plains, securing shelves and loose objects inside and around the home, developing and enforcing effective building codes and standards, using fire-retardant materials ... and the list goes on and on.

Remember... the more you prepare BEFORE disaster strikes, the better off you and your loved ones will be financially, emotionally and physically.

FEMA's Mitigation Directorate

The Federal Emergency Management Agency's Mitigation Directorate manages the National Flood Insurance Program and oversees a number of FEMA's programs and activities like the National Hurricane Program, National Dam Safety Program, National Earthquake Hazards Reduction Program and others. Plus the Division provides citizens information about safe rooms and flood insurance, and small businesses can learn about Pre-Disaster Mitigation (PDM) loans and other cost-saving mitigation tips for structures and property. Learn more at www.fema.gov

Soon we'll explain what to do BEFORE, DURING and AFTER specific types of natural and man-made disasters and emergencies. But first there are some things you should do in advance that take time and planning... otherwise known as prevention or mitigation tips. Also review the BEFORE sections of specific topics for additional tips.

MITIGATION TIPS TO HELP PREVENT DAMAGE AND LOSS

AIR QUALITY MITIGATION

We want to briefly mention indoor air quality here since it affects so many people at home, school and work (especially children and the elderly). Poor air quality often results naturally from many environmental and weather-related factors.

There are things people can do like install a **High Efficiency Particulate Air (HEPA)** filter in your central heating and cooling system (or get a portable filter) to remove contaminants. There are also kits available for testing home, work and school environments so please learn more about carbon monoxide, mold, and radon by visiting or calling ...

EPA's Indoor Air Quality: www.epa.gov/iaq or call 1-800-438-4318

Center for Disease Control's National Center for Environmental Health Air Pollution & Respiratory Health: www.cdc.gov/nceh/airpollution

National Radon Info Line: 1-800-SOS-Radon or www.epa.gov/radon

EARTHQUAKE MITIGATION

A lot of the ongoing research by scientists, engineers and emergency preparedness officials has resulted in improvements to building codes around the world. Proven design and construction techniques are available that help limit damage and injuries. There are some things you can do to reduce risk in earthquake-prone areas:

Consider retrofitting your home
There are options to retrofit or reinforce your home's foundation and frame available from reputable contractors who follow strict building codes. Other earthquake-safety measures include installing flexible gas lines and automatic gas shutoff valves. Changes to gas lines and plumbing in your house must be done by a licensed contractor who will ensure that the work is done correctly and according to code. This is important for your safety.

Secure loose stuff
- Use nylon straps or L-braces to secure cabinets, book-cases and other tall furniture to the wall.

- Secure heavy appliances like water heaters, refrigerators, etc. using bands of perforated steel (plumber's tape).
- Use buckles or safety straps to secure computers, TVs, stereos and other equipment to tabletops.
- Use earthquake or florist putty to tack down glassware, heirlooms and figurines.

FIRE MITIGATION

Home fire protection is very important and covered on pages 52-53. Also see Wildfire Mitigation to learn additional ways to protect your home.

FLOOD MITIGATION

Flood damage is normally the **second** most common disaster-related expense of insured losses reported worldwide. Many natural disasters like hurricanes, rain, thunderstorms, and melting snow cause flooding. Living near a dam or levee also increases flood risks.

According to FEMA, everyone lives in a flood zone - it's just a question of whether you live in a low, moderate or high risk area. There are certain parts of North America known as "flood plains" that are at high risk of floods. Consider contacting your local emergency management official to use the Flood Insurance Rate Maps (FIRMs) or to develop a community-based approach since there may be funds available to assist you and your area.

Some examples of State grant programs officials can access include the Hazard Mitigation Grant Program (**HMGP**), Flood Mitigation Assistance (**FMA**) Program, and the Pre-Disaster Mitigation (**PDM**) Program. Individual citizens cannot apply for grant money but local agencies or nonprofit organizations may apply on behalf of citizens.

But I have insurance...

Insurance companies will cover some claims due to water damage like a broken water main or a washing machine that goes berserk. However, standard home insurance policies DO NOT generally cover flood (or mud) damage caused by natural events or disasters!

The U.S. offers a **National Flood Insurance Program** available in most communities and there is a waiting period for coverage. Talk to your insurance agent or call NFIP at 1-888-379-9531 or visit www.floodsmart.gov.

Currently Canadians do not have a national flood program, however certain parts of Canada offer limited flood-damage coverage but it must be purchased year-round and rates are relatively high. Visit www.ibc.ca

Move valuables to higher ground

If your home or business is prone to flooding, you should move valuables and appliances out of the basement or ground level floors.

Elevate breakers, fuse box and meters

Consider phoning a professional to elevate the main breaker or fuse box and utility meters above the anticipated flood level so flood waters won't damage your utilities. Also consider putting heating, ventilation and air conditioning units in the upper story or attic to protect from flooding.

Protect your property

Build barriers and landscape around homes or buildings to stop or reduce floodwaters and mud from entering. Also consider sealing basement walls with waterproofing compounds and installing "check valves" in sewer traps to prevent flood water from backing up into drains.

LIGHTNING MITIGATION

Here are some safety tips to prepare your home for lightning.

Install a Lightning Protection System

A lightning protection system does not prevent lightning from striking but does create a direct path for lightning to follow. Basically, a lightning protection system consists of air terminals (lightning rods) and associated fittings connected by heavy cables to grounding equipment. This provides a path for lightning current to travel safely to the ground.

Install surge protectors on or in home

Surge protection devices (SPDs) can be installed in the electrical panel to protect your entire home from electrical surges. Sometimes it may be necessary to install small individual SPDs in addition to the home unit for computers and television sets due to different ratings and voltage levels.

If a home unit is too expensive, consider getting individual SPDs that plug into the wall for the refrigerator, microwave and garage door openers. Appliances that use two services (cable wire and electrical cord) may require combination SPDs for computers, TVs, and VCRs. (Better yet - consider getting an uninterrupted power supply [UPS] with surge protection and battery backup so you can shut down computers safely.)

POWER LOSS MITIGATION (TIPS ON GENERATORS)

Many disasters (including human error) can cause a loss of power for hours, days or weeks. One way to prepare for a power outage is to have a generator on-hand, but be aware of the potential hazards that come with it and learn how to use it properly!

Find the right size for your home or business

Generators come in many shapes and sizes. Permanent standby generators are connected to the main electrical supply of your home or building and must be installed by a qualified, licensed electrician. Portable generators are more convenient and less expensive, but you should determine how much power is needed for your facility before you buy something.

Make a list of the items you'll need to run during a power outage, then total up the watts needed for each device. (Check the manufacturer's paperwork for each unit or hire an electrician to help you calculate this total.) Also remember to include both "starting" and "running" wattage requirements. Starting amounts may only last a few seconds but can cause overloading and damage your generator or appliances if not calculated properly.

Generator safety tips

- Do not plug a generator into a wall outlet or main electrical supply coming into a building since it could backfeed and kill utility workers repairing the lines!
- NEVER use generators in homes/offices, garages, basements or partially enclosed places. Keep them outdoors and away from windows, doors and vents.
- Read the manual that comes with your unit and follow the manufacturer's instructions.
- Shut off generator and let it cool before refueling, and store fuel outside of living areas.
- Install carbon monoxide (CO) alarms in your home and office and test them often.

The U.S. Fire Administration (USFA) has two fact sheets about generator safety and the dangers of carbon monoxide. Download both at www.usfa.dhs.gov/citizens/co/index.shtm

WILDFIRE MITIGATION

As our population continues to grow, more and more people are building homes in places that were once pristine wilderness areas. Homeowners who build in remote and wooded areas must take responsibility for the way their buildings are constructed and the way they landscape around them.

Use Fire Resistant Building Materials

The roof and exterior structure of your home and other buildings should be constructed of non-combustible or fire-resistant materials. If wood siding, cedar shakes or any other highly combustible materials are used, they should be treated with fire retardant chemicals.

Landscape wisely

Plant fire-resistant shrubs and trees to minimize the spread of fire and space your landscaping so fire is not carried to your home or other surrounding vegetation. Remove vines from the walls of your home.

Create a "safety zone" around the house

- Mow grass regularly.
- Stack firewood at least 30 to 100 feet (10 to 30 m) away and uphill from home.
- Keep roof and gutters free of pine needles, leaves, and branches and clear away flammable vegetation at least 30 to 100 feet (9 to 30 m) from around structures.
- Thin a 15-foot (4.5 m) space between tree crowns and remove limbs within 10-15 feet (3 - 4.5 m) of the ground.
- Remove dead branches that extend over the roof.
- Prune tree branches and shrubs within 10 feet (3 m) of a stovepipe or chimney outlet.
- Remove leaves and rubbish from under structures.
- Ask power company to clear branches from power lines.
- Keep combustibles away from structures and clear a 10-foot (3 m) area around propane tanks, boats, etc.

Protect your home

- Install smoke detectors, test them each month and change batteries once a year.
- Install protective shutters or fire-resistant drapes.
- Inspect chimneys twice a year and clean every year.
- Cover chimney and stovepipe flue openings with 1/2 inch (1 cm) or smaller non-flammable mesh screen.
- Use same mesh screen beneath porches, decks, floor areas and home itself. Also screen openings to attic and roof.
- Soak ashes and charcoal briquettes in water for two days in a metal bucket.
- Keep a garden hose connected to an outlet.
- Have fire tools handy (ladder, shovel, rake, ax, etc.)
- Put address on all structures so it can be seen from road.

WIND MITIGATION

Wind damage is the **most common** disaster-related expense and usually accounts for **70% or more** of the insured losses reported worldwide. Many natural disasters like hurricanes, tornadoes, microbursts or thunderstorms, and winter storms include damaging winds. And certain parts of the world experience high winds on a normal basis due to wind patterns.

Realize when extreme winds strike they are not constant - they rapidly increase and decrease. A home in the path of wind causes the wind to change direction. This change in wind direction increases pressure on parts of the house creating stress which causes the connections between building components to fail. For example, the roof or siding can be pulled off or the windows can be pushed in.

Strengthen weak spots on home

Experts believe there are four areas of your home that should be checked for weakness -- the roof, windows, doors and garage doors. Homeowners can take some steps to secure and strengthen these areas but some things should be done by an experienced builder or contractor.

ROOF:
- Truss bracing or gable end bracing (supports placed strategically to strengthen the roof)
- Anchors, clips and straps can be installed (may want to call a professional since sometimes difficult to install)

WINDOWS and DOORS:
- Storm shutters (for windows, French doors, sliding glass doors, and skylights) or keep plywood on hand
- Reinforced bolt kits for doors

GARAGE DOORS:
- Certain parts of the country have building codes requiring garage doors to withstand high winds (check with local building officials)
- Some garage doors can be strengthened with retrofit kits (involves installing horizontal bracing onto each panel)

Secure mobile homes

Make sure your trailer or mobile home is securely anchored. Consult the manufacturer for information on secure tiedown systems.

Secure or tie down loose stuff

Extreme winds can also cause damage from flying debris that can act like missiles and ram through walls, windows or the roof if the wind speeds are high enough. You should consider securing large or heavy equipment inside and out to reduce some of the flying debris like patio furniture, barbeque grills, water heaters, garbage cans, bookcases and shelving, etc.

Consider building a shelter or "safe room"

Shelters or "safe rooms" are designed to provide protection from the high winds expected during hurricanes, tornadoes and from flying debris. Shelters built below ground provide the best protection, but be aware they could be flooded during heavy rains.

FEMA provides an excellent free booklet called "Taking Shelter From the Storm: Building a Safe Room Inside Your House" developed in association with the Wind Engineering Research Center at Texas Tech University. Learn more by visiting www.fema.gov *[do a search on safe rooms]*

WINTER STORM & EXTREME COLD MITIGATION

Severe winter weather causes deterioration and damage to homes every year. There are many things you can do to prepare for the bitter cold, ice and snow in advance to save you money and headaches in the long run. Some of these tips should be used by apartment dwellers too.

"Winterize" your home

- Insulate walls and attic.
- Caulk and weather-strip doors and windows.
- Install storm windows or cover windows with plastic film from the inside to keep warmth in.
- Detach garden hoses and shut-off water supply to faucets.
- Install faucet covers or wrap with towels and duct tape.
- Show family members the location of your main water valve and mark it so you can find it quickly.
- Drain sprinkler lines or well lines before the first freeze.
- Keep inside temperature of your home at 68 degrees Fahrenheit (20 degrees Celsius) or higher.
- Wrap pipes near exterior walls with towels or heating tape.
- Change furnace filters regularly and have it serviced.
- Make sure you have good lighting from street and drive-ways to help others see snow and ice patches and try to keep paths clear of drifts.
- Remove dead tree branches since they break easily.
- Cover fireplace openings with fire-resistant screens.
- Check shingles to make sure they are in good shape.

Preventing "ice dams"

A lot of water leakage and damage around outside walls and ceilings are actually due to "ice dams". Ice dams are lumps of ice that form on gutters or downspouts and prevent melting snow from running down. An attic with no insulation (like a detached garage) or a well-sealed and insulated attic will generally not have ice dams. But if the roof has peaks and valleys, is poorly insulated, or has a large roof overhang, ice dams usually happen.

Some tips to prevent ice dams:

- Keep gutters and downspouts clear of leaves and debris.
- Find areas of heat loss in attic and insulate it properly.
- Wrap or insulate heating duct work to reduce heat loss.
- Remove snow buildup on roof and gutters using snow rake or soft broom.
- Consider installing roof heat tapes (electric cables) that clip onto shingles' edges to melt channels in ice. (Remember, cables use a lot of energy and may not look pretty but could help on homes with complicated roofs.)

Preventing frozen pipes

- Keep doors open under sinks so heat can circulate.
- Run a slow trickle of lukewarm water and check water flow before going to bed and when you get up. (First sign of freezing is reduced water flow so keep an eye on it.)
- Heat your basement or at least insulate it well.
- Close windows and keep drafts away from pipes since air flow can cause pipes to freeze more often.

MITIGATION TIPS SUMMARY...

Take responsibility...

Basically, no matter where you live, YOU should take personal responsibility and prepare yourself, your family and your property BEFORE disasters or natural hazards strike.

...and learn more!

After reviewing the remainder of this manual, please contact your local emergency officials or your local building department to learn about all the risks in your area and what to expect if disaster strikes.

Or visit FEMA's "Plan & Prepare" section at www.fema.gov

Remember ... it's not a matter of IF but rather WHEN a disaster of some type will affect you or a loved one. The best thing you can do to deal with ANY type of disaster is...

<u>**BE AWARE**</u>... <u>**BE PREPARED**</u>... and... <u>**HAVE A PLAN**</u>!

If you do these 3 things, the life and property you save could be your own... because what you <u>don't</u> know <u>CAN</u> hurt you!

Now we are going to briefly summarize some key players involved in the response process.

Then we'll cover what to do **BEFORE, DURING** and **AFTER** specific types of natural and man-made disasters (sorted alphabetically).

We then cover some tips on **RECOVERING FROM A DISASTER** (includes many "AFTER" tips that apply to most every type of disaster) and on **SHELTER LIVING**.

We also offer some tips on **USING HOUSEHOLD FOODS, WATER PURIFICATION,** and **SANITATION OF HUMAN WASTE** followed by tips for **HELPING OTHERS** and **DEALING WITH DEATH OR MASS CASUALTIES** at the end this Section.

Section 3 covers a variety of basic First Aid topics (sorted alphabetically) that may be necessary to use during a major disaster or just for the minor injury at home.

Section 4 contains many helpful telephone numbers and web sites of various agencies and organizations.

And finally, we ask you please take some time to review the Appendixes, resources and web sites near the back of this manual.

As mentioned in the Introduction, a majority of this data was compiled from various publications provided by the U.S. Department of Homeland Security and FEMA, the CDC, Public Safety Canada, the Red Cross and others to assist you in preparing for various disasters.

We realize you may not experience every type of disaster or emergency in your part of the world but, if you ever travel away from home, you could potentially be placed in a disaster situation so please educate yourself and your family.

Knowledge is power and can help reduce fear and anxiety.

WHO RESPONDS DURING A DISASTER OR EMERGENCY?

During a crisis, government agencies, volunteers, nonprofits, churches, the private sector and citizens come together to help communities devastated by a disaster or emergency. We don't have enough space to acknowledge all the amazing groups who contribute their time and energy during the response and recovery phases, but here are some of the key players involved.

Local Fire - provides fire protection and response, EMS support, Search and Rescue and hazardous materials (HAZMAT) response among many other roles. Volunteers make up 90% of fire companies nationwide.

Local Law enforcement - work closely with agencies on scene to secure the area, gather data, maintain order, enforce laws and protect communities.

Local Emergency Management - runs the emergency operations center (EOC) and manages response and recovery efforts. The EM office also works closely with state and Federal officials.

Local EMS - are paramedics and emergency medical technicians who can provide immediate medical assistance to the wounded. Disaster medical assistance teams (or DMATs) made up of EMS professionals are often deployed to assist areas overwhelmed by an emergency or disaster.

Local Public Health - supports EMS by sending in doctors and nurses who care for patients while health-care workers (like psychologists, social workers and others) assist with recovery.

State agencies - provide support for above local agencies, especially when a crisis overwhelms an area. They also help interface with Federal officials.

National Guard - can be called up by the Governor to support fire, police, EMS and health officials during a disaster. They can provide manpower by helping distribute food, water and medicine or aid with law enforcement efforts. The NG also has heavy equipment that can help with debris removal or deliver supplies using air support.

Federal agencies - respond once a Governor has requested their assistance. FEMA reviews the request and, if merited, recommends action to the White House for the President to decide if it should be declared a major disaster.

Nonprofits, volunteers, faith-based groups, businesses and citizens - donate money, time, supplies and services to victims and communities.

What are YOU gonna do about...
AVALANCHES, LANDSLIDES & MUDFLOWS?

Avalanches - masses of loosened snow or ice that tumble down the side of a mountain, often growing as it descends picking up mud, rocks, trees and debris triggered by various means including wind, rapid warming, snow conditions and humans.

Landslides - masses of rock, earth or debris that move down a slope and can be caused by earthquakes, volcanic eruptions, and by humans who develop on land that is unstable.

Mudflows - rivers of rock, earth, and other debris soaked with water mostly caused by melting snow or heavy rains and create a "slurry". A "slurry" can travel several miles from its source and grows in size as it picks up trees, cars, and other things along the way just like an avalanche!

Please note, first we cover some very basic things on avalanches then we'll cover landslides and mudflows.

Avalanche Basics
Snow avalanches are a natural process and happen about a million times per year worldwide. Contrary to what is shown in the movies, avalanches are <u>not</u> triggered by loud noises like a shout or a sonic boom -- it's just not enough force. An avalanche is actually formed by a combination of several things -- a steep slope (the terrain), the snowpack, a weak layer in the snowpack, and a natural or artificial "trigger".

Nearly everyone caught in an avalanche is skiing, snowboarding, riding a snowmobile, snowshoeing, hiking or climbing in the backcountry and they, or someone in their party, almost always trigger the avalanche. According to the American Avalanche Association, the majority of victims are white, educated men between the ages of 18-35 who are very skilled at their sport.

BEFORE AN AVALANCHE:

<u>Learn risks</u> - Ask about local risks by contacting your local emergency management office *(see Section 4 for State and Provincial listings),* especially if visiting or moving to an "avalanche-prone" area.

<u>Take a course</u> - Professional trainers and educators offer a variety of avalanche safety training courses and levels ranging from recreational novices to backcountry experts. To learn more visit <u>www.avalanche.org</u>

Know your colors - Learn the Avalanche Danger Scales and corresponding colors used where you live or plan to visit.

Get equipped - Carry gear like portable shovels, collapsible probes, high frequency avalanche beacons (transceivers), etc. and learn how to use it!

Check it out - Check forecasts and avalanche advisories before going out.

Turn it on - Switch beacon on prior to entering the backcountry! Check the battery strength and verify the "transmit" and "receive" functionality with everyone in your group to ensure beacons are picking up both signals.

Secure it - Before crossing a snow covered slope in avalanche terrain, fasten clothing securely to keep snow out and remove your ski pole straps.

DURING AN AVALANCHE:

Bail - Try to get out of the way if possible! (For example, if a skier or boarder - ski out diagonally... if on a snowmobile - drive downhill, etc.)

If YOU are caught in the avalanche...

Scream and drop it - Yell and drop your ski poles (or anything in your hands) so they don't drag you down.

Start swimming - Use "swimming" motions, thrusting upward to try to stay near the surface of the snow.

Prepare to make an air pocket - Try to keep your arms and hands moving so the instant the avalanche stops you can make an air pocket in front of your face by punching in the snow around you before it sets.

If you see SOMEONE ELSE caught in the avalanche...

Watch - Keep an eye on victim as they are carried downhill esp the last point you saw them.

AFTER AN AVALANCHE:

If YOU are caught in the avalanche...

Make an air pocket ASAP! - The INSTANT the avalanche stops try to maintain an air pocket in front of your face by using your hands and arms to punch in the snow and make a pocket of air. (You only have 1-3 seconds before the snow sets -- most deaths are due to suffocation.)

<u>Stick it out</u> - If you are lucky enough to be near the surface, try to stick out an arm or a leg so that rescuers can find you.

<u>Don't panic</u> - Keep your breathing steady to help preserve your air space and help your body conserve energy.

<u>Listen for rescuers</u> - Since snow is a good insulator, rescuers probably won't even hear you until they are practically on top of you, so don't start yelling until you hear them. (This conserves your precious air.)

If you see SOMEONE ELSE caught in the avalanche...

<u>Watch</u> - Keep watching the victim(s) as they are carried downhill, paying particular attention to the last point you saw them.

<u>DO NOT go for help!</u> - Sounds crazy but the victim only has a few minutes to breathe under the snow, so every second counts. Spend 30 minutes to an hour searching before going for help.

<u>Be aware</u> - Assess the situation and dangers... in many cases it is safe to go in after the avalanche settles but proceed with caution.

<u>Look for clues</u> - Look for signs on the surface (like poles, a hand or foot, etc.) where victim was last seen. Equipment and clothing can be ripped off during the avalanche but can help determine the direction they were carried.

<u>Switch to "receive"</u> - Turn all transceivers to "receive" to try to locate victim's signal (in the event victim is wearing one and has it set correctly.)

<u>Mark the spot</u> - If you lost sight of the victim or can't find any visible clues on the surface, mark the spot where victim was last seen.

<u>Probe in a line</u> - When searching with probes, stand shoulder to shoulder in a line across the slope and repeatedly insert probes moving down the slope.

<u>Listen</u> - Make sure you listen for any muffled sounds as you search.

<u>Find them...dig 'em out!</u> - If you find the victim, dig them out as quickly as possible. Survival chances reduce the longer they are buried.

Now we'll briefly cover **LANDSLIDES** and **MUDFLOWS**. Realize many types of disasters like earthquakes, volcanic eruptions, rain and wind erosion can cause land, rocks and mud to shift and move, sometimes at rapid speeds. Compound that with gravity and these earth movements can become extremely destructive.

Another major factor is the world's growing population is sprawling out of major cities and developing in high-risk areas. There are some warning signs to indicate if you have a potential problem.

BEFORE A LANDSLIDE OR MUDFLOW:

Learn risks - Ask your local emergency management office *(see Section 4 for State & Provincial listing)* if your property is a "landslide-prone" area.

Recent fires? - Be aware that areas hit by wildfires have an increased risk of landslides and mudflows once the rainy season starts.

Get insurance...? - Talk to your agent and find out more about the **National Flood Insurance Program** since mudflows <u>are</u> covered by NFIP's flood policy. *(Visit www.floodsmart.gov - also see FLOOD MITIGATION)*

Be prepared to evacuate - Listen to local authorities and leave if you are told to evacuate. *(see EVACUATION)*

Where would we go? - Decide in advance where you would go in case you can't return home for weeks or months .. or ever. If your home is damaged or destroyed or you're forced to leave your home due to on-going threats (like mudslides or flooding), you'll need to find temporary or permanent living quarters. This could mean staying in a public shelter or hotel, living with friends or relatives, or renting a home or apartment in the middle of all the chaos, so discuss several options now. Then, write down those options and share them with relatives and friends.

Reduce risks - Plant ground cover on slopes and build retaining walls.

Inspect - Look around home and property for landslide warning signs:
- cracks or bumps appear on hill slopes, ground or roads
- water or saturated ground in areas not normally wet
- evidence of slow, downhill movement of rock and soil
- tilted trees, poles, decks, patios, fences or walls
- doors and windows stick or cracks appear on walls, etc.

Call an expert...? - Consult a professional for advice. Or visit the National Landslide Information Center at http://landslides.usgs.gov/nlic/

DURING A LANDSLIDE OR MUDFLOW:

Strange sounds - Listen for trees cracking, rocks banging together or water flowing rapidly (esp if near a stream or river) - debris flow may be close by.

Move it! - Whether you are in a vehicle, outside, or in your home – GET TO SAFER GROUND!

Be small - If there is no way to escape, curl into a tight ball and protect your head the best you can.

(Since most other disasters cause landslides and mudflows, we'll discuss them further in those specific cases - please see other topics to learn more.)

AFTER A LANDSLIDE OR MUDFLOW:

Listen - Local radio and TV reports will keep you posted on latest updates or check with your local police or fire departments.

Don't go there - Stay away from the area until authorities say all is clear since there could be more slides or flows.

Things to watch for:
- **flooding** - usually occur after landslides or debris flows
- **damaged areas** - roadways and bridges may be buried, washed-out or weakened -- and water, gas & sewer lines may be broken
- **downed power lines** - report them to power company

Inspect - Look for damage around home and property and watch for new landslide warning signs:
- check foundation, chimney, garage and other structures
- report any broken utility lines or damaged roads to local authorities
- watch for tilted trees, poles, decks, patios, fences or walls
- notice doors or windows stick, cracks appear, etc.

Replant - Try to fix or replant damaged ground to reduce erosion, possible flash flooding or future landslides.

Call an expert...? - Consult a professional landscaping expert for opinions and advice on landslide problems. Also call an expert out if you discover structural damage to home, chimney or other buildings.

Insurance - If your home suffers any damage, contact your insurance agent and keep all receipts for clean-up and repairs.

Recovery tips - Review TIPS ON RECOVERING FROM A DISASTER at the end of this section.

What are YOU gonna do about...
CIVIL DISTURBANCES OR CIVIL UNREST?

Civil disturbances (also called civil unrest or riots) can happen for many different reasons like frustration with the government, a bad court decision, drunken mayhem after sporting events, or racial tensions in a neighborhood. Or sometimes a peaceful rally, concert or party can turn violent and spill over into neighborhoods or business districts. Sometimes authorities can block off the affected areas -- other times things may just go crazy.

DURING A RIOT OR CIVIL UNREST:

Stay calm & be aware - If possible, avoid contact with rioters and keep a low profile. And leave the area as quickly and safely as possible.

Listen - If officials tell you to leave or to shelter-in-place ... DO it! Stay updated with local radio and TV reports since rumors may be flying around.

Evacuate? – If you are told to leave - do so ... and IF you have time...
- Secure your home or business. Lock doors and windows, back up files if possible, take valuables and important papers with you (or lock them up), etc.
- Don't try to drive through a crowd -- find another way out.

Things to watch for:
- **flying objects or gas** - rioters may throw rocks, bottles, bricks, cans, fireworks, molatov cocktails ... and police may have to use rubber bullets, bean bags or tear gas for crowd control
- **damaged areas** - drunks and rioters may smash windows, burn tires, overturn cars and set buildings or homes on fire
- **suspicious packages** - rioters may call in bomb threats

Firearms - Sometimes looting occurs but be smart about protecting your property, it's not worth getting hurt or shot defending it. (Learn more about firearm safety from local law enforcement officials or at www.nra.org.)

Don't go there - Stay away from the area until authorities say all is clear.

National Guard - If things get out of hand, local law enforcement may request the National Guard come in and help so don't be alarmed if you see uniformed armed forces on the streets.

What are _YOU_ gonna do about...
AN EARTHQUAKE?

Earthquakes can cause buildings and bridges to collapse, down telephone and power lines, and result in fires, explosions and landslides. Earthquakes can also cause huge ocean waves, called tsunamis [soo-nah'-mees], which travel long distances over water until they hit coastal areas.

Our planet's surface is actually made up of slowly-moving sections (called "tectonic plates") that can build up friction or stress in the crust as they creep around. An earthquake occurs when this built up stress is suddenly released and transmitted to the surface of the earth by earthquake waves (called seismic waves).

There are actually millions of small earthquakes, or seismic tremors, per year around the world. Many earthquakes are too small to be felt, but when they happen, you will feel shaking, quickly followed by a rolling motion that can rotate up, down, and sideways that lasts from a few seconds to several minutes.

BEFORE AN EARTHQUAKE:

Learn the buzzwords - Learn the terms / words used with earthquakes...

- **Earthquake** - a sudden slipping of the earth's crust that causes a series of vibrations
- **Aftershock** - usually not as strong as earthquake but can occur for hours, days, months or years after a main quake
- **Fault** - area of weakness where two sections of crust have separated
- **Subduction zone** - where 2 tectonic plates collide and one plate dives or "subducts" underneath the other
- **Epicenter** - area of the earth's surface directly above the crust that caused the quake
- **Seismic Waves** - vibrations that travel from the center of the earthquake to the surface
- **Magnitude** - used to define how much energy was released (A Richter Scale is the device used to measure this energy on a scale from 0-10 ... each whole number equals an increase of about 30 times the energy released meaning a 5.0 is about 30 times stronger than a 4.0.)
- **Liquefaction** - when water-saturated ground loses strength and acts as a muddy fluid

Prepare - See EARTHQUAKE and POWER LOSS MITIGATION at the beginning of this Section. Also visit www.shakeout.org

Reduce risks - Look for things that could be hazardous...
- Place large or heavy objects on lower shelves and fasten shelves to walls, if possible.
- Hang heavy pictures and mirrors away from beds.
- Store bottled foods, glass, china and other breakables on low shelves or in cabinets that can fasten shut.
- Repair faulty electrical wiring and leaky gas connections.

Learn to shut off - Know where and how to shut off electricity, gas and water at main switches and valves -- ask local utilities for instructions.

Do drills - Hold earthquake drills with your family to learn what to do...
- **DROP** - drop down to the floor
- **COVER** - get under heavy desk or table or against inside wall protecting head and neck with your arms
- **HOLD ON** - grab something sturdy, be ready to move with it and hold on until shaking stops!

Make a plan - Review Section 1 and develop a **Family Emergency Plan.**

Check policies - Review your insurance policies. Some damage may be covered even without specific earthquake insurance.

DURING AN EARTHQUAKE:

Stay calm & be aware - Watch for falling objects and find a safe spot! Realize most injuries happen when people are hit by things when running IN or OUT of buildings.

IF INDOORS – Stay inside and ...
- Avoid danger zones like glass, windows, heavy things that can fall over or down on you.
- **DROP**, **COVER** and **HOLD ON** until the shaking stops. If there isn't a table or desk near you, cover face and head with arms and crouch in an inside corner of the building.

IF IN A HIGH-RISE BUILDING – Stay on the same floor!
- Move away from outside walls and windows.
- Stay on the same floor - you may not have to evacuate.
- Realize electricity may go out and alarms and sprinkler

systems may go on.
- DO NOT use the elevators!

IF OUTDOORS - Stay outside and, if possible, move away from buildings, signs, trees, power lines and street lights.

IF IN A MOVING VEHICLE - Stop as quickly and safely as you can!
- Try not to stop near buildings, trees, overpasses, or power lines and stay in vehicle until shaking stops.
- Watch for road and bridge damage and be ready for aftershocks once you drive again.

If you are trapped in an area:
- **light** - use a flashlight (if you have one) – do not use matches or lighters in case of gas leaks
- **be still** - try to stay still so you won't kick up dust
- **breathing** - cover your mouth with a piece of clothing
- **make noise** - tap on a pipe or wall so rescuers can hear you (shouting may cause you to inhale a lot of dust)

AFTER AN EARTHQUAKE:

Aftershocks - Usually not as strong but can cause more damage to weakened structures and may continue for days, months or even years.

Injuries - Check yourself and people around you for injuries - do not try to move seriously injured people unless they are in danger. If you must move a person who is passed out keep their head and neck still and call for help! *(see Section 3 – TIPS ON BASIC FIRST AID)*

Light - Never use candles, matches or lighters since there might be gas leaks. Use flashlights or battery powered lanterns.

Check home - Look for structural damage -- call a professional if needed.

Check chimney - First check from a distance to see if chimney looks normal and have a professional check it if it looks strange. Check out the Chimney Safety Institute of America's homeowner tips at www.csia.org

Clean up - Any flammable liquids (bleaches, gasoline, etc.) should be cleaned up immediately.

Inspect - Check all utility lines and appliances for damage:
- **smell gas or hear hissing** - open a window and leave

quickly. Shut off main valve outside, if possible, and call a professional to turn it back on when it's safe

- **electrical damage** - switch off power at main fuse box or circuit breaker
- **water pipes** - shut off water supply at the main valve
- **toilets** - do not use until you know sewage lines are okay

Water - If water is cut off or contaminated then use water from your **Disaster Supplies Kit** or other clean water sources. *(see TIPS ON WATER PURIFICATION)*

Power - If you use a generator, keep it outside and follow manufacturer's instructions. *(see some safety tips in POWER LOSS MITIGATION)*

Phones - Keep calls to a minimum to report emergencies since most lines will be down.

Listen - Keep up on news reports for the latest information.

Things to avoid:
- **going out** - try to stay off the roads to reduce risk
- **stay away** - unless emergency crew or First Responders ask for your help stay away from damaged areas
- **downed power wires**

Tsunami - If you live near the coast, a tsunami can crash into the shorelines so listen for warnings by local authorities. *(see section on TSUNAMIS)*

RED or GREEN sign in window – After a disaster, Volunteers and Emergency Service personnel will be going door-to-door to check on people. By placing a sign in your window that faces the street near the door, you can let them know if you need them to STOP HERE or MOVE ON.

Either use a piece of RED or GREEN construction paper or draw a big RED or GREEN "X" (using a crayon or marker) on a piece of paper and tape it in the window.
- RED means STOP HERE!
- GREEN means EVERYTHING IS OKAY…MOVE ON!
- Nothing in the window would also mean STOP HERE!

Recovery tips - Review TIPS ON RECOVERING FROM A DISASTER at end of this Section.

What are YOU gonna do about...
AN EVACUATION?

Evacuations are quite common and happen for a number of reasons – fires, floods, mudflows, hurricanes, or chemical spills on the roads or railways.

When community evacuations become necessary, local officials provide information to the public usually through the media. Government agencies, the Red Cross, churches and other relief organizations provide emergency shelter and supplies. But, as we have said before, you should have enough food, water, clothing and emergency supplies for days or weeks (or more) in case you cannot be reached by relief efforts.

The amount of time to evacuate obviously depends on the type of disaster. Hurricanes can be tracked and allow a day or two notice to get ready, but many types of disasters happen without much notice... so prepare NOW!!

BEFORE AN EVACUATION:

<u>Ask & learn</u> - Ask emergency management officials about community evacuation plans and learn the routes that should be used. Also learn the signs used for your area - and, if you're traveling, make a mental note what evacuation signs look like in case something happens while on the road. And ask if your local officials have developed pet-friendly shelters and pet-related disaster plans through the 2006 PETS Act.

<u>Make a plan</u> - Review Section 1 and develop a **Family Emergency Plan** (so you know where to meet if separated, how to contact everyone, have a **Disaster Supplies Kit** ready to go, etc.) If you don't have a car, make arrangements with friends, neighbors or local officials so you have a way to evacuate.

<u>Think about your pets</u> - Make a plan for your critters. Review Tips for Pets or Livestock / Large Animals on page 11 and pack supplies for them in your **Disaster Supplies Kit**.

<u>Where do we go?</u> - Talk with your family members and decide in advance where you would go in case you can't return home for weeks or months. If your home is damaged or destroyed or you're forced to leave your home due to on-going threats (like mudslides or flooding), you will need to find temporary or permanent living quarters. This could mean staying in a public shelter or hotel, living with friends or relatives, or renting a home or apartment in the middle of all the chaos, so discuss several options. Then, write down your various options and share them with relatives and friends.

Paperwork & money - As discussed in Section 1, put important paperwork (wills, photo I.D.s, insurance policies, list of bank and credit card numbers, etc.) in a portable fireproof container (and have copies in an off-site safety deposit box) so you have identification to get access to your bank or to set up new accounts if you have to relocate long-term to another town. Also keep copies on a CD, flash drive or external drive and store media in a safe place off-site or in a locked fireproof container. Or consider using a service that allows you to upload scans and securely store your documents on their servers.

Fill 'er up - Keep car fueled up -- stations may close during an emergency. (Try to stay in the habit of having at least half a tank of gas at all times.)

Learn to shut off - Know where and how to shut off electricity, gas and water at main switches and valves -- ask local utilities for instructions (and keep a wrench handy).

Review tips on basic needs - Please review TIPS ON SHELTER LIVING, TIPS ON USING HOUSEHOLD FOODS, TIPS ON WATER PURIFICATION and TIPS ON SANITATION OF HUMAN WASTE near end of this section to prepare yourself and family for what to expect.

DURING AN EVACUATION:

Listen - Keep up on news reports for the latest information.

Grab & Go - Grab your **Disaster Supplies Kit** (has water, food, clothing, emergency supplies, insurance and financial records, etc. ready to go).

What do I wear? - Put on protective clothing (long sleeve shirt and pants) and sturdy shoes - may even want to grab a jacket, hat or cap.

Shut off utilities - Turn off main water valve and electricity (if authorities tell you to do so).

Secure home - Close and lock doors and windows, unplug appliances, protect water pipes (if freezing weather), tie down boats, etc. *(See specific types of disaster for additional tips on securing home.)*

Take quick pics - Use your camera phone to take some shots of your home and property for a last minute inventory of things.

Pets - Make sure you take pets in secure carriers and bring food, water and leashes or harnesses with you. Grab medical records so you can prove immunizations are current. Realize some shelters may not accept pets so have a backup plan on where you'll go. If you have no alternative but to leave your pet at home, confine it to a safe area inside with dry food and plenty of water. Leave bathroom door open and toilet lid up (or remove lid completely) so they can access additional water (but only if toilet is free of chemicals.) If you must leave your pet outside -- don't chain it!

Large animals - Hopefully you made arrangements in advance to evacuate livestock and/or large animals. If you must turn them loose, prepare halters for horses that include your name and phone numbers or spray paint your number on the animals and leave lots of food and water out.

Alert family / friends - Let others know where you are going (or at least leave a message or note in clear view explaining where you can be found). If pets are left on the property, put a note on door to alert rescue workers.

Twitter, Flickr, etc - Social networking sites allow users to stay current on evacuation and recovery efforts. You may not have access to the Internet during or after a crisis, but text messages can sometimes get through when cell and phone systems are down. The Red Cross, FEMA, local emergency officials and other relief groups use Twitter to send instant messages (called Tweets) about evacuations and shelter information. And FEMA and DHS partnered with Facebook and MySpace so users can get emergency broadcast warnings and stay updated on friends and families displaced by storms. Social media sites are also a great way to post photos and videos.

Things to avoid:
- **bad weather** - leave early enough so you're not trapped
- **shortcuts** - may be blocked -- stick to the recommended Evacuation routes
- **flooded areas** - roadways and bridges may be washed-out
- **downed power lines**

Review tips on basic needs - Make sure you review tips on SHELTER LIVING, USING HOUSEHOLD FOODS, WATER PURIFICATION and SANITATION OF HUMAN WASTE at end of this section to prepare your family for the unexpected.

What are YOU gonna do about...
EXTREME HEAT?

What is Extreme Heat? Temperatures that hover 10 degrees or more above the average high temperature for that area and last for several weeks are considered "extreme heat" or a **heat wave**. Humid and muggy conditions can make these high temperatures even more unbearable. Really dry and hot conditions can cause dust storms and low visibility. **Droughts** occur when a long period passes without enough rainfall. A heat wave combined with a drought is a very dangerous situation!

Doing too much on a hot day, spending too much time in the sun or staying too long in an overheated place can cause **heat-related illnesses**. Know the symptoms of heat illnesses and be ready to give first aid treatment. *(see HEAT-RELATED ILLNESSES in Section 3)*

BEFORE EXTREME HEAT HITS:

<u>Keep it cool</u> - Tips to keep hot air out and cool air inside include...
- Close any floor heat vents nearby.
- Seal gaps around window units with foam or duct tape.
- Use a circulating or box fan to spread the cool air around.
- Use aluminum foil covered cardboard in windows to reflect heat back outside.
- Use weather-stripping on doors and windowsills.
- Keep storm windows up all year to help keep cool in.

DURING EXTREME HEAT:

<u>Protect windows</u> - If you hang shades, drapes, sheets, or awnings on windows you can reduce heat from entering home by as much as 80%.

<u>Conserve power</u> - During heat waves there are usually power shortages since everyone is trying to cool off, so stay indoors as much as possible.

<u>Conserve water</u> - Tips to lower water usage, esp. during drought conditions
- Check plumbing for leaks.
- Replace toilet and shower head with "low flow" versions.
- Don't leave water running while shaving, brushing teeth, washing dishes, cleaning fruit or veggies, etc.

- If washing dishes or clothes, make sure it's a full load.
- Take short showers rather than filling up a bathtub.
- Limit watering lawn or washing cars.

No A/C..? - If you have no air conditioning, try to stay on the lowest floor out of the sunshine and use electric fans to help keep yourself cool.

Cars - Never leave children or pets in vehicles on warm or hot days!!

Eat light - Light meals are best, especially fresh fruits and veggies.

Drink WATER - Increase your daily intake of water, esp. in dry climates (deserts and high elevations) -- you don't realize how dehydrated you get And don't forget your pets!

Limit booze - Even though beer and alcoholic beverages may be refreshing on a hot day, they actually cause your body to dehydrate more.

What to wear - Light-colored (to reflect heat) loose-fitting clothes are best… and cover as much skin as possible. Dark colors absorb the sun's heat. Also, wear a wide-brimmed hat to protect face and neck.

Use sunscreen - Apply lotion or cream at least 20 minutes before going out-side so skin can absorb and protect, esp. face and neck (SPF 30 to 50 with a 3 or 4 star UVA protection is best). You usually burn within the first 10 minutes outside, so take care of your skin… especially children! A sunburn slows the body's ability to cool itself and can be extremely dangerous.

Working outdoors - If you have to do yard work or other outdoor work, try to do it in the early morning hours to limit exposure in the sun. The most powerful sun is between 10 a.m. and 3 p.m. (when you burn the quickest) so limit outdoor activity during the heat of the day, if possible.

Ozone alerts - These can cause *serious* danger to people with breathing and respiratory problems (especially children and the elderly) so limit your time outdoors when alerts are announced on the radio, newspapers or TV.

- **ozone** - a colorless gas that is in the air we breathe and is a major element of urban smog.
- **ground-level ozone** - an air pollutant that can lower resistance to colds, cause problems for people with heart and lung disease, and cause coughing or throat irritation
- **ozone levels** - Air Quality Index between 0-50 is fine, but anything above 100 is extremely dangerous!

Heat Index - Visit NOAA's heat safety page at www.weather.gov/om/heat

What are YOU gonna do about...
FIRES & WILDFIRES?

Since fire spreads so quickly, there is <u>NO</u> time to grab valuables or make a phone call! In just <u>two</u> minutes a fire can become life threatening! In <u>five</u> minutes a house can be engulfed in flames.

A fire's heat and smoke are more dangerous than the actual flames since you can burn your lungs by inhaling the super-hot air. Fire produces a poisonous gas that makes you drowsy and disoriented (confused). Instead of being awakened by a fire, you could fall into a deeper sleep.

First we will discuss **FIRES** like you might encounter in your home or apartment, then we will cover **WILDFIRES** since there are many things people need to think about when living near wilderness areas.

BEFORE A FIRE (FIRE SAFETY TIPS):

<u>Install smoke and carbon monoxide (CO) detectors!</u> - Test alarms 1-4 times a month, replace batteries once a year, and get new units every 10 years.

<u>Make a plan</u> - Review Section 1 and create an Escape Plan that includes two escape routes from every room in the house and walk through the routes with your entire family. Also...

- Make sure your windows are not nailed or painted shut.
- Make sure security bars on windows have a fire safety opening feature so they can be easily opened from the inside…and teach everyone how to open them!
- Teach everyone how to stay LOW to floor (air is safer).
- Pick a spot to meet after escaping fire (meeting place).

<u>Clean up</u> - Keep storage areas clean - don't stack up newspapers & trash.

<u>Check power sources</u> - Check electrical wiring and extension cords -- don't overload cords or outlets. Make sure there are no exposed wires anywhere and make sure wiring doesn't touch home insulation.

<u>Use caution</u> - Never use gasoline or similar liquids indoors and never smoke around flammable liquids!

<u>Check heat sources</u> - Check furnaces, stoves, cracked or rusty furnace parts, and chimneys. Always be careful with space heaters and keep them at least 3 feet (1 m) away from flammable materials.

Know how to shut off power - Know where the circuit breaker box and gas valve is and how to turn them off, if necessary. (And always have a gas company rep turn on a main gas line.)

Install & learn A-B-C - Install A-B-C fire extinguishers in the home and teach family members how to use them. (A-B-C works on all types of fires and recommended for home - please read label.)

Call local fire - Ask local fire department if they will inspect your home or business for fire safety and prevention.

Teach kids - Explain to children that matches and lighters are TOOLS, not toys... and if they see someone playing with fire they should tell an adult right away! And teach them how to report a fire and when to call 9-1-1.

Prevent common fires - Pay attention when cooking & don't smoke in bed!

DURING A FIRE:

If only a small fire that's not spreading too fast ...

Try to put out...? - Use a fire extinguisher or water (unless it's an electrical or grease fire) ... and never try to put out a fire that's getting out of control!

- **electrical fire** - never use water… use a fire extinguisher approved for electrical fires
- **oil or grease fire in kitchen** - smother fire with baking soda or salt (or, if burning in pan or skillet, carefully put a lid over it -- but don't try to carry pan outside!)

If fire is spreading ...

GET OUT - DO NOT take time to try to grab anything except your family members! Once outside, do NOT try to go back in (even for pets) - let the firemen do it! Ask a neighbor to call fire department if not already called.

GET DOWN - Stay low to the ground under smoke by crawling on your hands and knees or squat down and walk like a duck… but keep moving to find a way out!

Closed door - Using the back of your hand (not your palm) always feel the top of the door, doorknob, and the crack between the door and door frame before you open a closed door!

- **if door is cool** - leave quickly, close door behind you and crawl to an exit
- **if door is hot** – DO NOT open it ... find another way out

No way out - If you can't find a way out of the room you're trapped in (door is hot and too high to jump) then hang a white or light-colored sheet, towel or shirt outside a window to alert firemen.

Use stairs - Never take the elevator during a fire ... always use stairs!

If YOU are on fire - If your clothes ever catch fire, **STOP** what you're doing, **DROP** to the ground, cover your face and **ROLL** until the fire goes out. Running only makes the fire burn faster!

Toxic gas - Plastics in household goods create deadly fumes when burned.

AFTER A FIRE:

Don't go in there - Never enter a fire-damaged building until officials say it's okay and watch for signs of smoke in case the fire isn't totally out. Even if a fire's out, hydrogen cyanide and other toxic fumes can remain.

Utilities - Have an electrician check your household wiring before you turn the power back on and DO NOT try to reconnect any utilities yourself!

Damage - Look for structural damage (roof, walls, floors, etc.) since they may be weak.

Call for help - Local disaster relief service (Red Cross, Salvation Army, etc.) can help provide shelter, food, or personal items that were destroyed.

Insurance - Call your insurance agent or representative and...
- Keep receipts of all clean-up and repair costs (for both insurance and income taxes).
- Do not throw away any damaged goods until an official inventory has been taken by your insurance company.

If you rent - Contact your landlord since it is the owner's responsibility to prevent further loss or damage to the site.

Move your stuff - Secure your personal belongings or move them to another location, if possible.

Recovery tips - Review TIPS ON RECOVERING FROM A DISASTER at end of this Section.

To learn more about fire safety and fire prevention visit the U.S. Fire Administration's web site www.usfa.dhs.gov or contact your local fire department, emergency official, or your insurance agent / representative.

Wildfires are intense fires that are usually caused by careless humans or lightning. Campfires, children playing with matches or lighters, and cigarettes are the most common things that cause brush fires or wildfires so please be careful when you're out in deserts, mountains, or any other heavy vegetation areas. And please don't toss cigarettes out when driving!

NEVER leave a campfire burning - make sure it is completely out using plenty of water before leaving the area. Stir the coals around with a stick or log while pouring water over them to ensure all the coals get wet and they are no longer hot. Any hot coals left unattended can be easily ignited by wind since they can stay hot for 24 - 48 hours.

When building a campfire, always choose a level site, clear away any branches and twigs several feet from the fire, and never build a fire beneath tree branches or on surface roots. Also, build at least 10 feet (3 m) from any large rocks that could be blackened by smoke or cracked from a fire's heat.

See your local Forest Service office or Ranger Station for more information on campfires and permits. Or visit www.fs.fed.us or www.pc.gc.ca

BEFORE A WILDFIRE (FIRE SAFETY TIPS):

Prepare - See WILDFIRE MITIGATION at beginning of this Section.

Learn fire laws - Ask fire authorities or the forestry office for information on fire laws (like techniques, safest times to burn in your area, etc.)

Could they find & reach you? - Make sure that fire vehicles can get to your property and that your address is clearly marked.

Safety zone - Create a 30-100 foot (9-30 m) safety zone around your home. *(see WILDFIRE MITIGATION)*

Teach kids - Explain to children that matches and lighters are TOOLS, not toys... and if they see someone playing with fire tell an adult right away. And teach kids how to report a fire and when to call 9-1-1.

Tell authorities - Report hazardous conditions that could cause a wildfire.

Be ready to evacuate - Listen to local authorities and leave if you are told to evacuate. *(see EVACUATION)*

DURING A WILDFIRE:

Listen - Have a radio to keep up on news, weather and evacuation routes.

<u>Evacuate?</u> – If you are told to leave - do so ... and <u>IF</u> you have time also…

- Secure your home - close windows, vents, all doors, etc.
- Turn off utilities and tanks at main switches or valves.
- Turn on a light in each room to increase the visibility of your home in heavy smoke.
- See WILDFIRE MITIGATION at front of this section.

<u>Head downhill</u> – Fire climbs uphill 16 times faster than on level terrain (since heat rises) so always head down when evacuating the area.

<u>Food & water</u> - If you prepared ahead, you'll have your **Disaster Supplies Kit** handy to **GRAB & GO**… if not, gather up enough food and water for each family member for at least 3 days or longer!

<u>Be understanding</u> - Please realize the firefighters main objective is getting wildfires under control and they may not be able to save every home. Try to understand and respect the firefighters' and local officials' decisions.

AFTER A WILDFIRE:

<u>Don't go there</u> - Never enter fire-damaged areas until authorities say it's okay and watch for signs of smoke or heat in case the fire isn't totally out.

<u>Critters</u> - Don't try to care for a wounded critter -- call Animal Control.

<u>Utilities</u> - Have an electrician check your household wiring before you turn the power back on and DO NOT try to reconnect any utilities yourself!

<u>Damage</u> - Look for structural damage (roof, walls, floors) -- may be weak.

<u>Call for help</u> - Local disaster relief services (Red Cross, Salvation Army, etc.) can help provide shelter, food, or personal items that were destroyed.

<u>Insurance</u> - Call your insurance agent or representative and…

- Keep receipts of all clean-up and repair costs
- Do not throw away any damaged goods until an official inventory has been taken by your insurance company.

<u>If you rent</u> - Contact your landlord since it is the owner's responsibility to prevent further loss or damage to the site.

<u>Move your stuff</u> - Secure belongings or move them to another location.

<u>Recovery tips</u> - See TIPS ON RECOVERING FROM A DISASTER.

What are <u>YOU</u> gonna do about...
A FLOOD?

Floods are the most common natural disaster. Some floods develop over a period of several days, but a flash flood can cause raging waters in just a few minutes. Mudflows are another danger triggered by flooding that can bury villages without warning, especially in mountainous regions.

Everyone is at risk from floods and flash floods, even in areas that seem harmless in dry weather. Always listen to the radio or TV to hear the latest updates. Some other types of radios are the NOAA Weather Radio and Environment Canada Weatheradio with battery backup and tone-alert feature that alert you when a Watch or Warning has been issued.

BEFORE A FLOOD (OR HEAVY RAIN):

<u>Prepare</u> - Review FLOOD MITIGATION at beginning of this Section.

<u>Learn the buzzwords</u> - Learn the terms / words used with floods...
- **Flood watch** - flooding is possible
- **Flash flood watch** - flash flooding is possible so move to higher ground if in a low-lying area
- **Flood warning** - flooding is occurring or will occur soon so listen to radio or TV for updates or evacuation alerts
- **Flash flood warning** - flash flood is occurring so seek higher ground on foot immediately
- **Urban and Small Stream Advisory** - flooding of small streams, streets and low-lying areas is occurring

<u>Learn risks</u> - Ask local emergency management office if your property is a flood-prone or high-risk area and what you can do to reduce risks to your property and home. Find out what official flood warning signals are and what to do when you hear them. Ask if there are dams or levees nearby and if they could be hazards. *(also see Landslides & Mudflows on pages 39-41.)*

<u>Be ready to evacuate</u> - Listen to local authorities and leave if you are told to evacuate. *(see EVACUATION)*

<u>Make a plan</u> - Review Section 1 to develop a **Family Emergency Plan** and **Disaster Supplies Kit**. And download Iowa Conservation and Preservation Consortium's "Flood Recovery Booklet" to learn how to dry materials like artwork, books, photographs, etc. at <u>www.iowaconserveandpreserve.org</u>

Learn to shut off - Know where and how to shut off electricity, gas and water at main switches and valves -- and ask local utilities for instructions.

Get insurance...? - Talk to your agent and find out more about the **National Flood Insurance Program**. *(see FLOOD MITIGATION)*

Did you know…

>   … you can buy federal flood insurance through most major insurance companies and licensed agents?!
>
>   … you do not have to own a home to have flood insurance as long as your community participates in the **NFIP**?!
>
>   … **NFIP** offers coverage even in flood-prone areas and offers basement and below ground level coverage?!

Put it on film/chip/drive - Either videotape or take pictures of home and personal belongings and store them in a safe place with important papers.

DURING A FLOOD (OR HEAVY RAIN):

Be aware - Listen to local news and watch for flash floods especially if near streams, drainage channels, and areas known to flood. Be prepared to fill and place sandbags in areas as instructed to help combat rising waters.

Get to higher ground - If in a low-lying area, move to higher ground.

Prepare to evacuate – *(see EVACUATION)*, and IF time also…

- Secure home and move important items to upper floors.
- Turn off utilities at main switches or valves if instructed by authorities and DO NOT touch electrical equipment if you are wet or standing in water!
- Fill up your car with fuel.

Obey warnings - If road signs, barricades, or cones are placed in areas - DO NOT drive around them! Find another way or you may get fined.

Things to avoid:
- **moving water** - 6 inches (15 cm) of moving water can knock you off your feet and 2 ft (0.6 m) can float a car
- **flooding car** - if flood waters rise around your car, get out and move to higher ground if you can do it safely
- **bad weather** - leave early enough so you're not trapped
- **flooded areas** - roadways and bridges may be washed-out
- **downed power lines** - extremely dangerous in floods!!

AFTER A FLOOD (OR HEAVY RAIN):

Things to avoid:

- **flood waters** - avoid since they may be contaminated by oil, gasoline or raw sewage or may be electrically charged from underground or downed power lines - local authorities will say when it's okay to return
- **moving water** - 6 inches (15 cm) can knock you off your feet and 2 ft (0.6 m) can float a car
- **flooded areas** - roadways and bridges may be washed-out
- **downed power lines** - extremely dangerous and report them to the power company

Obey warnings - If road signs, barricades, or cones are placed in areas - OBEY THEM! Most areas fine people who ignore posted warnings. DO NOT drive around barricades... find another way to get there!

Strange critters - Watch out for snakes and other wildlife in areas that were flooded. Don't try to care for a wounded critter since it may try to attack you... call your local animal control office or animal shelter.

Flooded food - Throw away food that has come into contact with flood waters since eating it can make you sick.

Drinking water - Wait for officials to advise when water is safe to drink. If you have a well that gets contaminated, find another source or boil water.

Wash your hands - Wash hands often with clean water and soap since flood waters are dirty and full of germs!

Use bleach – The best thing to use for cleaning up flooded areas is household bleach since it helps kill germs.

Sandbags - If any sandbags come into contact with floodwaters, wear rubber gloves when removing them and follow officials' instructions on where to discard them since they're most likely contaminated.

Listen - Continue listening to radio or TV for updates on weather and tips on getting assistance for housing, clothing, food, etc.

Insurance - Call your insurance agent or representative to discuss claims.

Mold - Consider asking a restoration professional to inspect your house for mold. *(see AIR QUALITY MITIGATION)*

Recovery tips - See TIPS ON RECOVERING FROM A DISASTER.

What are <u>YOU</u> gonna do about...
HAILSTORMS?

Hail is the largest form of precipitation that begins as tiny ice pellets and grows by colliding with supercooled water droplets as it gets tossed around violently in strong updraft winds. As the pellet continues to be tossed, it builds layer by layer until it becomes so heavy that it drops out of the sky as hailstones.

Hailstone diameters can range from 1/16 of an inch to 5 inches (2 mm to 13 mm) - basically meaning they can range in size from tiny pebbles to golf balls to softballs. One of the largest hailstones ever recorded in the U.S. weighed 1 pound 15 ounces and had a 18.62 inch (47 cm) circumference.

Hail is usually present in powerful storms like tornadoes, thunderstorms and even some winter storms mainly due to the strong winds and rapidly rising air masses needed to form hailstones.

The U.S. averages about 3,000 hailstorms each year across the country and a majority of the storms occur between March and June. Hail occurs all across Canada but more frequently in the Canadian Prairies (particularly the Calgary-Medicine Hat area). This region can expect up to 10 hailstorms a year and most damaging hailstorms generally occur from May to October.

BEFORE A HAILSTORM:

Since hailstorms are pretty localized events, it is difficult to prepare for "hail", however please review the other topics that create hailstorms (Thunderstorms, Tornadoes and Winter storms) to learn what to do and how to protect yourselves during these events.

<u>Listen</u> - Keep up on local radio or TV weather forecasts and updates.

<u>Park it</u> - If possible, secure vehicles in a garage or under substantial cover.

<u>Bring 'em in</u> - Put pets and livestock in a shelter for their safety.

<u>Stay put</u> - Stay inside until the entire storm system passes.

DURING A HAILSTORM:

<u>Listen</u> - Keep radio or TV tuned in for more information and updates on weather conditions and other types of warnings.

IF INDOORS - Stay inside until the storm passes and don't try to go out and protect your property.

IF OUTDOORS - Take shelter under the strongest structure you can find (especially if hailstones are large!)

IF IN A VEHICLE - Carefully pull over to the shoulder and seek shelter under an overpass or the closest substantial structure available.

AFTER A HAILSTORM:

<u>Listen</u> - Continue listening to radio or TV for updates on weather.

<u>Check it out</u> - Check for damage to trees and shrubs because, if damaged, your roof most likely is too. Also check your vehicles and structures for damage but don't put yourself in danger if storms are still active!

<u>Stop leaks</u> - Cover up holes in your roof and broken windows in your car and home to keep water out.

<u>Insurance</u> - Call your insurance agent or representative to set up a visit to your home or to take your vehicle down for inspection.

<u>Recovery tips</u> - Review TIPS ON RECOVERING FROM A DISASTER at end of this Section.

What are <u>YOU</u> gonna do about...
HAZARDOUS MATERIALS?

Chemical plants are one source of hazardous materials, but there are many others that exist in large industry, small businesses, and homes. There are about 500,000 products that could pose a physical or health hazard -- things ranging from waste produced by a petroleum refinery to materials used by the dry cleaners to pesticides stored in your home.

Most hazardous materials are transported around the country by road, rail and through pipelines potentially causing spills on highways, near railroad tracks or underground. Many U.S. communities have a **Local Emergency Planning Committee (LEPC)** that keeps local planners, companies and members of the community informed of potential risks. All companies that have hazardous chemicals must report to the LEPC every year and the public is encouraged to get involved. We [the public] should all learn more about hazardous materials and how they can affect our lives so contact your emergency management office to learn more.

We're going to cover two topics here -- **HAZARDOUS MATERIALS DISASTER** (where a spill or incident affects an area or community) and **HOUSEHOLD CHEMICAL EMERGENCIES** (how to handle products and react if there's an emergency in the home). Also, please review the **TERRORISM** topic since it covers several chemical and biological agents that are also classed as "hazardous materials".

BEFORE A HAZARDOUS MATERIALS DISASTER:

<u>Learn the buzzwords</u> - Ask your local officials about emergency warning procedures and terms...

- **Outdoor warning sirens or horns** - ask what they mean and what to listen for
- **Emergency Alert System (EAS)** - information and alerts via TV and radio
- **"All-call" telephoning** - an automated system for sending recorded messages via telephone
- **Residential route alerting** - messages announced from vehicles equipped with public address systems (loud speakers on top of car or van)

<u>Learn risks</u> - Ask Local Emergency Planning Committee (LEPC), Emergency Management Office, or Fire Department about community plans for responding to a hazardous materials accident at a plant or a

transportation accident involving hazardous materials. Ask about the Emergency Planning and Community Right To Know Act (or EPCRA) and help your community become better informed.

Make a plan - Use LEPC's or agency's information to determine if your family is at risk (especially people living close to freeways, railroads, or factories which produce or transport toxic waste). And review Section 1 to develop a **Family Emergency Plan** and **Disaster Supplies Kit**.

Take a tour - LEPCs sometimes visit facilities that produce or transport toxic waste and include community groups, local officials and the media.

Pick a room - It could take authorities time to determine what the hazardous material is (if any) so pick a room in advance that your family could use as "shelter-in-place" if told to stay indoors for several hours. It's best to pick an internal room where you could block out air, if instructed to do so. To save critical time consider measuring and cutting plastic sheets in advance for each opening (vents, windows, and doors). Remember, toilets / drains are vented meaning outside air comes in constantly or when flushed / open (depends on design) - in case using bathroom as safe room.

Calculate air for room - Keep in mind people can stay in a sealed off room for only so long (or you'll run out of air.) FEMA suggests 10 square feet of floor space per person (like 5ft x 2ft / 1.5m x 0.6m) will provide enough air to prevent carbon dioxide buildup for up to 5 hours.

Be ready to evacuate - Listen to local authorities and leave if you are told to evacuate. *(see EVACUATION)*

DURING A HAZARDOUS MATERIALS DISASTER:

Call for help - If you see a hazardous materials accident, call 9-1-1, local emergency number, or the fire department.

Listen - Keep radio or TV tuned in for more information, especially if you hear a warning signal... and stay calm!

IF INDOORS – If instructed to stay inside, prepare to "shelter-in-place"...
- Close windows, vents, and fireplace dampers and turn off A/C or heat and fans to reduce air drawn in from outside.
- Keep a radio with you at all times.
- Grab **Disaster Supplies Kit** and get to a closed off room.
- Seal gaps under doorways and windows with wet towels or plastic and duct tape (see above tips on picking a room and calculating air!)

IF OUTDOORS - Stay upstream, uphill, or upwind from the disaster since hazardous materials can be carried by wind and water quickly. Try to get at least 1/2 mile or kilometer away or as far away as possible!

IF IN A VEHICLE - Close your windows and shut off vents to reduce risk.

Stay away - Get away from the accident site to avoid contamination.

Evacuate...? - If told to leave… DO it! If officials say you have time, close windows, shut vents and turn off attic fans. *(see EVACUATION)*

What to wear - Keep your body fully covered and wear gloves, socks and shoes. (Even though these may not keep you totally safe, it can help.)

Things to avoid:
- **chemicals** - spilled liquid materials or airborne mists
- **contaminated food or water** - don't eat or drink food or water that may have been exposed to hazardous materials

AFTER A HAZARDOUS MATERIALS DISASTER:

Don't go there - Do not return home until local authorities say it is safe.

Air out - Open windows, vents and turn on fans in your home.

Listen - Keep up with local reports from either the radio or TV.

Clean up - A person, critter or item that has been exposed to a hazardous chemical could spread it.
- **decontamination** - follow instructions from local authorities since it depends on the chemical. May need to rinse off or may be told to stay away from water - check first!
- **strange symptoms** - if unusual symptoms show up, get to a hospital or medical expert right away. Remove contaminated clothing and put on fresh, loose, warm clothing and listen to local reports on the radio.
- **store clothes & shoes** - put exposed clothing and shoes in tightly sealed containers/bags without touching other materials and ask local authorities how to get rid of them
- **tell people you've been exposed** - tell everyone who comes in contact with you that you may have been exposed to a toxic substance
- **land and property** - ask authorities how to clean area

Strange vapors or danger - Report any strange vapors or other dangers to the local authorities immediately.

To learn more about hazardous materials, check out the Programs under the U.S. Environmental Protection Agency's Office of Emergency Management at www.epa.gov/emergencies ... or visit the U.S. Department of Transportation's Office of Hazardous Materials Safety at http://hazmat.dot.gov/

Or visit Environment Canada at www.ec.gc.ca ... or the Canadian Transport Emergency Centre of the Department of Transport at www.tc.gc.ca/canutec/

BEFORE A HOUSEHOLD CHEMICAL EMERGENCY:

Learn risks - Call your local public health department or the Environmental Protection Agency for information about hazardous household materials. And check out the National Library of Medicine's Household Products Database that provides information on over 8,000 common household products and their potential health effects at http://householdproducts.nlm.nih.gov/

Read labels - Always read product labels for proper use, safe storage and disposal of chemicals.

Recycle it? - Call your local recycling center or collection site to ask what chemicals can be recycled or dropped off for disposal -- many centers take things like car batteries, oil, tires, paint or thinners, etc.

Store it - Keep all chemicals and household cleaners in safe, secure locations out of reach of small children.

Put it out - Don't smoke while using household chemicals.

DURING A HOUSEHOLD CHEMICAL EMERGENCY:

Call for help - Call your local Poison Control Center (or 1-800-222-1222), 9-1-1, fire department, hospital or emergency medical services. If possible, have container handy since medical professionals may need specific data from label.

First aid tips - Follow instructions on label and see Basic First Aid tips for POISONING in Section 3.

What are YOU gonna do about...
HURRICANES, CYCLONES & TYPHOONS?

Hurricane season in North America is generally between June and November. Hurricanes are tropical cyclones with torrential rains and winds of 74 - 155 miles per hour (120 - 250 km/h) or faster. These winds blow in a counter-clockwise direction (or clockwise in the Southern Hemisphere) around a center "eye". The "eye" is usually 20 to 30 miles (32 to 48 km) wide, and the storm may be spread out as far as 400 miles (640 km)!

As the hurricane approaches the coast, a huge dome of water (called a storm surge) will crash into the coastline. Nine out of ten people killed in hurricanes are victims of storm surge. Hurricanes can also cause tornadoes, heavy rains and flooding.

What's with all the different names?

You may have heard different words used to describe storms depending on where you live in the world. It's a little confusing but hopefully this explains the various names.

Cyclone - an atmospheric disturbance with masses of air rapidly rotating around a low-pressure center... (sort of like a dust devil or a tornado)

Tropical Depression - maximum surface winds of less than 39 miles per hour (62 km/h) over tropical or sub-tropical waters with storms and circular winds

Tropical Storm - a tropical cyclone is labeled a Tropical Storm if winds are between 39-73 mph (62 - 117 km/h) and given a name to track it

Hurricane, Typhoon, Tropical cyclone - surface winds are higher than 74 mph (120 km/h)... and depending on where it is happening will determine what it is called

Where in the world do they use these names?

(Please note: We are only listing a few major countries or areas for each name.)

Cyclone - used in several parts of the world - **Indian Ocean, Australia, Africa, SW and southern Pacific Ocean**

Hurricane - used in North Atlantic Ocean, Northeast Pacific Ocean (east of the dateline), or South Pacific Ocean (east of 160) - **both coasts of North America, Puerto Rico, Caribbean Islands, and Central America**

<u>Typhoon</u> - used in Northwest Pacific Ocean west of the dateline - **Guam, Marshall Islands, Japan, Philippines, Hong Kong, coastal Asia**

<u>Tropical cyclone</u> - used in Southwest Pacific Ocean west of 160E or most of Indian Ocean - **Australia, Indonesia, Africa, Middle East**

Hurricanes are classed into five categories based on wind speeds, central pressure, and damage potential. The chart below is the Saffir-Simpson Hurricane Wind Scale with examples of damage provided by NOAA:

Scale # (Category)	Sustained Winds	Wind Damage (examples of potential damage)
1	74-95 mph 119-153 km/h	Dangerous winds will produce some damage (Untied mobile homes, vegetation & signs)
2	96-110 mph 154-177 km/h	Extremely dangerous winds/extensive damage (All mobile homes, roofs, small crafts, floods)
3	111-129 mph 178-208 km/h	Devastating damage will occur (Small buildings, low-lying roads cut off)
4	130-156 mph 209-251 km/h	Catastrophic damage will occur (Roofs and mobile homes destroyed, trees down, beach homes flooded)
5	> 156 mph > 251 km/h	Catastrophic damage will occur (Most bldgs and vegetation destroyed, major roads cut off, homes flooded)

BEFORE A HURRICANE:

<u>Prepare</u> - Review FLOOD, LIGHTNING, POWER LOSS and WIND MITIGATION at beginning of this Section.

<u>Learn the buzzwords</u> - Learn the terms / words used with hurricanes...

- **Hurricane/Tropical Storm Watch** - hurricane/tropical storm is possible within 48 hours so listen to TV and radio updates
- **Hurricane/Tropical Storm Warning** - hurricane/tropical storm is expected within 36 hours -- may be told to evacuate (if so, do it) and listen to radio or TV for updates
- **Short term Watches and Warnings** - warnings provide detailed information on specific hurricane threats (like flash floods and tornadoes)
- **Storm surge** - large dome of water formed as the winds push water towards the shore. Surges can be up to 20 feet (6 meters) tall and 50 to 100 miles (80-160 km) wide.

- **Eye wall** - area that circles the eye of the storm and contains the most damaging winds and heaviest rains
- **Outer bands** - the outer rings or bands of thunderstorms that make landfall first

Listen - Keep local radio or TV tuned in for weather forecasts and updates. (Some other radios to consider are Environment Canada's Weatheradio and NOAA's Weather Radio with battery backup and tone-alert feature that automatically alert you when a Watch or Warning has been issued.)

Be ready to evacuate - Listen to local authorities and leave if you are told to evacuate. *(see EVACUATION)*

Pets & large animals - Make arrangements for pets since shelters may not allow them. If you have horses or livestock, make a plan for an alternate site in case they must be evacuated. *(see tips on page 11 and in EVACUATION)*

Make a plan - Review Section 1 to develop a **Family Emergency Plan** and **Disaster Supplies Kit**.

Learn to shut off - Know where and how to shut off electricity, gas and water at main switches and valves -- ask local utilities for instructions.

Batten down - Make plans to protect your property with storm shutters or board up windows with plywood that is measured to fit your windows. Tape does not prevent windows from breaking. *(see WIND MITIGATION)*

Get insurance...? - Talk to your agent and find out more about the **National Flood Insurance Program**. *(see FLOOD MITIGATION)*

Put it on film/chip/drive - Either videotape or take pictures of home and personal belongings and store them in a safe place (like a fireproof box or a safety deposit box) along with important papers.

DURING A HURRICANE THREAT:

Listen - Have a battery-operated radio available to keep up on news reports, tornado warnings and evacuation routes.

Evacuate? – If you are told to leave - do it! *(see EVACUATION)* And if you have time also…
- Secure your home - close storm shutters or put up boards on windows, moor your boat, and secure outdoor objects or put them inside since winds will blow them around.
- Turn off utilities at main switches or valves, if instructed.

- Fill up your car with fuel.
- Make arrangements for pets in case you can't take them with you.

<u>Food & water</u> - If you prepared ahead, you'll have your **Disaster Supplies Kit** handy to GRAB & GO... if not, gather up enough food and water for each family member for at least 3 days!

IF INDOORS – Stay inside!
- Find a SAFE SPOT - get to small interior room, closet or hallway ... or lie on the floor under a heavy desk or table.
- Move away from windows and glass doors.

IF IN A MULTI-STORY BUILDING – Go to the first or second floor!
- Find a SAFE SPOT - get to a small interior room or hallway ... or lie on the floor under a heavy desk or table.
- Move away from outside walls and windows.
- Realize electricity may go out and alarms and sprinkler systems may go on.

<u>Things to avoid</u>:
- **moving water** - 6 inches (15 cm) can knock you off your feet and 2 ft (0.6 m) can float a car
- **flooding car** - if flood waters rise around your car, get out and move to higher ground if you can safely
- **bad weather** - leave early enough so you are not trapped
- **flooded areas** - roadways and bridges may be washed-out
- **downed power lines** - extremely dangerous in floods!!

<u>Stay indoors</u> - If you do not evacuate, stay indoors and stay away from glass doors and windows. Keep curtains and blinds closed and remember, a lull in the storm could only be the middle of the storm (the "eye") and winds can start again. Keep listening to radio or TV reports.

<u>Nasty weather</u> - Be aware of other hazards like high winds, heavy rain, flooding and tornadoes. And realize weather can move hundreds of miles into the mainland too.

<u>Right front quadrant</u> - The northeast part or right front quadrant of a hurricane typically has the strongest winds and highest storm surge. If it's a high tide when the storm slams ashore you could have serious problems.

<u>Limit phone calls</u> - Only use phones in an emergency so it keeps lines open for local authorities.

AFTER A HURRICANE:

Stay put - Stay where you are (if you're in a safe location) and don't return home (if you've been evacuated) until local authorities say it's okay. Realize it may take weeks, months or years before some areas will be classed as "safe" due to health hazards or massive destruction from the storm.

Listen - Continue listening to your battery-powered radio for updates on weather and tips on getting assistance for housing, clothing, food, etc.

Stick together - Keep family together since this is a very stressful time. Try to find chores for children so they feel they're helping with the situation.

Things to avoid:

- **flood waters** - stay away from flood waters since it may be contaminated by oil, gasoline or raw sewage or may be electrically charged from underground or downed power lines - wait for local authorities to approve returning to flooded areas
- **moving water** - 6 inches (15 cm) can knock you off your feet and 2 ft (0.6 m) can float a car
- **flooded areas** - roadways and bridges may be washed-out or weakened
- **downed power lines** - extremely dangerous and report them to power company

Things to watch out for:

- **weak structures** - be careful since buildings and homes could have been weakened by wind or floods
- **looting, guns and panicked people** - be aware people may become violent trying to find loved ones, water or food (or there may be criminals and jerks out stealing whatever they can)
- **bodies** - strong storm surges, floods, and high winds may cause deaths so be aware there may be dead human and animal carcasses scattered around

Drinking water - Use bottled water or purify water until officials advise it is okay to drink out of the tap. *(see TIPS ON WATER PURIFICATION)*

Flooded food - Throw away any food that has come into contact with flood waters since eating it can make you sick!

Wash your hands - Use **clean** water and soap when washing hands.

<u>Use bleach</u> – The best thing to use for cleaning up flooded areas is house-hold bleach since it will help kill germs.

<u>Insurance</u> - Call your insurance agent to set up a visit to your home.

<u>Mold</u> - Consider asking a restoration professional to inspect your house for mold. *(see AIR QUALITY MITIGATION)*

<u>No power?</u> - If you use a generator, keep it outside and follow the manufac-turer's instructions. *(see some safety tips in POWER LOSS MITIGATION)*

<u>Donations</u> – Lots of people want to help victims of a hurricane and here are some tips...

- **wait & see** - don't donate food, clothing or personal items unless they are specifically requested
- **money** - donations to a known disaster relief group, like the Red Cross, Salvation Army, churches, etc. is always helpful
- **volunteers** - if local authorities ask for your help, bring your own water, food and sleeping gear

<u>Recovery tips</u> - Review TIPS ON RECOVERING FROM A DISASTER at end of this Section.

What are YOU gonna do about...
A NUCLEAR POWER PLANT EMERGENCY?

Please note: Nukes [nuclear devices] and dirty bombs [radiological dispersion devices or RDDs] are both covered in the next topic called TERRORISM, but review next several pages before moving on.

The World Nuclear Association reports as of December 2010 there are 441 commercial nuclear power reactors in 30 countries with 537 more reactors under construction or planned. The U.S. has over 100 commercial power plants and Canada has 20 power stations meaning millions of citizens live within 10 miles (16 km) of an operating reactor. And WNA reports there are 280 research reactors (54 in the U.S.) mainly on university campuses.

Even though governments and associations monitor and regulate construction and operation of plants, accidents are possible and do happen. An accident could result in dangerous levels of radiation that could affect the health and safety of the public living near a nuclear power plant, as well as people many miles away depending on winds and weather - so millions of North Americans could potentially be affected.

Some other incidents involving possible radiation exposure may be a nuclear missile or suitcase nuke (plutonium creates massive energy and destruction) or a "dirty bomb". (Again, these are covered in TERRORISM.)

How is radiation detected?
You cannot see, feel, taste or smell radiation, but special instruments can detect even the smallest levels of it. If radiation is released, authorities will monitor levels of radioactivity to determine the potential danger so they can alert and protect the public. *Learn about detection devices on page 112.*

What is best way to reduce radiation exposure?
Limit the amount of radiation you are exposed to by doing 3 things ...

Distance - The more distance between you and the source of radiation, the less you'll receive. During a serious accident you may be told to evacuate.

Shielding - Heavy, dense materials between you and radiation is best - this is why you want to stay indoors since the walls in your home should be good enough to protect you in some cases... but listen to radio and TV to learn if you need to evacuate.

Time - Most radioactivity loses its strength rather quickly. Limiting your time near the source of radiation reduces the amount you receive.

What is the most dangerous part of a nuclear accident?

Radioactive iodine - nuclear reactors contain many different radioactive products, but a dangerous one is radioactive iodine which, once absorbed, can damage cells of the thyroid gland. The greatest population that suffers in a nuclear accident is **children** (including unborn babies) since their thyroid is so active, but all people are at risk of absorbing radioactive iodine.

How can I be protected from radioactive iodine?

Potassium iodide (KI) - can be purchased over-the-counter now (usually from companies selling disaster-related kits) and is known to be an effective thyroid-blocking agent. In other words, it fills up the thyroid with good iodine that keeps radioactive iodine from being absorbed into our bodies.

What if I am allergic to iodine?

According to the United States Nuclear Regulatory Commission Office of Nuclear Material Safety and Safeguards, the FDA suggests that risks of allergic reaction to potassium iodide are minimal compared to subjecting yourself to cancer from radioactive iodine. Ask your doctor or pharmacist what you should keep on hand in the event of an allergic reaction.

Many European countries stockpile potassium iodide (KI), especially since the Chernobyl incident. Several states are considering or already have stockpiles of KI ready in case of an accident or incident.

As of 2005, the FDA has approved 3 KI products - Iosat, ThyroSafe, and ThyroShield. Learn more at www.fda.gov (do a search on KI) or www.bt.cdc.gov/radiation/ki.asp. In an emergency, other options may be taking KIO3, applying iodine solution to your skin, or taking kelp or seaweed pills.

Community Planning for Emergencies (U.S. and Canada)

Local, state and provincial governments, Federal agencies and utilities have developed emergency response plans in the event of a nuclear power plant accident.

United States' plans define 2 "emergency planning zones" (EPZs)

- **Plume Exposure EPZ** - a 10-mile radius from nuclear plant where people may be harmed by radiation exposure
  NOTE: People within a 10-mile radius are given emergency information about radiation, evacuation routes, special arrangements for handicapped, etc. via brochures, phone books, and utility bills.

- **Ingestion Exposure EPZ** - about a 50-mile radius from plant where accidentally released radioactive materials could contaminate water supplies, food crops and livestock

Canada's Provincial Nuclear Emergency Response Plans define 3 "zones"

- **Contiguous Zone** - approximately 3 kilometres from nuclear facility where evacuation and sheltering may be ordered

- **Primary Zone** - approximately 10 kilometres from the nuclear facility where evacuation and sheltering may be ordered

- **Secondary Zone** - approximately 50 kilometres from the nuclear facility where radioactive contamination could cause monitoring and/or bans on some food and water sources
  NOTE: Public Education brochures are available to residents and businesses within the Primary Zone (10 km) of each nuclear facility.

BEFORE A NUCLEAR POWER PLANT EMERGENCY:

Learn the buzzwords - Know terms used in both countries to describe a nuclear emergency at a plant: **U.S.** / **(Canada)**...

- **Notification of Unusual Event / (Reportable Event)** - a small problem has occurred. No radiation leak is expected. Federal, state/provincial and county/municipal officials will be told right away. No action on your part will be necessary.

- **Alert / (Abnormal Incident)** - a small problem has occurred, and small amounts of radiation could leak inside plant. This will not affect you and you shouldn't have to do anything.

- **Site Area Emergency / (Onsite Emergency)** - a more serious problem... small amounts of radiation could leak from the plant. If necessary, officials will act to ensure public safety. Area sirens may be sounded and listen to your radio or TV for information.

- **General Emergency / (General Emergency)** - the MOST serious problem... radiation could leak outside the plant and off the plant site. In most cases sirens will sound so listen to local radio or TV for reports and updates. State/Provincial and county/municipal officials will act to assure public safety and be prepared to follow their instructions!

Learn signals - Ask about your community's warning system and pay attention to "test" dates to learn if you can HEAR it. Nuclear power plants are required to install sirens and other warning devices to cover a 10-mile area around the plant in the U.S. (If you live outside the 10-mile area you will probably learn of the event through local TV and radio, but just be aware winds and weather can impact areas as far as 200 miles [320 km] away!!)

Learn risks - Ask the company operating the plant for brochures and data.

<u>Make a plan</u> - Review Section 1 to develop a **Family Emergency Plan** and **Disaster Supplies Kit**. Double check on emergency plans for schools, day cares or places family may be and where they'll go if evacuated. And <u>please</u> review the Nuclear section in TERRORISM topic to learn more about long-term sheltering, protection from fallout, radiation detection devices, etc.

<u>Go?</u> - Listen to authorities and leave if told to go. *(see EVACUATION)*

DURING A NUCLEAR POWER PLANT EMERGENCY:

<u>Stay calm</u> - Not all accidents release radiation - may be contained in plant.

<u>Listen</u> - Turn on radio or TV. Authorities will give specific instructions and information... pay attention to what THEY tell you rather than what is written in this Manual since they know the facts for each specific incident.

<u>Stay or go..?</u> - Evacuate if told to do so by local authorities ... and ...
- Grab your **Disaster Supplies Kit**.
- Close doors, windows and fireplace damper.
- Cover your mouth and nose with face mask or cloth.
- Close car windows and vents and use "re-circulating" air.
- Keep listening to radio for evacuation routes & updates.

As long as you are NOT told to evacuate, do the following...

IF INDOORS - Stay inside and prepare to "shelter-in-place"...
- Close doors and windows and your fireplace damper.
- Turn off air conditioner, ventilation fans, furnace and other intakes (they pull in air from outside).
- Go to a basement or underground area (if possible).
- Keep a battery-operated radio with you to hear updates.
- Stay inside until authorities tell you it is safe to go out!

IF OUTDOORS - Get indoors as soon as possible!
- Cover mouth and nose with a cloth or napkins and find shelter.
- Once inside, remove clothing, shower & wash hair and put on fresh clothing and different shoes. Put clothes and shoes you were wearing in plastic bags, seal and store. Local authorities can tell you what to do with bags.

IF IN A VEHICLE - Keep windows up, close vents, use "recirculating" air and keep listening to radio for updates. If possible, drive away from site.

Pets & livestock - Get them in shelters with clean food and water that has not been exposed to air-borne radiation, especially milk-producing animals.

Food - Put food in covered containers or in refrigerator -- any food that was not in a covered container should be washed first.

Take potassium iodide..? - IF radioactive iodine has been released into the air from a power plant accident, some states *may* decide to provide KI pills mentioned at beginning of this topic to people in a 10-mile radius.

(In June 2002 President George W. Bush signed a provision that gave state and local governments supplies of potassium iodide for people within 20 miles of a nuclear power plant, increasing protection beyond the Nuclear Regulatory Commission's current 10-mile radius.[5] This is at the option of state and local government and realize it will take time for them to disperse to citizens ... unless you prepare in advance and keep KI handy.)

NOTE: Take KI pills ONLY as directed by local public health authorities and follow instructions on the package exactly! (see page 73)

AFTER A NUCLEAR POWER PLANT EMERGENCY:

Listen - Keep radio and TV tuned in -- stay in until authorities say all clear.

Clean up - If you were possibly exposed to radiation...

- **store clothes & shoes** - put clothing and shoes in tightly sealed containers or plastic bags and ask health officials what to do with them
- **shower** - wash your body and hair to remove radioactive particles
- **land and property** - ask authorities how to clean up area

Weird symptoms - Seek medical attention if you have symptoms like upset stomach or feel queasy after a reported incident since it could be related to radiation exposure. *(see page 114 for more about radiation sickness)*

Gardens & crops – Authorities will provide information concerning safety of farm and homegrown products -- or check with agricultural extension agent. Unharvested crops are hard to protect but crops that are already harvested should be stored inside, if possible.

Milk - Local officials should inspect cows' and goats' milk before using.

Recovery tips - Review TIPS ON RECOVERING FROM A DISASTER

More tips - See TERRORISM for more information about a nuke crisis.

What are <u>YOU</u> gonna do about...
TERRORISM?

Terrorism is the use of force or violence against persons or property usually for emotional or political reasons or for ransom. The main goal of terrorists is to create public fear and panic.

Obviously there is a lot of anxiety since the September 11, 2001 attacks on the U.S., however, being afraid or worrying is very unhealthy - especially about something you have little control over. But remember, terrorist attacks are a very <u>low risk</u> possibility.

Let's put a few "risks" in perspective ... the chances of having high blood pressure is 1 in 4 ... the odds of dying from cancer is 1 in 500 ... and the odds of dying from anthrax is 1 in 56 <u>million</u>!

People need to remain calm about the threat of terrorist attacks and learn about some of the types, how to prepare for them, and what to expect in some cases. Discuss this with everyone - even the kids so they can talk about their feelings too. Stay current on news but don't obsess over it ... and just be aware of your surroundings as you go about your daily routines.

One type of terrorism that we can help prevent is the use of guns and bombs by children and youth against other groups of children at schools. A key solution to stopping this type of school violence is through communication, education and awareness – and it starts within <u>the FAMILY</u>! *(see also APPENDIX C - SCHOOL SAFETY RESOURCES)*

The Federal Bureau of Investigation categorizes terrorism in two ways:

<u>Domestic terrorism</u> - terrorist activities are directed at certain groups or parts of the government within the U.S. without foreign direction.

> Some examples of domestic terrorism include shootings and bomb threats at schools, the Oklahoma City bombing of the Federal Building, and the letters mailed to various groups with a white powdery substance (anthrax scares).

<u>International terrorism</u> - terrorist activities are foreign-based by countries or groups outside the U.S.

> Some examples of international terrorism include bombings like the U.S.S. Cole in Yemen and U.S. Embassies in other countries, the attacks on the Pentagon and World Trade Center, hostage situations with civilians in various countries, or threats with weapons of mass destruction.

Until recently, most terrorist attacks involved bombs, guns, kidnappings and hijackings, but some other forms of terrorism involve cyber attacks or CBRN (chemical or biological agents, radiological or nuclear devices).

Cyber attacks - computer-based attacks from individuals, networking groups, terrorist groups or nations causing severe problems for government, businesses and public in general (sometimes causing or leading to injury and death)

Chemical agents - poisonous vapors, liquids or solids that can kill or slow down or weaken people, destroy livestock or crops -- can be absorbed through the skin, swallowed or inhaled

Biological agents - infectious microbes (tiny life forms), germs or other substances that occur naturally or are "designed" to produce illness or death in people, animals or plants -- can be inhaled, enter through a cut in the skin, or swallowed when eating or drinking

Radiological threat or device - a "dirty bomb" or RDD uses conventional explosives to spread radioactive materials over a general or targeted area

Nuclear device - a bomb or missile using weapons grade uranium or plutonium -- requires long-term sheltering from the deadly fallout. And devices can range in size and yield from suitcase-sized nukes to Intercontinental ballistic missiles (ICBMs).

Terrorism is quite an extensive topic now -- below we are listing some basic things to do before ANY type of terrorist attack followed by several pages explaining the **National Terrorism Advisory System** (NTAS).

Then we will cover specific types of potential terrorist attacks shown above in red - including what to do BEFORE, DURING and AFTER each and where to find more information. We also threw in some tips for handling "bomb threats" or "suspicious packages" and suggest some sheltering and shielding tips in the event of a nuclear crisis.

Keep in mind, the best thing you can do about terrorism is prepare yourself and your family for the unexpected, so please review this entire topic. By learning about potential threats, we are all better prepared to know how to react if the unthinkable happens.

Americans are very fortunate since we have a strong, talented network of First Responders who rapidly respond to threats and incidents.

But let's look at some statistics. The U.S. has approximately 800,000 active Law Enforcement Officials (includes Police & Sheriff), 1.1 million

Firefighters (over 70% are volunteers) and 210,000 EMT / paramedics.

That means there are about **2.1 million** First Responders supporting over **300 million** people..!

And there are millions of active military personnel, Federal agents and observant citizens you could add to the mix ... but the numbers of eyes and ears could increase exponentially if more people would pay attention

BEFORE <u>ANY</u> TYPE OF TERRORIST ATTACK:

<u>Be alert</u> - You should always be aware of your surroundings and report any suspicious activities to local authorities.

<u>Be vigilant</u> - Dictionary.com defines vigilant as "keeping careful watch for possible danger or difficulties". It also is defined as "watchful, alert, observant, guarded, attentive, awake, cautious, careful, wary, on the alert, on the lookout" ... among other things. We are not implying you become a snitch or panicked, but just be aware of your surroundings as you go through your day to day activities. Some things you can do to be more vigilant include...

- **Stay calm** - As mentioned at the beginning of this topic, terrorist attacks are a very low risk possibility so there is no need to worry or panic.

- **Be aware & watch** - Stay current on news, alerts and threats – but don't obsess over them – then start making a habit of being aware of your surroundings. You don't have to be paranoid or obvious – just watch for things that look strange or out of place especially if you walk or drive the same route day after day.

- **If you see something, say something**™ - This program is spreading across the nation, and it's a good suggestion. We are not implying you spy on your neighbors, but as you go about your day, watch for suspicious activities -- like someone wearing a heavy coat on a hot day or unattended bags, briefcases or backpacks in odd places -- and report anything that seems out of the ordinary. It may be completely harmless ... but it might not. Many crimes and plots have been thwarted by citizens who saw something weird and reported it to officials.

- **Know the targets** - Terrorists prefer areas that are easy to access by the public like airports, train or bus stations, military and government buildings, major events, schools, malls, etc. Some other high risk targets include water and food supplies, nuclear power plants, and high-profile landmarks. When you are at these types of facilities, try to pay more attention to activities going on around you.

- **Get involved** - Talk to your local Fire, Police, Health, Sheriff and Emergency Management offices and ask if they have volunteer programs available for citizens and businesses. *(Learn about Citizen Corps or CERT on pages 222-224)* Some agencies even have safety classes and programs for youth and children too.

Stay current on threats - Both U.S. Department of Homeland Security www.dhs.gov and Public Safety Canada www.publicsafety.gc.ca post alerts online.

Things to watch out for:
- **unknown packages** - DO NOT accept a package or case from a stranger
- **unattended bags** - report unattended bags or backpacks to authorities and don't ask strangers to watch your stuff or leave bags or purses alone (esp. when traveling)
- **emergency exits** - always be aware of where EXITS are... just casually look around for signs since most are marked well in public places

Make a plan - Review Section 1 to develop a **Family Emergency Plan** and **Disaster Supplies Kit**. And Appendix B has plans and suggestions for businesses.

ABOUT THE NATIONAL TERRORISM ADVISORY SYSTEM

The National Terrorism Advisory System, or NTAS, replaced the color-coded Homeland Security Advisory System (HSAS) as of 2011. NTAS will more effectively communicate information about terrorist threats by providing timely, detailed information to the public, government agencies, first responders, airports and other transportation hubs, and the private sector.

It recognizes that Americans all share responsibility for the nation's security, and should always be aware of the heightened risk of terrorist attack in the United States and what they should do.

NTAS Alerts

Imminent Threat Alert - Warns of a credible, specific, and impending terrorist threat against the United States.

Elevated Threat Alert - Warns of a credible terrorist threat against the United States.

The NTAS Alerts will be based on the nature of the threat: in some cases, alerts will be sent directly to law enforcement or affected areas of the private sector, while in others, alerts will be issued more broadly to the American people through both official and media channels.

Additionally, NTAS has a **sunset provision** meaning individual threat alerts will be issued with a specific end date. Alerts may be extended if new information becomes available or if the threat evolves significantly.

How does the new NTAS system work?

When there is credible information about a threat, an NTAS Alert will be shared with the American public. It may include specific information, if available, about the nature of the threat, including the geographic region, mode of transportation, or critical infrastructure potentially affected by the threat, as well as steps that individuals and communities can take to protect themselves and their families, and help prevent, mitigate or respond to the threat.

The advisory will clearly indicate whether the threat is **Elevated** (if DHS has no specific information about the timing or location) or **Imminent** (if officials believes the threat is impending or very soon).

How can you help?

Citizens should report suspicious activity to their local law enforcement authorities. The **"If You See Something, Say Something™"** campaign across the U.S. encourages all citizens to be vigilant for indicators of potential terrorist activity, and to follow NTAS Alerts for information about threats in specific places or for individuals exhibiting certain types of suspicious activity. Visit www.dhs.gov/ifyouseesomethingsaysomething to learn more.

Learn more and find NTAS print materials and tools at www.dhs.gov/alerts or follow DHS on FB at www.facebook.com/NTASAlerts or on Twitter http://twitter.com/NTASAlerts

ABOUT CYBER ATTACKS

There are 3 key risk factors related to information technologies systems:

- A direct attack against a system "through the wires" alone (called hacking) -- meaning an attacker or user "hacks" in or gains **"access"** to restricted data and operations.

- An attack can be a physical assault against a critical IT element meaning an attacker changes or destroys data, modifies programs or takes control of a system (basically can cause a loss of data "**integrity**" = data is no good).

- The attack can be from the inside -- meaning private information could get in the wrong hands and become public or identities stolen (basically "**confidentiality**" is broken = data is no longer secure or private).

Cyber attacks target computer networks that run government, financial, health, emergency medical services, public safety, telecommunications, transportation and utility systems - also known as "critical infrastructure". Because technologies have improved our access to information, we have opened ourselves up for attacks by our enemies to destroy or alter this data.

Cyberterrorism is different than computer crime or "hacktivism" (which can be costly and a pain to fix but doesn't threaten lives or public safety.)

Cyberterrorism is usually done with a minimal loss of life but there are some groups that could use cyber attacks or cyber warfare to cause human casualties or fear by disrupting transportation or public safety systems.

For example, prior to Russia invading Georgia in 2008, Georgian Internet servers were overloaded by multiple coordinated distributed denial of service (or D.D.O.S.) attacks. These attacks crippled Georgia's government, media, communications and transportation web sites before and after Russian troops entered South Ossetia. It's the first time a cyberattack coincided with a shooting war according to some Internet experts.[6]

We are not trying to cause worry or panic, but understand the possibility exists and services could be disrupted or cut off or man-made disasters could happen due to cyber attacks. For example, services like banking, gas pumps, or internet access could be down or slow. And some emergency planners are concerned a cyber attack combined with a physical act of terrorism (like a "dirty bomb" or releasing a chemical or biological agent) could potentially interfere with response capabilities.

As we have seen in news reports, many systems (including military and government systems) have been breached repeatedly and over the course of many years or even decades by rogue hackers and nations. Many experts feel the next major conflict could be a cyberwar rather than conventional warfare.

Most countries have agencies committed to securing and monitoring critical infrastructure and share information on a regular basis. Businesses and consumers can help too by taking some preventative measures.

Before a Cyber Attack:

Protect computers - Make sure your computers and wireless devices have current anti-virus software and firewalls, and update and scan them often.

Learn about US-CERT - Consumers and businesses should take some time to visit the United States Computer Emergency Readiness Team and learn more about Internet security at www.us-cert.gov

Stay current on threats & alerts - The Department of Homeland Security www.dhs.gov and Public Safety Canada www.publicsafety.gc.ca post alerts and news about national security online.

What .. no services? - Think about how you would handle not having access to the Internet, phones, ATMs and other electronic devices you use daily. A cyber attack could disrupt or crash systems so have a backup plan and listen to authorities for updates.

Business Continuity tips - See APPENDIX B to learn about resources that can help businesses and employees prepare for the unexpected.

About Chemical Agents

Chemical agents are toxic vapors (gas), sprays (aerosols), liquids or solids that can poison people, animals and the environment. Some compounds or agents do have industrial uses, but many are man-made substances designed, developed and stockpiled as military weapons around the world.

A known terrorist tactic combines bombs and chemical trucks to spread deadly fumes. Most chemical agents are difficult to produce and very hard to deliver in large quantities since they scatter so quickly. Most are liquids and some may be odorless and tasteless. They could be inhaled, absorbed into the skin, or swallowed from a contaminated food or water source. Chemical agents can take effect immediately or over several hours or days - and can be deadly if exposed to enough of the agent. If exposed, the best thing to do is distance yourself from the agent and area and get fresh air.

What chemical agents could be used in an attack?

According to the CDC, there are several **categories** of chemical agents that could potentially be used in a terrorist attack - some common ones include:

- **Blister Agents / Vesicants** (Sulfur Mustard / Mustard Gas or Lewisite) - primarily cause blisters but can also damage eyes, airways, and digestive system
- **Blood Agents** (Arsine or Cyanide) - gets in blood stream and prevents cells from absorbing oxygen so cells die

- **Choking / Lung / Pulmonary Agents** (Ammonia or Chlorine) - cause breathing problems and lack of oxygen damages organs
- **Incapacitating Agents** (BZ or LSD) - disrupts central nervous system, causes confusion, and slows breathing (makes you woozy or knocks you out)
- **Nerve Agents** (Sarin, Soman, Tabun or VX) - the most toxic agents -- basically turns "off" the body's ability to stop muscles and glands from twitching (body goes into convulsions). Most agents were originally developed as pesticides / insecticides.

Some other categories include ... **Biotoxins** (like Abrin or Ricin), **Caustics** (Hydrofluoric Acid), **Metals** (Arsenic or Mercury), **Organic Solvents** (Benzene), **Riot Control Agents / Tear Gas** (CS or CN), **Toxic Alcohols** (Ethylene Glycol), and **Vomiting Agents** (Adamsite).

Remember, many chemical weapons - or chemical warfare - have been around since World War I ... it's unfortunate we have to even discuss it but try not to let this topic frighten you. Educate yourselves about the types and where to find more information so you are prepared to react in the event of a chemical threat or attack.

How could chemical agents be used in an attack?

There are several ways chemical agents could be spread:
- **Vapors / Gas / Aerosols** - spread into air by a bomb or from aircraft, boats or vehicles -- could spread for miles
- **Liquids** - could be released into the air, water or soil or touched by people or animals
- **Solids** - could be absorbed into water, soil or touched

Some chemical agents can remain in the environment and cause problems long after they are released. Keep in mind, both the Center for Disease Control and Environmental Protection Agency are working closely with various Departments of Defense and Energy and officials around the country to monitor systems and security and develop plans. The same goes for Health Canada and other Canadian government agencies.

In the event of a public health emergency, officials will tell people what actions need to be taken. But learn as much as you can before a crisis to help alleviate some stress, fear and problems.

What are the names of some chemical agents and what can they do?

According to the CDC's Emergency Preparedness and Response site, there are many types of chemical agents - too many to list here. We're only mentioning several common agents in alphabetical order, but there are many others we are not covering that could potentially be used. Always listen to authorities for instructions in the event of a chemical threat or attack.

BZ **(Incapacitating)** - and other stun agents (LSD, etc.) disrupt the central nervous system causing confusion, short-term memory loss and immobility (means you can't move or are incapacitated).

How it spreads: BZ could be released by a bomb or sprayed into the air as an aerosol but has been proven unpredictable if used outdoors.

Signs & Symptoms: Depends on how person is exposed to BZ and varies by person -- basically it disrupts your nervous system causing confusion, dream-like feelings or strange visions (called hallucinations), dilation of the pupils (means pupils bigger than normal), slurred speech, and loss of motor skills (can't move). It can also slow down breathing and heart rate.

Treatment: BZ is treated with an antidote that reverses symptoms for an hour. May need repeated doses since effects can last for hours or days.

Chlorine **(Choking / Lung / Pulmonary)** - is used in industry (to bleach paper or cloth), in water (to kill germs), and in household products. Chlorine can be in the form of a poisonous gas or gas can be pressurized and cooled into a liquid. When gas comes in contact with moist tissues (eyes, throat, or lungs), an acid is produced that can damage these tissues. Chlorine is not flammable but reacts explosively if mixed with certain liquids. Terrorists use bombs on chlorine trucks to spread deadly fumes.

How it spreads: Chlorine could be released into water, food or air. People can be exposed by drinking or eating something contaminated with excess amounts of chlorine or by inhaling the poisonous gas. Chlorine gas is yellow-green, smells like bleach, and stays close to the ground as it spreads.

Signs & Symptoms: Depends on how much and how exposed but signs may show up during or right after exposure to dangerous amounts of chlorine:

- Skin - *if gas:* burning pain, redness, and blisters
  if liquid: skin white or waxy, numbness (like frostbite)
- Eyes - burning feeling, blurred vision, watery eyes
- Nose, throat & lungs (respiratory tract) - burning feeling in nose and throat, tightness in chest, coughing, hard time breathing or shortness of breath, fluid builds up in lungs within 2 to 4 hours
- Stomach / gastrointestinal: puking, sick to stomach

Treatment: - There is no antidote for chlorine exposure -- main things are to remove it from body and seek medical attention as soon as possible.

- First - leave area as quickly as possible
  ... if outdoors - get to high ground (avoid low-lying areas)
  ... if in building - get outside to high ground and upwind
- If inhaled - get fresh air as quickly and calmly as possible
- If on clothing or skin - remove clothes and shoes that are contaminated but don't pull anything over head - cut it off body. If possible, seal clothing in plastic bag, then seal that bag in a bag. Immediately wash body with clean water and soap. Ask officials how to dispose of bags.
- If in eyes - remove contacts and put in a bag - do not put back in eyes! If eyes burning or vision blurred, rinse eyes with plain water for 10 to 15 minutes. If wearing glasses, wash them with soap and water before putting back on.
- If swallowed - if someone drinks or eats something exposed to chlorine, do NOT make them puke or drink fluids - call 9-1-1

Cyanide (Blood) - is a very fast acting and potentially deadly chemical that exists in several forms. The CDC categorizes cyanide as "blood" agents but sometimes called "cyanide or cyanogen" agents. Cyanide can be a colorless gas (cyanogen chloride or hydrogen cyanide) or a crystal solid form (like potassium or sodium cyanide). It may smell like "bitter almonds" but most often is odorless. Cyanide is naturally present in some foods or plants - it's also in cigarette smoke or given off when some plastics burn. It is also used to make paper or textiles and in chemicals used to develop photos.

How it spreads: Cyanide could enter water, soil or air as a result of natural or industrial processes or be spread indoors or outdoors as a weapon. People can be exposed by breathing gas or vapors or cigarette smoke, by drinking or eating something contaminated (either accidentally or on purpose) or by touching soil or clothing that was exposed to cyanide. The gas disappears quickly and rises (less dense than air) so pretty useless outdoors.

Signs & Symptoms: Basically cyanide prevents the cells from absorbing oxygen so cells die. No matter how exposed (breathing, absorbed through skin, or eating / drinking) some or all signs show up within minutes:

- Exposed to small amount - rapid breathing, gasping for air, dizziness, weakness, headache, sick to stomach, puking, restlessness, rapid heart rate, bluish skin or lips (due to lack of oxygen in blood)
- Large amount - above signs plus convulsions, low blood pressure, slow heart rate, passes out, stops breathing

leading to death. Survivors of serious poisoning may develop heart and brain damage due to lack of oxygen.

Treatment: Cyanide poisoning is treated with antidotes and supportive medical care (mainly to help symptoms). The main things are to avoid area where it was released and seek medical attention as soon as possible.

- First - leave area as quickly as possible
  ... if outdoors - move upwind and stay low to ground
  ... if in building - get outside and get upwind
- If inhaled - get fresh air as quickly and calmly as possible
- If on clothing or skin - remove contaminated shoes and clothes but don't pull anything over head - cut it off. Seal all in a bag then put that bag in a bag - ask how to dispose of. Immediately wash body and hair with soap & water.
- If in eyes - remove contacts if necessary. If eyes burning or vision blurred, rinse eyes with water for 10-15 minutes.
- If swallowed - if someone drinks or eats something exposed to cyanide, do NOT make them puke or drink fluids - call 9-1-1

Sarin (**Nerve**) - is a clear, colorless, odorless and tasteless liquid that could evaporate into a vapor (gas) and contaminate the environment. It is man-made and originally developed to kill insects. Nerve agents basically turn "off" the body's ability to stop muscles and glands from twitching.

How it spreads: Sarin could be released into the air, water, or soil as a weapon. People can be exposed by breathing vapors, by drinking or eating something contaminated, or by touching water, soil or clothing exposed to sarin. A person's clothing can release sarin for about 30 minutes after being exposed to vapor. Because sarin vapor is heavier than air, it settles in low-lying areas creating a greater exposure hazard.

Signs & Symptoms: Depends on how much, what form, and how people are exposed to sarin. No matter how exposed (breathing, absorbed through skin, or eating / drinking it), the following may show up within seconds (vapor or gas) or within minutes to 18 hours (liquid)...

- Head - runny nose, drooling or excess spittle, headache
- Eyes - watery, small pupils, blurred vision, eye pain
- Lungs - cough, tight feeling in chest, fast/rapid breathing
- Nervous system - confusion, drowsiness, weakness
- Heart/blood - slow/fast pulse, rise/drop in blood pressure
- Stomach/gastrointestinal - abdominal pain, puking, sick to stomach, diarrhea, pee lot more than normal
... plus ...

- If exposed to small amount - just a drop of sarin on skin can cause sweating and muscle twitching
- If large amount - can cause convulsions (body can't stop the muscles and glands from twitching), paralysis (can't move), pass out, stops breathing leading to death

Treatment: Sarin poisoning is treated with antidotes and supportive medical care. Mainly want to avoid area where released, get decontaminated (strip & wash), and seek medical attention as soon as possible.

- First - leave area as quickly as possible
  ... if outdoors - move to higher ground and stay upwind
  ... if in building - get outside to highest ground possible
- If inhaled - get fresh air as quickly and calmly as possible
- If on clothing or skin - remove contaminated clothes and shoes but don't pull anything over head - cut it off body. Seal all in plastic bag, then seal that bag in a bag and ask how to dispose of. Immediately wash body with clean water and soap.
- If in eyes - remove contacts if any. If eyes burning or vision blurred, rinse eyes with water for 10 -15 minutes.
- If swallowed - if someone drinks or eats something exposed to sarin, do NOT make them puke or drink fluids - call 9-1-1

Sulfur Mustard / Mustard gas (**Blister/Vesicant**) - (also known as mustard agent) can be in the form of a vapor, an oily-textured liquid or a solid and be clear to yellow or brown when in liquid or solid form. It is not normally found in the environment, however, if released, can last for weeks or months under very cold conditions. During normal weather conditions, it usually only lasts a day or two.

Mustard gas is fairly easy to develop so many countries that decide to have chemical warfare agents usually stock up on this one. Sulfur mustard was originally produced in the 1800's but first used as chemical warfare in World War I and in many wars since. Exposure to mustard gas is usually not fatal but could have long-term health effects.

How it spreads: Sulfur mustard / mustard gas can be released into the air as a vapor or gas and enter a person's body by breathing or get on skin or in eyes. The vapor would be carried for long distances by wind so could affect a wide area. Sulfur mustard is heavier than air so vapors will settle in low-lying areas. A liquid or solid form could be released into water and a person could be exposed by drinking it or absorbing it through the skin. Since it often has no smell or smell doesn't raise a red flag (can smell like garlic, onions or mustard), people may not realize they have been exposed.

Signs & Symptoms: Depends on how much, what form, and how a person is exposed to sulfur mustard / mustard gas and may not occur for 2 to 24 hours ... some immediate signs include ...

- Skin - redness and itching of skin may occur 2 to 48 hours after exposure -- changes to yellow blistering of skin
- Eyes - a mild case causes irritation, pain, swelling and watery eyes within 3 to 12 hours -- a more severe case causes same within 1 to 2 hours - may also include light sensitivity, severe pain or temporary blindness (lasting up to 10 days)
- Nose & lungs (respiratory tract) - runny nose, sneezing, sinus pain, bloody nose, short of breath, may get hoarse, and cough (mild exposure shows within 12 to 24 hours -- severe shows within 2 to 4 hours)
- Digestive tract - abdominal pain, sick to stomach, diarrhea, puking, and fever

Some long-term health effects may include ...

- Burns or scarring - exposure to the liquid (not gas) may produce second- and third-degree burns and later scarring
- Breathing problems or disease - severe exposure could cause chronic respiratory disease, infections, or death
- Blindness - severe exposure can blind you permanently
- Cancer - may increase risk of lung or respiratory cancer

Treatment: There is no antidote for sulfur mustard / mustard gas exposure - the best thing to do is avoid it by leaving the area where it was released.

- First - leave area as quickly as possible
  ... if outdoors - move upwind and get to higher ground
  ... if inside - get outside, upwind and to higher ground
- If inhaled - get fresh air as quickly and calmly as possible
- If on clothing or skin - remove everything that got contaminated. Seal clothing and shoes in plastic bag, then seal that bag in a bag - ask how to dispose of later. Immediately wash exposed body parts (eyes, skin, hair, etc.) with plain, clean water.
- If in eyes - remove contacts if any. Flush eyes with water for 5 - 10 minutes but do NOT cover eyes with bandages - put on shades or goggles to protect them.
- If swallowed - if someone drinks or eats something contaminated with sulfur mustard (mustard gas), do NOT make them puke it up -- give the person some milk to drink and call 9-1-1

VX **(Nerve)** - is an oily liquid that is odorless, tasteless, amber or honey-yellow in color, and evaporates about as slowly as motor oil. VX is the most potent of all nerve agents, which basically turn "off" the body's ability to stop muscles and glands from twitching. Like other nerve agents, VX is a man-made chemical originally developed to kill insects and pests.

How it spreads: VX could be released into the air or water as a weapon, however it does not mix with water as well as other nerve agents. If VX gas or vapors are released into the air, people can be exposed by breathing or eye or skin contact and a person's clothing can release VX for about 30 minutes after being exposed. If VX liquid is put in food or water source, people could get it from eating, drinking or touching something exposed to the liquid.

VX vapor is heavier than air so settles in low-lying areas. Under average weather conditions, VX can last for days on objects that come in contact with the agent, but in cold weather it could last for months. The liquid takes time to evaporate into a vapor so could be a long-term threat to the environment.

Signs & Symptoms: VX is similar to sarin - depends on how much, what form, and how people are exposed. No matter how exposed (breathing, absorbed through skin, or eating / drinking it) the following may show up within seconds to hours ...

- Head - runny nose, drooling or excess spittle, headache
- Eyes - watery, small pupils, blurred vision, eye pain
- Lungs - cough, tight feeling in chest, fast/rapid breathing
- Nervous system - confusion, drowsiness, weakness
- Heart/blood - slow/fast pulse, rise/drop in blood pressure
- Stomach/gastrointestinal - abdominal pain, puking, sick to stomach, diarrhea, pee more than normal

... plus ...

- If exposed to small amount - a tiny drop of VX on skin can cause sweating and muscle twitching
- If large amount - can cause convulsions (body can't stop the muscles and glands from twitching), paralysis (can't move), may pass out, stops breathing leading to death

Treatment: VX poisoning can be treated with antidotes but must be given shortly after exposure to be effective. The main things are avoid area where agent was released, get decontaminated (strip & wash), and seek medical care as soon as possible.

- First - leave area as quickly as possible
    ... if outdoors - move to higher ground and stay upwind

... if in building - get outside to highest ground possible

- **If inhaled** - get fresh air as quickly and calmly as possible
- **If on clothing or skin** - remove clothes and shoes contaminated with VX but don't pull anything over head - cut it off body. Seal all in plastic bag, then seal that bag in a bag and ask how to dispose of. Immediately wash body with clean water and soap.
- **If in eyes** - remove contacts if any. If eyes burning or vision blurred, rinse eyes with water for 10 to 15 minutes.
- **If swallowed** - if someone drinks or eats something exposed to VX, do NOT make them puke or drink fluids - call 9-1-1

BEFORE A CHEMICAL ATTACK:

Watch & listen for signs - Many chemical agents can cause watery eyes, choking, trouble breathing, coughing or twitching. If you see or hear a lot of people doing this or see a bunch of birds, fish or critters sick or dead, it should raise a red flag. Learn about some common potentially hazardous chemical agents (see previous pages) and stay current by listening to radio and TV to hear what local authorities tell people to do -- and DO it!

Report strange things - Be aware of your surroundings -- watch for strange or suspicious packages, luggage or backpacks ... or spray trucks or crop dusters in weird places at strange times ... and report suspicious activities to local authorities.

Make a plan - Review Section 1 to develop a **Family Emergency Plan** and **Disaster Supplies Kit**. Some key items include a battery-powered radio (with extra batteries), food and drinking water, duct tape, plastic and scissors, first aid kit, and sanitation items (soap, extra water and bleach).

Pick a room - It could take authorities time to determine what (if any) agent was used so pick a room in advance your family could use if told to "shelter-in-place" for several hours. It's best to pick an internal room where you could block out air <u>IF</u> told to do so. To save time consider measuring and cutting plastic sheets in advance for openings (vents, windows, and doors). Remember, toilets / drains may be vented meaning outside air comes in constantly or when flushed / open (depends on design) - in case you're using a bathroom as a safe room.

Calculate air for room - Keep in mind people can stay in a sealed off room for only so long (or you'll run out of air.) FEMA suggests 10 square feet of floor space per person (like 5ft x 2ft / 1.5m x 0.6m) will provide enough air to prevent carbon dioxide buildup for up to 5 hours.

<u>Be ready to evacuate</u> - Listen to local authorities and leave if you are told to evacuate. *(see EVACUATION)*

DURING A CHEMICAL ATTACK:

During any type of chemical attack, local authorities will instruct the public on where to go and exactly what to do if exposed to an agent (which may require immediate attention with professional medical staff).

<u>Watch for signs</u> - If you see or hear a lot of people choking, coughing or twitching or see a bunch of sick or dead critters - leave area quickly!

<u>Don't panic -- Listen</u> - Stay calm and listen to radio, TV and officials to ...
- Determine if your area is or was in danger.
- Learn signs and symptoms of some agents (see previous pages briefly describing **BZ**, **chlorine, cyanide, sarin, sulfur mustard / mustard gas**, and **VX**).
- Find out if and where antidotes are being distributed.

IF INDOORS – Stay inside and prepare to "shelter-in-place"...
- Close your windows, vents and fireplace damper and turn off A/C and fans to reduce air drawn in from outside.
- Seal gaps under doorways and windows with wet towels, plastic (if available) and duct tape.
- If you picked a safe room in advance, grab your **Disaster Supplies Kit** and seal off that room - remember, you can only stay there for so many hours or you'll run out of air.
- Some vapors and gases may sink so avoid basements (unless instructed otherwise).

IF OUTDOORS - Stay upwind from the disaster area since many agents can be carried by wind. Try to find a shelter as quickly as possible.

IF IN A VEHICLE - Close your windows and shut off vents to reduce risk and drive away and upwind from the attack site, if possible.

<u>Cover up</u> - Cover mouth and nose to filter air but still let you breathe (like a T-shirt or towel or several layers of paper towel, napkins or tissues).

<u>Feel sick...?</u> - Some agents can cause immediate symptoms and some take a while to show up so watch family members for signs of illness.

<u>Evacuate...?</u> - If you are told to evacuate... DO it! If officials say you have time, close windows, shut vents and turn off attic fans. *(see EVACUATION)*

Things to avoid:
- **chemicals** - any spilled liquid materials, vapors or gas
- **contaminated food or water** - don't eat or drink any food or water that may have been exposed to materials

Stay away - Get away from the attack site to avoid contamination.

AFTER A CHEMICAL ATTACK:

Feel sick...? - In some cases, people won't be aware they have been exposed to an agent -- most cause immediate symptoms and some take a while to show up so continue watching for signs of illness.

Don't panic -- Listen - Stay calm and listen to radio, TV and officials to ...
- Determine if your area is or was in danger.
- Learn signs and symptoms of specific chemical agent(s).
- Find out if antidotes are being distributed by authorities and, if so, where you can get them.

Don't go there - Don't return home until local authorities say it is safe.

Air out - Open windows, vents and turn on fans to air things out.

Clean up - A person, critter or item that has been exposed could spread it...
- **decontamination** - follow instructions from authorities since it depends on chemical. May need to shower with or without soap or may be told to avoid water - check first
- **strange symptoms** - if unusual symptoms show up, get to a hospital or medical expert right away
- **store clothes & shoes** - put exposed clothing and shoes in tightly sealed containers or bags and ask local authorities how to get rid of them
- **tell people you've been exposed** - tell everyone who comes in contact with you that you may have been exposed to a chemical agent
- **land and property** - ask local authorities how to clean up

Strange vapors or danger - Report these to local authorities immediately.

*For more information about **chemical agents**, visit the CDC Emergency Preparedness & Response site at www.bt.cdc.gov .. or .. call CDC Hotline at 1-800-CDC-INFO (1-800-232-4636) or 1-888-232-6348 (TTY).*

ABOUT BIOLOGICAL AGENTS

Biological agents are actually tiny life forms or germs that can occur naturally in plants, animals and soils or can be developed for scientific or military purposes. Many biological agents affect humans by being inhaled, absorbed into the skin through a cut, or by swallowing contaminated food or water. But there are things that make it difficult for some biological agents to live like sunlight (ultraviolet light) or dry conditions. Wind could carry agents long distances but also spreads it out making it less effective.

Many animals and insects carry diseases that affect humans but most don't make us sick when eaten or inhaled because our immune systems are strong enough to fight them. But, if a person's immune system is weak (like in babies or the elderly), it's possible that person could become sick or die.

What biological agents could be used in an attack?

There are **3 basic groups** of biological agents that could be weaponized and used in an attack (but realize there are some that occur naturally too):

- **Bacteria** - tiny life forms that reproduce by simple division and are easy to grow -- diseases they spread are killed by strong or boosted immune system or antibiotics
- **Viruses** - organisms that need living cells to reproduce and are dependent on the body they infect -- most diseases caused by viruses don't respond to antibiotics but sometimes antiviral drugs work (and a boosted immune system may fight invading organisms - depends on type of virus)
- **Toxins** - poisonous substances found in and extracted from living plants, animals or microorganisms; some toxins can be produced or altered -- some toxins can be treated with specific antitoxins and selected drugs

Remember, biological weapons - or germ warfare - have been around for centuries so it's not anything new ... it's unfortunate we have to discuss it at length, but try not to let this topic frighten you. Educate yourself about the types and where to find more information so you are prepared to react.

How could biological agents be used in an attack?

As mentioned earlier, most biological agents break down when exposed to sunlight or other conditions, and they are very hard to grow and maintain.

There are 3 ways biological agents could be spread:

- **Aerosols** - dispersed or spread into air by a number of methods forming a fine mist that could drift for miles
- **Animals and insects** - some diseases can be carried and

spread by critters like birds, mice or rodents, mosquitoes, fleas, or livestock -- called bioterrorism or agroterrorism

- **Food and water contamination** - most organisms and toxins are killed or deactivated when we cook food and boil or treat water but some may continue living

Some biological agents could remain in the environment and cause problems long after they are released. Again, keep in mind both the CDC and EPA work closely with Departments of Defense and Energy and many other agencies to monitor systems and security and develop plans. The same goes for Health Canada and many Canadian government agencies.

What are the names of some biological agents and what can they do?

According to CDC's Emergency Preparedness and Response site, there are many types of biological diseases and agents - in fact, too many to list here. The CDC has categorized biological agents into 3 groups (A, B and C). The diseases and agents listed in Category A are considered "highest priority". Since most agents were also listed on Public Health Agency of Canada's Emergency Preparedness site, we are covering 7 specific agents (6 in Category A plus ricin from Category B) in alphabetical order.

<u>Anthrax</u> - is an infection caused by bacteria (*Bacillus anthracis*) found naturally in soil where it can live for years. The bacteria form a protective coat around themselves called spores which are very tiny, invisible to the naked eye, and odorless. Anthrax is most common in cows and sheep but can also infect humans (primarily people who work with hoofed animals).

How it spreads: Anthrax <u>cannot</u> spread person to person. People come into contact with bacteria by breathing in spores (**inhalation**), by getting it through a cut in skin (**cutaneous**) or by eating something containing bacteria - like undercooked meat from an infected animal (**gastrointestinal**).

Signs & Symptoms: Signs depend on type of anthrax you're exposed to:
- <u>Inhalation</u> - most serious form - first signs similar to cold or flu (sore throat, fever and extremely tired but <u>no</u> runny nose) -- after several days may lead to severe breathing problems, shock, then possibly death
- <u>Cutaneous</u> - least serious form - first symptom is a small sore that turns into a blister -- a day or two later blister turns into a skin ulcer with a black area in the center. The sore, blister and ulcer do not hurt.
- <u>Gastrointestinal</u> - first nausea, loss of appetite, bloody diarrhea and fever -- followed by bad stomach pain

Symptoms for all 3 types can appear within 7 days of coming in contact with anthrax, but inhalation symptoms may take up to 42 days to appear.

Treatment: All three forms of anthrax are treatable with antibiotics. Chances of coming into contact with anthrax are very low, and your body naturally fights off bacteria so you may not even become ill.

Botulism - is a muscle-paralyzing disease caused by a toxin made by a bacterium called *Clostridium botulinum*. *C. botulinum* occurs naturally and can be found in soil, water, animals, contaminated foods or crops. According to Health Canada, the toxin produced by *C. botulinum* is the most potent toxin known and can affect humans, animals and even fish. There is only one form of human-made botulism known to date.

How it spreads: Botulism <u>cannot</u> spread person to person. People come into contact with the naturally formed bacteria by eating something (**food-borne** - usually due to improper storage or home canning methods), through a cut in the skin (**wound**), or a small number of infants (typically less than a year old) can eat bacterial spores that get into intestines (**infant botulism**). The only human-made form has been known to be transmitted from monkeys to veterinarians and lab workers (**inhalation**).

Signs & Symptoms: Depends on type of botulism you're exposed to and the degree of exposure to the toxin but generally ...

- <u>Foodborne</u> - rare - signs usually appear in 6 to 36 hours
- <u>Wound</u> - first signs usually appear in 4 to 8 days
- <u>Infant botulism</u> - signs usually appear in 6 to 36 hours
- <u>Inhalation</u> - first signs usually appear in 72 hours

Early symptoms for <u>ALL</u> forms of botulism include double vision, blurred vision, drooping eyelids, hard to speak or swallow, dry mouth and fatigue (very tired). Muscle weakness starts at top of body and goes down causing nerve damage that results in paralysis of face, head, throat, chest, arms and legs -- could possibly lead to death since breathing muscles do not work.

Treatment: There is an antitoxin for botulism, but it must be treated as quickly as possible since it may or may not reverse effects of the disease but can stop further paralysis. Antibiotics are not effective against toxins.

Plague - is caused by a bacterium called *Yersinia pestis* that affects animals and humans. *Y. pestis* is found in rodents and their fleas in many areas of the world, including the U.S. The bacterium is easily killed by sunlight and drying but could live up to an hour when released into the air depending on weather conditions.

How it spreads: There is only one cause of plague but three different types of illness the infection can cause. One type of infection comes from the bite of an infected flea or gets in through a cut in the skin by touching material infected with bacterium (**bubonic**), another can be spread through the air and inhaled (**pneumonic**), and a third occurs when plague bacteria multiplies in the blood of a person already infected with plague (**septicemic**).

Signs & Symptoms: Plague types may occur separately or in combination with each other ... and all start with fever, headache, weakness, chills (possibly puking and diarrhea) usually within 1 to 10 days of being exposed.

- Bubonic - most common - also develop swollen, tender lymph glands (called buboes). Does <u>not</u> spread person to person.

- Pneumonic - least common but most deadly -- could be used in attack but hard since sunlight kills it. Also get rapidly developing pneumonia with shortness of breath, chest pain, cough, and sometimes bloody or watery spittle. May cause respiratory failure, shock or death. <u>Can</u> spread person to person through air (inhaling droplets from a cough, sneeze, etc.)

- Septicemic - can occur with either bubonic or pneumonic plague due to bacteria multiplying in blood. Also develop abdominal pain, shock, and bleeding into skin and other organs. Does <u>not</u> spread person to person.

Treatment: There are several antibiotics that can effectively treat plague. (It is very important to get treatment for <u>pneumonic</u> plague within 24 hours of first symptoms to reduce the chance of death.)

<u>Ricin</u> - is said to be one of the most toxic natural poisons made very easily from the waste left over from processing castor beans. A castor bean plant is a shrub-like herb with clustered seed pods containing bean-like seeds. Accidental poisoning by ricin is unlikely -- it would have to be a planned act to make and use the toxin as a weapon. Ricin can be in many forms and is not weakened much by extreme hot or cold temperatures. (Note: Ricin is also classed as a "biotoxin" under the CDC's chemical agents' list.)

How it spreads: Ricin <u>cannot</u> spread person to person. People come into contact with ricin by breathing in a mist or powder spread into the air (**inhalation**), by eating or drinking something containing toxin (**ingestion**), or by having a ricin solution or pellet stuck into the body (**injection**). It can also irritate skin and eyes if exposed to the powder or mist.

It is hard to say how much ricin could kill a person since it depends on how that person was exposed to the toxin. For example, about 500 micrograms (about the size of the head of a pin) could kill a person if injected into the body, but it would take a lot more if inhaled or swallowed. Ricin prevents cells from making proteins they need when toxin gets inside the body. Cells will die without proteins and eventually entire body shuts down and dies.

Signs & Symptoms: Depends on how much ricin a person is exposed to -- in large amounts death could occur within 36 to 72 hours. If a person lives more than 3-5 days without problems, there's a good chance they'll survive:

- <u>Inhalation</u> - within a few hours of breathing in large amounts of ricin, the first signs are usually coughing, tightness in the chest, hard time breathing, fever, nausea (sick to stomach), and heavy sweating. In the next few hours excess fluid would build up in lungs making it even harder to breathe and skin may turn blue. Finally, blood pressure drops and breathing will stop leading to death.

- <u>Ingestion</u> - if a large amount of ricin is swallowed it will cause internal bleeding of the stomach and intestines, leading to puking and bloody diarrhea within 2 to 6 hours -- and most likely lead to liver, spleen and kidneys shutting down, and person could die within several days

- <u>Injection</u> - if enough ricin is injected into a person, it immediately kills muscles and lymph nodes around area where it entered body ~ eventually organs will shut down

- <u>Skin or eyes</u> - mist or powder can cause redness and pain

Treatment: There is no antidote for ricin exposure. Supportive medical care can be given based on how a person was exposed to ricin (like oxygen [if inhalation] or I.V. fluids or flushing stomach with activated charcoal [if ingestion]), but care mainly helps symptoms.

If a mist or powder was released, get the ricin off or out of body asap:

- <u>First - leave area as quickly as possible</u>
  ... if outdoors - move away and upwind from area
  ... if in building - get outside to high ground and upwind

- <u>If inhaled</u> - get fresh air as quickly and calmly as possible

- <u>If mist or powder on clothing or skin</u> - remove contaminated clothes and shoes but don't pull anything over head - cut it off. Seal items in a bag, then seal that bag in a bag. Immediately wash body with clean water and soap.

- <u>If mist or powder in eyes</u> - remove contacts and put in bags with clothing. If eyes burn or vision is blurred, rinse eyes with water for 10 to 15 minutes. If wearing glasses, wash them with soap and water before putting back on.

Smallpox - is a very serious, highly contagious and sometimes deadly disease caused by the variola virus. The most common form of smallpox causes raised bumps on the face and body of an infected person. There has not been a case of smallpox in the world since 1977, however in the 1980s all countries consolidated their smallpox stocks in two government-controlled laboratories in the U.S. and Russia. These secured laboratories still have the virus in quantities for research purposes, but it is very possible some vials have gotten or could get into the hands of terrorist groups.

Smallpox disease killed over 300 million people in the 20th century and experts say it is the most dangerous infectious disease ever. There is no cure for smallpox and most patients infected with the disease recover, but death may occur in as many as 3 of every 10 persons infected.

How it spreads: Smallpox is primarily spread person to person through droplets that are inhaled but usually requires close contact. It can also be spread by infected bodily fluids (especially fluid from bumps) or from bed linens or clothing from an infected person. It is very rare but the virus could carry in the air of an enclosed area like a train or building. Smallpox only infects humans and is not known to be transmitted by insects or animals.

Someone carrying the virus may not even know they have it since it lies dormant (incubation period) for up to 17 days. A person with smallpox is most contagious from the time the rash starts until the last scab falls off (usually about 1 month). Anyone face-to-face with an infected person (within 6 - 7 feet / 2 meters) will most likely get the virus by inhaling droplets or dried fluids or by touching infected materials.

Signs & Symptoms: According to the CDC, exposure to the smallpox virus has an incubation period of 7 to 17 days (average is 12 to 14 days) where people feel fine, show no symptoms and are not contagious, then...

- Prodrome phase - first symptoms of smallpox include fever, weird or uneasy feeling (malaise), head and body aches, and sometimes puking. Fever may be high (between 101F-104F or 38C-40C) -- may be contagious. Phase can last 2 - 4 days.

- Spotty mouth - small red spots appear on the tongue and in the mouth (this is start of the "early rash phase")

- Spots become sores - spots turn into sores that break open and spread large amounts of the virus into the mouth and throat -- person is VERY contagious at this point!

- Rash - as sores in mouth break down, a rash starts on the face and spreads to arms and legs, then hands and feet -- usually takes about 24 hours to cover body. As the rash appears, fever drops, and person may feel a little better.

- Raised bumps - by third day, rash turns into raised bumps

- Bumps fill up - by fourth day, bumps fill with a thick, clear fluid -- each bump has a dent in center (like a bellybutton)

- Bumps become pustules - fever returns and bumps become pustules (which is a raised bump, usually round, firm and feels like there's something hard inside - like a BB pellet) -- lasts about 5 days

- <u>Pustules become scabs</u> - fever still high, next the pustules form a crust turning into scabs - lasts about 5 days -- about 2 weeks after rash first appears most of the sores will be scabbed over
- <u>Scabs fall off</u> - takes about 6 days for all the scabs to fall off leaving a scar or dent in the skin where each scab was (most are gone about 3 weeks after early rash first appears). Person is no longer contagious when <u>all</u> scabs have fallen off.

<u>Treatment:</u> There is no cure or treatment for smallpox. A vaccination within 4 days of being exposed could help stop disease but, if vaccinated years ago, it's doubtful you'd be protected now. Many countries are stockpiling vaccine and considering vaccinations for all citizens, but many experts feel that may not be necessary yet. There are certain people who should not get the vaccine. If you do decide to take vaccination, consider boosting your immune system before getting shots -- may help your body fight any adverse reactions.

*If you have concerns or questions about **smallpox**, visit the CDC's Emergency Preparedness & Response site at <u>www.bt.cdc.gov/agent/smallpox</u> or the Public Health Agency of Canada's Emergency Preparedness site at <u>www.phac-aspc.gc.ca/ep-mu/smallpox-eng.php</u>*

<u>Tularemia</u> - (also known as "rabbit fever") is a disease caused by a strong bacterium, *Francisella tularensis*, found in wild animals and some insects (especially rabbits, hares, beavers and other rodents, mosquitoes, deerflies or ticks) and found in soil, water sources and vegetation in those critters' habitats. *F. tularensis* is one of the most infectious bacteria known and it doesn't take much to cause the disease, plus it can remain alive for weeks in water and soil. Tularemia has been considered useful as an airborne weapon worldwide since the 1930s which is why there's valid concern it could be used today in a terrorist attack.

<u>How it spreads:</u> Tularemia is not known to spread person to person. Some wild animals carry the disease - usually because they were bitten by an infected bug or drank or ate from contaminated water or soil. Hunters and people who spend a lot of time outdoors can get the disease from critters through a bite or handling a diseased carcass (**skin**), from eating an infected animal not properly cooked or by drinking contaminated water (**stomach**), or from breathing in dust from contaminated soil (**lungs**).

<u>Signs & Symptoms:</u> Depends on how person is exposed to tularemia and all symptoms may not occur -- all 3 usually appear in 3 to 5 days (or take

up to 14 days) ... may include fever, chills, joint pain, weakness, and ...

- <u>Skin</u> - may also include a bump or ulcers on bite, swollen and painful lymph glands
- <u>Stomach</u> - may also include sore throat, abdominal pain, ulcers on or in mouth, diarrhea or puking
- <u>Lungs</u> - may also include dry cough, chest pain, bloody spittle, trouble breathing or stops breathing

Treatment: Tularemia can be treated with antibiotics but exposure to *F. tularensis* should be treated as soon as possible since it can be deadly.

Viral hemorrhagic [hem-o-RAJ-ik] **fevers (VHFs)** - are a group of diseases or illnesses caused by several families of viruses. There are many types of VHFs - some the public may recognize are Ebola, Marburg or hantavirus. Some VHFs cause mild reactions or illnesses while others are deadly. Most VHFs are highly contagious and associated with bleeding (hemorrhage), but that's usually not life-threatening. In severe cases, the overall vascular - or blood vessel - system is damaged so the body can't regulate itself thus causing organs to shut down.

Viral hemorrhagic fevers (VHFs) are quite an extensive and complex topic so we are only mentioning it here since it's on the CDC's Category A list. Both the CDC and the Public Health Agency of Canada cover VHFs at length on their web sites if you would like to learn more. We're just briefly explaining how it can spread and listing some general signs and symptoms in the event you ever hear about "viral hemorrhagic fevers" in the news.

How it spreads: Most viruses associated with VHFs naturally reside in animals (mice or other rodents) or insects (ticks or mosquitoes). Some VHF viruses could spread to humans by the bite of an infected insect or by breathing in or touching an infected animal's pee, poop, or other body fluids. (For example, a person crawling in a rat-infested area could stir up and breathe in a virus, or someone slaughtering livestock infected by an insect bite could also spread the virus.) Some other viruses spread person to person through close contact with an infected person's body fluids.

Signs & Symptoms: Signs vary (from minor to deadly) by the type of VHF, but first symptoms often include sudden fever, fatigue (very tired), dizziness, weakness and headache. Person could also have a sore throat, abdominal pain, puking, and diarrhea. Severe cases often show signs of bleeding under the skin, in internal organs, or from the mouth, eyes, or ears. Blood loss is not usually life-threatening, but the damaged vascular system can cause shock, coma, seizures, organ failure or death.

Treatment: There is no specific cure or vaccine for most VHFs.

Hospitalization and supportive care can be given in strict isolation to prevent the virus from spreading to others, but care mainly helps symptoms. Keeping rodents and mosquitoes out of your home is good prevention.

BEFORE A BIOLOGICAL ATTACK:

Watch & listen for signs - Many biological agents do not give immediate "warning signs" -- and most symptoms show up hours or days later so it's hard to say what to watch for, but learn about some common agents (see previous pages) and stay current by listening to radio and TV reports to hear what local authorities tell people to do -- and DO it!

Report strange things - Be aware of your surroundings -- watch for strange or suspicious packages ... or spray trucks or crop dusters in weird places at strange times ... and report suspicious activities to local authorities.

Make a plan - Review Section 1 to develop a **Family Emergency Plan** and **Disaster Supplies Kit**.

Get rid of pests - Keep home clean and put food away that might attract rats or mice and get rid of "standing water" sources around yard (like buckets, tires, pots, or kiddie pools) since they are breeding grounds for mosquitoes.

Be ready to evacuate - Listen to local authorities and leave if you are told to evacuate. *(see EVACUATION)*

DURING A BIOLOGICAL ATTACK:

During any type of biological attack, local authorities will instruct the public about where to go and exactly what to do if exposed to an agent (which may require immediate attention with professional medical staff). It's possible there may be signs (as seen with the anthrax mailings), but more likely it would be discovered after the fact when local health care workers have a wave of sick people seeking emergency medical attention or there are reports of unusual illnesses or symptoms.

Don't panic -- Listen - Stay calm and listen to radio, TV and officials to ...

- Determine if your area is in danger or if you were in the area when it was contaminated.
- Learn signs and symptoms of agent or disease (see previous pages briefly describing **anthrax**, **botulism**, **plague**, **ricin**, **smallpox**, **tularemia**, and **viral hemorrhagic fevers** [**VHFs** - like Ebola or Marburg]).
- Find out if medications or vaccines are being distributed

by authorities and, if so, where you can get them.

<u>Cover up</u> - Cover your mouth and nose with layers of fabric to filter air but still let you breathe (like 2-3 layers of cotton T-shirt or towel or several layers of paper towel, napkins or tissues).

<u>Clean up</u> - Wash with soap and water to keep from spreading germs.

<u>Stay away</u> - Get away from the attack site to avoid contamination.

<u>Evacuate...?</u> - If you are told to leave... DO it! If officials say you have time, close windows, shut vents and turn off attic fans. *(see EVACUATION)*

<u>Things to avoid:</u>
- **powder** - white powdery substance in strange places
- **aerosol mists** - could drift for miles / may be hard to see
- **contaminated food or water** - don't eat or drink any food or water that may have been exposed to agents

<u>Feel sick...?</u> - Many symptoms from biological agents take time to show up so watch family members for signs of illness.

AFTER A BIOLOGICAL ATTACK:

<u>Don't panic -- Listen</u> - Stay calm and listen to radio, TV and officials to ...
- Determine if your area is or was in danger.
- Learn signs and symptoms of specific agent or disease.
- Find out if medications or vaccines are being distributed by authorities and, if so, where you can get them.

<u>Feel sick...?</u> - In most cases, people won't be aware they have been exposed to an agent -- some cause immediate symptoms but many take a while to show up so keep watching for signs of illness.

<u>Don't go there</u> - Do not return home until local authorities say it is safe.

<u>Don't spread it</u> - A person, critter, or item that has been exposed to a disease or biological agent may spread it so...
- **clean up** - if your skin or clothing comes in contact with a suspected visible powder or liquid, wash with soap and water to keep from spreading germs
- **store clothes & shoes** - put exposed clothing and shoes in tightly sealed containers without touching other materials and call local authorities to ask how to get rid of them

- **strange symptoms** - if unusual symptoms show up, get to a hospital or medical expert right away!
- **tell people you've been exposed** - tell everyone who comes in contact with you that you may have been exposed to a biological agent
- **land and property** - ask how to clean up (if needed)

*For more information about **biological agents** or **bioterrorism**, visit the CDC's Emergency Preparedness & Response site at www.bt.cdc.gov or Public Health Agency of Canada's Emergency Preparedness site at www.phac-aspc.gc.ca/ep-mu/index.html or call the CDC Public Response Hotline at 1-800-CDC-INFO (1-800-232-4636) or 1-888-232-6348 (TTY).*

ABOUT RADIOLOGICAL THREAT OR DEVICE

Also review NUCLEAR THREAT OR DEVICE (covered next) since it contains additional information about radiation and e-bombs.

Another known terrorist tactic uses explosives on chemical trucks to spread deadly fumes. See previous pages covering Chemical Agents.

What is a "dirty bomb"?

A radiological dispersion device (**RDD**) - also known as a "dirty bomb" - uses conventional explosives (such as dynamite) to spread radioactive materials in the form of powder or pellets over a targeted area.

A terrorist's main reasons for using a "dirty bomb" is to cause damage to buildings, contaminate an area, and spread fear or panic. This type of attack appeals to terrorists since it doesn't require a lot of technical know-how to build and use ... plus low-level radioactive materials are pretty easy to obtain since they are used in many fields like agriculture, research and medicine.

The most harmful, high-level radioactive materials would be found in nuclear power plants and at nuclear weapons sites, but with the heightened state of alert at many of these locations, it'd be hard for terrorist organizations to get them within the U.S. *Note, nuclear power plant accidents are covered on pages 72-76 and nukes are covered next.*

What are the dangers of an RDD ("dirty bomb")?

According to the Center for Disease Control, the primary danger from a dirty bomb would be the blast itself - not necessarily the radiation. Knowing how much (if any) radiation might be present at the attack site is difficult when the source of the radiation is unknown until site is tested. However, since many RDDs use low-level radioactive materials, there probably would not be enough radiation to cause severe illness.

Has anyone used a "dirty bomb" before?

According to a United Nations report, Iraq tested a dirty bomb device in 1987 but found the radiation levels were too low to cause significant damage. Thus, Iraq abandoned any further use of the device.[7]

What if you or your office receives a "bomb threat"?

Bomb threats are usually received by a telephone call or in the mail. It is highly unlikely a terrorist organization using a "dirty bomb" would give anyone advance warning or call with a bomb threat, however, in the event you or someone in your office receives a bomb threat, do the following...

- If you ever receive a bomb threat, get as much information from the caller as possible (e.g. what kind of bomb, what does it look like, where is it, when will it go off, etc.)
- Try to keep caller on phone as long as you can and write down everything that is said! (Since you'll be nervous or scared, good notes will be very helpful to officials later.)
- Notify the police and building management.
- Calmly evacuate the building, keep the sidewalks clear and stay away from windows.

What if you or someone in your office receives a "suspicious package"?

According to the United States Postal Service, the likelihood of you ever receiving a bomb in the mail is remote. But there have been a small number of explosive devices and biological agents that have surfaced in the mail over the years. Some possible motives for an individual or group sending a "suspicious package" include revenge, extortion, love triangles, terrorism, and business disputes.

The following are some unique signs or characteristics from the U.S. Postal Inspection Service that may help identify a "suspect" piece of mail ...

- Package may have restricted markings like "Personal" or "Private" to one who doesn't receive personal mail at office or to someone no longer working there.
- Package is sealed with excessive amounts of tape or has way too much postage on it.
- Postmark city different than Return Address city.
- Misspelled words, written badly or done with letters cut from newspaper or magazine and pasted on.

- Package has wires or aluminum foil sticking out, oil stains, smells weird or sounds funny (sloshing noise).
- Package may feel strange or look uneven or lopsided.

If you are unsure about a letter or package and are not able to verify the Sender or contents with the person it is addressed to then...

- DO NOT open it, shake it, bump it or sniff it!
- Cover it with a shirt, trash can or whatever is handy.
- Evacuate the area quickly and calmly.
- Wash your hands with lots of soap and water.
- Call building security, police and your postal inspector.
- List all the people who were near the package or letter in case they are needed for further questioning.

BEFORE A RADIOLOGICAL THREAT OR EVENT:

Make a plan - Review Section 1 and check emergency plans for schools, day care and nursing home to find out where everyone goes if evacuated. Find out if there are any below ground shelters near your home, school or office in case you need to take cover from radiation.

Learn more about radiation - Review pages 72-73 and 109-114.

Report strange things - Be aware of your surroundings -- watch for strange or suspicious packages, abandoned briefcases or backpacks and report suspicious activities to local authorities.

Stay current on threats - The Department of Homeland Security www.dhs.gov and Public Safety Canada www.publicsafety.gc.ca post alerts and news about national security online.

Be ready to evacuate - Listen to authorities -- if told to leave - DO it!

DURING A RADIOLOGICAL EVENT OR EXPLOSION:

Don't panic... - Stay calm and don't stop to retrieve personal items or make phone calls - get to a safe place.

Don't look... - Do not look directly at explosion, flash, blast or fireball!

Things to watch out for:

- **falling objects** - if things are falling off bookshelves or from the ceiling get under a sturdy table or desk

- **flying debris** - many blast injuries are caused by flying glass, metal and other materials
- **fires** - stay below the smoke (crawl or walk like a duck)
  - only use the stairs (don't use elevators)
  - check doors with back of hand before opening
    (If <u>HOT</u>, do NOT open - find another exit!)
- **weak structures** - be careful since floors, stairs, roofs or walls might be weakened by the blast

IF INDOORS - Stay put if building is not damaged but leave if warned of a radiation release inside. Cover nose and mouth and find shelter in a building not damaged by blast and prepare to "shelter-in-place".

IF OUTDOORS - Cover mouth and nose with a cloth or handkerchief and take shelter in a safe building as quickly as possible!

IF IN A VEHICLE - Keep windows up, close vents, use "recirculating" air and keep listening to radio for updates. If possible, drive away from site.

AFTER A RADIOLOGICAL EVENT OR EXPLOSION:

<u>If you are trapped in an area:</u>
- **light** - use a flashlight – never use matches or lighters in case there are gas leaks
- **be still** - try to stay still so you won't kick up dust
- **breathing** - cover your mouth with a piece of clothing
- **make noise** - tap on a pipe or wall so rescuers can hear you (shouting may cause you to inhale a lot of dust)

<u>Rescuing others</u> - Untrained persons should not try to rescue people who are inside a collapsed building… wait for emergency personnel to arrive – then, if they need you, they will ask.

<u>Avoid crowds</u> - Be aware large crowds may be targeted for a second attack.

<u>Reduce exposure</u> - Get out of area quickly and into nearest building to reduce chances of being exposed to radioactive materials (or chemicals). The less time you spend in a potentially contaminated area the better.

If radioactive materials were possibly present:

<u>Don't panic -- Listen</u> - Stay calm and listen to radio, TV and officials to ...
- Determine if your area is in danger or contaminated.
- Find out where to go for radiation monitoring and blood

tests to determine if you were exposed and what to do to protect your health if radioactive materials are found.

- Learn if **KI** (potassium iodide) is being passed out by authorities and, if so, find out where to get it. Or ask if you should take KI if in your **Disaster Supplies Kit** (more about KI on page 73). Dirty bombs don't normally have radioactive iodide so KI may not be needed.

As long as you are NOT told to evacuate:

Stay put – Stay inside and prepare to "shelter-in-place"!

- Close doors, windows, vents and fireplace damper.
- Turn off air conditioner, ventilation fans, furnace and other intakes (they pull in air from outside).
- Grab **Disaster Supplies Kit** and go to a basement or underground area (if possible).
- Keep a battery-operated radio with you to hear updates.
- Stay inside until authorities tell you it is safe to go out!

Clean up - If you were possibly exposed to radiation (or chemicals)...

- **store clothes & shoes** - put clothing and shoes in tightly sealed containers or plastic bags and ask health officials what to do with them
- **shower** - wash body and hair to remove particles / toxins

Will I get radiation sickness or cancer...? - Just because you were at the site of a dirty bomb does not mean you were exposed to radioactive materials. Radiation cannot be seen, smelled, felt, or tasted. Until doctors are able to check skin with sensitive detection devices or run blood tests to determine there was any radiation - no one really knows if they were exposed (unless you have your own detection devices - see page 112). And, even if you were exposed to small amounts of radioactive material, it does not mean you'll be sick or get cancer. Stay calm -- listen to and work with medical health professionals since it depends on each situation or incident.

For the CDC's information on "acute radiation syndrome" (radiation sickness) visit www.bt.cdc.gov/radiation/ars.asp

*For more information about **radiological emergencies** or **radiation emergencies**, visit the CDC's Emergency Preparedness & Response site at www.bt.cdc.gov or visit Health Canada's Emergencies & Disasters site at www.hc-sc.gc.ca*

ABOUT NUCLEAR THREAT OR DEVICE

No one wants to think about a nuclear crisis - and hopefully it will never happen - but we as a nation <u>must</u> accept the fact nuclear tensions are rising globally (plus Al-Qaeda and others are seeking nukes) so we should prepare ourselves and our loved ones in the event the unthinkable strikes our soil.

For decades, movies and some in the media have portrayed a nuclear attack as a "doomsday" event implying most people would be killed on impact ... and survivors would want to die once they come out of their shelters. In reality, unless you are actually at ground zero or within a several mile radius of the blast zone (depending on the size of the nuke, of course), there is a very high probability you will survive as long as you limit your exposure to the radiation, take shelter with proper shielding, and wait for the most dangerous radioactive materials to decay.

In other words, you CAN survive a nuke attack ... but you MUST make an effort to learn what to do!

By learning about potential threats, we are all better prepared to know how to react if something happens. Earlier we covered nuclear power plant accidents and RDDs (dirty bombs) explaining both scenarios would be fairly localized. We also listed sheltering tips and suggested items to be included in Disaster Supplies Kits for several days (in Section 1), however a nuclear attack could create more extensive damage and longer sheltering requirements meaning <u>more</u> preparation is needed.

In this topic we'll explain a nuke scenario, give some tips on sheltering and supplies, and suggest what to do BEFORE, DURING and AFTER an attack.

Please realize this topic is being written with small nuke devices in mind (like a 1-kiloton to 1-megaton device - similar to what a terrrorist group may try to obtain and use). A larger device or a nuclear war would cause more wide-spread damage but some of this data could still be helpful.

Again, these are some very basic things you can do to prepare yourself and your family so you <u>can</u> survive the unthinkable.

<u>What happens when a nuke explodes?</u>

A nuclear blast produces a blinding light, intense heat (called **thermal radiation**), **initial nuclear radiation**, 2 explosive shock waves (**blasts**), mass **fires**, and **radioactive fallout** (residual nuclear radiation). And, if a nuke is launched over our continent and explodes miles above the earth, it could create an **electromagnetic pulse** (**EMP**). Let's break this down a little further...

- **fireball / flash** - a combination of heat and light so intense the flash can be seen for hundreds of miles. Just looking at the flash or even reflected / diffracted light can cause temporary or permanent eye damage.

- **thermal radiation** - an intense heat that could cause fires for several miles around ground zero. The heat flash could cause severe burns from direct exposure or from burning objects like clothing, buildings, etc.

- **initial nuclear radiation** - penetrating invisible rays that can be lethal in high levels

- **blast** - explosive shock wave that happens a split second after the fireball. The blast could destroy most buildings for several miles depending on the size of the nuke and strength of the structures. A blast can also cause serious or lethal injuries to people from being thrown by the shock wave or getting hit by flying objects or debris.

- **radioactive fallout** (residual nuclear radiation) - created when the fireball vaporizes everything inside it (including dirt and water). Vaporized materials mix with radioactive materials in the updraft of air forming a mushroom cloud. Fallout can be carried by winds for hundreds of miles and begin falling to the ground within minutes of the blast or take hours, days, weeks or even months to fall. The heaviest fallout would hit ground zero and areas downwind of that, and 80% of fallout would occur within 24 hours. Most fallout looks like grey sand or gritty ash and the radiation given off cannot be seen, smelled, tasted or felt which is why it is so dangerous.

- **mass fires** - any size blast would cause fires due to the intense heat, and keep in mind gas lines, chemicals and other objects just add fuel to the fires

- **EMP** - an electromagnetic pulse is a split-second silent energy burst (like a stroke of lightning) that can fry electronics connected to wires or antennas like cell phones, cars, computers, TVs, etc. Unless electronics are grounded or hardened, North Americans could experience anything from minor interference to crippled power, transportation, banking and communications systems.

An EMP from a high-altitude nuke (where a nation or group succeeds in detonating a nuclear device carried miles into the atmosphere) could affect electronics within 1,000 miles or more as shown on next page. *(Evidence suggests some countries and groups are working on enhanced and non-nuclear EMP weapons or e-bombs.)*

EMP AREA BY BURSTS AT 30, 120 AND 300 MILES
Dr. Gary Smith "Electromagnetic Pulse Threats", testimony
to House National Security Committee on July 16, 1997

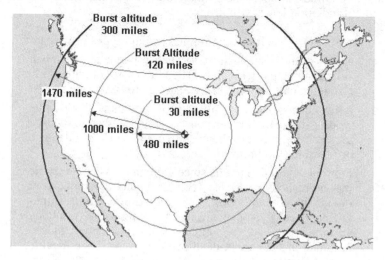

Sizes of nukes - Nuclear weapons are measured in kilotons (KT = 1,000 tons of TNT) or megatons (MT = 1,000,000 tons of TNT). According to FEMA, the most common weapons today range from 100KT to 1MT. A suitcase nuke or portable device would most likely be a 1KT to 10KT bomb. For some perspective, the device used on Hiroshima was about a 15KT bomb.

Damage estimates - Blast effects of a nuke depend on the size of the device and whether it's a surface blast or a high-altitude blast. For example, the number of miles affected by a 500KT blast is fairly small (< 6 mile radius) according to FEMA graphics from "Nuclear Attack Environment Handbook" (posted on www.radshelters4u.com).

Also realize a suitcase nuke or portable device used by a terrorist group would potentially be a 1KT to 10KT bomb reducing the blast zone immensely. In other words, if you are several miles away from Ground Zero your chances of survival are good if you take immediate actions to protect yourself.

Map impact - An interesting widget by Carlos Labs provides a visual map of the impact a nuclear device would have by entering a city anywhere on the planet. You can also choose a weapon size between a 1KT to 50MT. Check out Ground Zero II at www.carloslabs.com/index.php?q=node/20

What is the most dangerous part of a nuclear attack?

Both the initial nuclear radiation and residual nuclear radiation (also called radioactive fallout) are extremely dangerous. But as the materials decay or spread out radiation levels will drop.

Types of radiation - Nuclear radiation has 3 main types of radiation ...

- **alpha** - can be shielded by a sheet of paper or by human skin. If alpha particles are inhaled, ingested, or enter body through a cut, they can cause damage to tissues and cells.

- **beta** - can be stopped by skin or a thicker shield (like wood). Beta particles can cause serious damage to internal organs if ingested or inhaled, and could cause eye damage or possible skin burns.

- **gamma** - most dangerous since gamma rays can penetrate the entire body and cause cell damage throughout your organs, blood and bones. Since radiation does not stimulate nerve cells you may not feel anything while your body absorbs it. Exposure to high levels of gamma rays can lead to radiation sickness or death which is why it is critical to seek shelter from fallout in a facility with <u>thick</u> shielding!

Detecting radiation - You cannot see, smell, taste or feel radiation, but special instruments can detect even the smallest levels of radiation. After an incident, authorities will monitor levels of radioactivity to determine the potential danger. However, since it may take days or weeks before First Responders could get to you, <u>please</u> consider purchasing detection devices for your home and Disaster Supplies Kits. Having these devices handy during a crisis or attack could save your life!

- **survey meter** - measures rate of exposure or intensity of radiation at that specific location if you stayed there for an hour ... like a speedometer in a car (cost: $300-$1,000+)

- **dosimeter** - a pen-like device you can wear that measures total dose or accumulated exposure to radiation as you move around (needs a charger too - cost: $45-$65+ each)

- **KFM kit** - (Kearny Fallout Meter) measures radiation more accurately than most instruments since it's charged electrostatically. Free plans online or available as a low-cost kit ($40-$75). And a great science project for kids.

- **NukAlert**™ - a patented personal radiation meter, monitor and alarm small enough to fit on a key chain. The unit makes chirping sounds if it detects radiation. (cost: $160)

- **RADSticker**™ - postage stamp sized card (cost: $2-$5 ea)

Measuring radiation - Radiation was measured in units called roentgens (pronounced "rent-gens" and abbreviated as "R") ... or "rads" or "rem". An EPA document called "Planning Guidance for Response to A Nuclear Detonation 2nd Edition June 2010" explains ... 1 R (exposure in air) ≅ 1 rad (absorbed dose) ≅ 1 rem (whole-body dose).

Although many measuring devices and older documentation use R and rem, officials and the media now use sievert (Sv) which is the System International or SI unit of measurement of radiation. The formula to convert sieverts to rems is quite simple ... 1 Sv = 100 R (rem).

Radiation detection devices measure the amount of radiation at a specific location or display the total amount of radiation you've been exposed to over a period of time. Exposure limits vary from person to person. Some people can handle higher amounts of rad exposure than others, but the key thing to remember is the less radiation you are exposed to the better.

How many rads are bad? - High doses of radiation in a short span of time can cause radiation sickness or even death, but if that high dose is spread out over a long period of time, it's not as bad.

According to FEMA, an adult could tolerate and recover from an exposure to 150R (1.5 Sv) over a week or 300R (3 Sv) over a 4-month period. But 300R (3 Sv) over a week could cause sickness or possibly death. Exposure to 30R (0.3 Sv) to 70R (0.7 Sv) over a week may cause minor sickness, but a full recovery would be expected. But radioactive fallout decays rapidly so staying in a shelter with proper shielding is critical!

The "seven-ten" rule - An easy way to estimate the decay of radioactive materials is to use the "seven-ten" rule. For every sevenfold increase in time after the initial blast, there is a tenfold decrease in the radiation rate. There is a small fraction of fallout that remains radioactive for many years, but the majority will decay more rapidly than most people think.

Per FEMA's "Preparedness Planning for a Nuclear Crisis" handbook, the below table shows how fast radiation drops from a level of 1,000 rads (10 Sv) per hour:

Hours after detonation	Fraction Remaining	Level of Radiation
1	-------	1000 R / hr (10 Sv)
7	1/10	100 R / hr (1 Sv)
49 (2 days)	1/100	10 R / hr (0.1 Sv)
346 (2 weeks)	1/1000	1 R / hr (0.01 Sv)

In other words, if you have shelter with good shielding and stay put for even just 7 hours ... you've really increased your chances of survival!

<u>Reduce exposure</u> - Protect yourself from radioactive fallout with ...

- **distance** - the more distance between you and the fallout particles, the better
- **shielding** - heavy, dense materials (like thick walls, earth, concrete, bricks, water and books) between you and fallout is best. Stay indoors or below ground.
- **time** - most fallout loses its strength quickly. The more time that passes after the attack, the lower the danger.

<u>Protect your thyroid</u> - Slow down the absorption of radioactive iodine by taking **potassium iodide (KI)**. KI can be purchased over-the-counter and is known to be an effective thyroid-blocking agent. In other words, it fills up the thyroid with good iodine that keeps radioactive iodine from being absorbed into our bodies. However, KI cannot protect the body from radioactive elements other than radioactive iodine. *(Learn more about KI on page 73.)* A few other options to protect your thyroid include taking KIO3, applying iodine solution to your skin, or taking kelp/seaweed pills.

<u>Radiation sickness</u> - Exposure to high levels of radiation (especially gamma rays) over a short period of time can cause severe illness or death.

- <u>First symptoms</u> - sick to stomach (nausea), puking and diarrhea can start within minutes to days after exposure. (Note: Keep in mind ... fear can cause similar symptoms.)
- <u>More serious symptoms</u> - person may look and feel healthy for a short time, then become sick again with loss of appetite, fever, nausea, puking, diarrhea, fatigue and possibly seizures and coma. This seriously ill stage may last from a few hours up to several months.
- <u>Skin</u> - damage can start to show up within a few hours after exposure and include swelling, itching, and redness of skin (like a bad sunburn). Complete healing may take several weeks to a few years depending on dose received.
- <u>Hair</u> - serious exposure could cause temporary hair loss

Please note, radiation sickness is <u>not</u> contagious so will not spread person to person. Consider storing immune-boosting supplements in your Disaster Supplies Kits to help strengthen immune system and rebuild any possible cell damage in the event you are exposed to radiation.

<u>Nuke versus dirty bomb</u> - A nuke creates a massive blast and dangerous radiation that could spread for hundreds of miles. A radiological dispersion device (RDD or dirty bomb) uses explosives (like dynamite) to spread low-level radioactive materials over a small, targeted area. The bomb blast itself may cause more damage than radiation. *(RDDs covered on pages 104-108)*

So how do I protect myself and my family?

Some communities provide 2 types of shelters for local citizens, but not all cities have them plus you may not be able to get to one during a crisis. Contact your local office of emergency management and ask if they have:

- **blast shelter** - specifically constructed to offer some protection against blast pressure, initial radiation, heat, and fire (but realize it can't take a direct hit from a nuke)
- **fallout shelter** - can be any protected space that has walls and materials thick and dense enough to absorb radiation given off by fallout. *(Note: we are mainly focusing on these types of shelters in this section.)*

Basic shelter requirements - Whether you build a shelter in advance or throw together an expedient last-minute shelter during a crisis, the area should protect you from radiation and support you for at least 2 weeks. Some basic requirements for a fallout shelter include ...

- shielding
- ventilation
- water and food
- sanitation and first aid products
- radiation monitoring devices, radio, tools, firearms, etc.

Shielding materials - All fallout shelters must provide good protection from radioactive particles. FEMA suggests having a minimum of several inches of concrete or 1 to 2 feet of earth as shielding around your shelter, and the more the better. Per FEMA, the following shows examples of shielding materials that equal the protection of **4 inches** (10 cm) of **concrete** ...

- **5 - 6 inches** (12 - 15 cm) of **bricks**
- **6 inches** (15 cm) of **sand** or **gravel**
- **7 inches** (18 cm) of **earth**
- **8 inches** (20 cm) of **hollow concrete block**
- **10 inches** (25 cm) of **water**
- **14 inches** (35 cm) of **books** or **magazines**
- **18 inches** (46 cm) of **wood**

Underground is best - Taking shelter in a basement or a facility below ground reduces exposure by **90%**. Less than 4 inches (10 cm) of soil or earth can reduce the penetration of dangerous gamma rays by half.

Prefab shelter - If you have money, time and land, there are many types of prefabricated shelters you can purchase and have buried on your property. Some have complete living quarters and come fully stocked with food and other items. Do your research and get references first though.

<u>Outside shelter</u> - There are free books and pamphlets with instructions on building underground fallout shelters by FEMA, Cresson Kearny (author of "Nuclear War Survival Skills"), Shane Connor (CEO of KI4U, Inc.) and others. If you have a few days, tools, property you can dig down into, and don't mind heavy labor ... check out <u>www.oism.org/nwss</u> or <u>www.ki4u.com</u>. (Both sites describe other shelters too like lean-tos, pole-covered trench shelters, etc.) You can also find several old FEMA booklets from 1980 if you do a web search on "FEMA home fallout shelter".

<u>Indoor shelter locations</u> - If you don't have a fallout shelter you can access safely and quickly, these options could provide protection from dangerous radiation by using shielding materials described on the next page.

- **basement** - find the corner that is most below ground level (the further underground you are the better)
- **1-story home / condo / apartment** - if no underground facility, find a spot in center of home away from windows
- **trailer home** - find sturdier shelter if at all possible (like a basement or a brick or concrete building)
- **multi-story building or high-rise** - go to center of the middle section of the building. Note: if the rooftop of a building next to you is on that same floor, move one floor up or down since radioactive fallout would accumulate on rooftops. Avoid the first floor (if possible) since fallout will pile up on the ground outside.

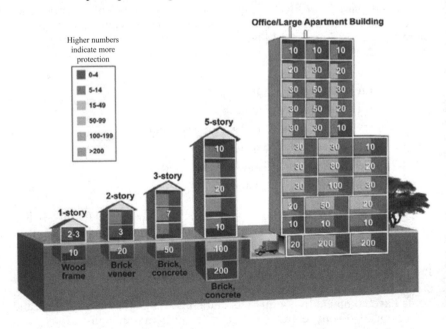

The numbers in the graphic (on previous page) stand for a 'dose reduction factor.' A dose reduction factor of 10 means that a person in that area would get 1/10th of the dose of a person in the open. A dose reduction factor of 200 means that a person in that area would receive 1/200th of the dose of a person out in the open. A color version of the graphic is available at www.ready.gov/america/beinformed/shelter.html

Indoor shelter shielding - Below are some ways to build an expedient last-minute shelter in your home, apartment or workplace. Please realize these tips are very basic things to help protect you from dangerous radiation.

- Set up a large, sturdy workbench or table in location you've chosen (see previous page). If no table, make one by putting doors on top of boxes, appliances or furniture.
- Put as much shielding - furniture, file cabinets, appliances, boxes or pillowcases filled with dirt or sand, boxes of food, water or books, concrete blocks, bricks, etc. - all around sides and on top of table, but don't put too much weight on tabletop or it could collapse. Add reinforcing supports, if needed. *(See page 115 for shielding materials and remember, the more shielding you use, the better protection you'll have from radioactive fallout.)*
- Leave a crawl space so everyone can get inside and be prepared to block opening with shielding materials.
- Leave 2 small air spaces for ventilation (about 4-6" each) - one low at one end and one high at other end. (This allows for better airflow since warm air rises.)
- If you have time and ability to do so, add more mass or shielding materials (like earth) on the floor above you. Support or brace floor from below for the added weight.
- Have water, detection devices, radio, food and sanitation supplies in case you have to shelter for days or weeks.

Ventilation - While inside a shelter you need to circulate fresh air in to reduce carbon dioxide buildup and help reduce heat. If shelter is above ground, the natural flow of air through cracks or windows outside shelter can help move stale warm air out, but basements and underground shelters may have trouble getting airflow. Some ways to improve airflow ...

- **open a door or window** - consider opening a door or window in another part of house or building to improve the natural air circulation (but don't expose yourself to fallout or high radiation levels and don't open window in shelter)
- **air pump** - by planning ahead you can purchase or make a portable pump (read App. B at www.oism.org/nwss)

- **directional fanning** - make a strong 2-handled fan using 2 sticks (or folded cardboard) and tie or tape a piece of cloth (or 2 pieces of cardboard) between sticks to make a rectangular fan. You want to push warm air out of the shelter so start with fan straight up in front of your face, then forcefully push it out and down with your arms completely extended until fan is parallel with floor (about waist high), pause then repeat often and as needed.

Water - As mentioned throughout this manual, water is critical for survival. In addition to water tips on page 152, some more suggestions include ...

- Store about 1 gallon (about 4 litres) of water per person per day for drinking, cooking and sanitation. It may be weeks or months before systems can be tested or they function properly so consider storing 55-gallon drums of water in advance. Or build or install a cistern or water catchment system and store various filtration options.

- Make sure all water containers have tight-fitting lids and cover supply to protect it from bacteria, bugs and dirt.

- Use water as extra shielding by lining cardboard boxes with 2 large trash bags and fill with water.

- If water contains fallout particles, filter it through several layers of clean cloth or paper towels ... or ... allow water to stand for several hours so particles settle to bottom of container. Only take water off the top (don't stir up the settled particles), then purify it using tips on page 152.

There are many types of water purification units on the market and keep in mind a stand-alone unit is the best option during a time of crisis. Some homes have purifiers hooked up to faucets, but remember they rely on functioning utilities. If you're on a limited budget, learn how to make a homemade purifier at http://life-linewaterpurifiers.com/homemade-water-filter-and-purifier/

Also it could be very difficult to store enough water to deal with long term sheltering so if you live in a rural environment, map out different sources of water that could be accessed quickly and easily. Same for city dwellers but finding useable water sources in urban areas could be tough. Kearney's ebook has an entire chapter about water at www.oism.org/nwss

Food, sanitation items & supplies - Please review pages 14-23 and 151-153 for suggestions and tips on gathering food, first aid items, tools, supplies and handling sanitation during a crisis. Store enough supplies for several weeks (or months or longer) in your basement or shelter since services may be disrupted for quite some time after a nuclear attack. Rotate supplies and test batteries every 6 months as discussed on page 23. And for safety's sake, don't tell others what you've stored since you may become a target for looters.

Firearms - If you decide to store guns and ammunition, learn possession laws of your state, make sure you know how to safely store and operate weapons, and ensure family members understand gun safety. Learn more about state laws and training programs for all ages at www.nra.org

Next we're mentioning some very basic things to think about and do BEFORE, DURING and AFTER a nuke attack (many covered in previous pages). Remember ... unless you are at ground zero or within a several mile radius of the blast zone (depending on the size of the nuke, of course), there is a very high probability you will survive as long as you limit your exposure to the radiation, take shelter with proper shielding, and wait for the most dangerous radioactive materials to decay.

BEFORE A NUCLEAR ATTACK:

Make a shelter - If you don't have a basement or underground shelter, think about how you would design a quick shelter with sufficient shielding to keep you safe from fallout. *(see page 117)*

Make a plan - Review Section 1 to develop a **Family Emergency Plan** and **Disaster Supplies Kit** (but expand supplies to have at least 2 to 4+ weeks worth on-hand.) Double check emergency plans for schools, day cares or places family may be and where they'll go if evacuated or sheltered.

Protect yourself - Purchase radiation detection devices from a reputable disaster supplies company. There are many that claim they will work but devices are known to have calibration problems so do your homework. *(see page 112)*

Protect electronics - An electromagnetic pulse could disrupt or fry systems that are not hardened or shielded. Unplugging devices is the best protection, but in most cases you won't get advance warning of an EMP. Electrical and hardware stores carry grounding supplies, surge protectors and battery backup units. Look for the strongest protection available, but realize electronics may still get fried. *(Tip: Do a web search on "Faraday cage" to learn more about shielding electronic devices.)*

Stay current on threats & alerts - The Department of Homeland Security www.dhs.gov and Public Safety Canada www.publicsafety.gc.ca post alerts and news about national security online.

Learn more - There are millions of websites, books and resources about long-term prepping, food storage, nuclear preparedness, survival and more so it can get very overwhelming. Try to stay focused on finding solutions for yourself and your loved ones and not get too burdened with the doomers.

Some examples of sites you may want to research include...

American Medical Association Journal of AMA (can search for data about nuclear war and radiation) http://jama.ama-assn.org

American Preppers Network (network and forum teaching self-reliance, sustainable living and preparedness) www.americanpreppersnetwork.net

Centers for Disease Control Emergency & Preparedness Response (data on Disasters, Chem/Bio/Radiological, etc.) www.bt.cdc.gov

Columbia University National Center for Disaster Preparedness (browse through their reports, videos, etc) www.ncdp.mailman.columbia.edu

Getprepared.ca (Public Safety Canada's family preparedness site) www.getprepared.ca

JP Labs (resources about SIRADs, RADsticker and other dosimeters) www.jplabs.com

Ready.gov (DHS's family preparedness site + pages for Seniors, kids, pets, etc) www.ready.gov

Survival Blog (resources, daily blog, forum, etc) www.survivalblog.com

TACDA (The American Civil Defense Association has resources to help communities prepare for disasters and emergencies) www.tacda.org

US Dept of Health & Human Services Radiation Emergency Medical Management Nuclear page www.remm.nlm.gov/nuclearexplosion.htm

Some examples of books, CDs, courses and magazines include...

Boy Scout Fieldbook (online version in PDF) www.bsafieldbook.org

Country Wisdom & Know-How Everything You Need to Know to Live Off the Land from the Editors of Storey Books (they have lots of great books) www.storey.com

Countryside & Small Stock Journal magazine www.countrysidemag.com

Crisis Preparedness Handbook: A Comprehensive Guide to Home Storage and Physical Survival by Jack A. Spigarelli (on Amazon.com)

Disaster Prep 101® The Ultimate Guide to Emergency Readiness by Paul Purcell www.disasterprep101.com

Emergency Preparedness Digital Library by Rich Fleetwood @ SurvivalCD.com (4 CD/1 DVD set) www.survivalcd.com

GRIT magazine Rural American Know-How www.grit.com

Handbook to Practical Disaster Preparedness for the Family by Arthur T Bradley, PhD www.disasterpreparer.com

LDS Preparedness Manual by Christopher M. Parrett (on Amazon but also available as PDF online) www.ldsavow.com/resources.html

Making the Best of Basics: Family Preparedness Guide by James T Stevens (over 500+ pages of resources, etc) www.makingthebestofbasics.com

Mother Earth News magazine www.motherearthnews.com

Nuclear War Survival Skills by Cresson Kearney (free ebook hosted on OISM site) www.oism.org/nwss

"Personal Radiation Detectors" by Shane Connor (brief paper about devices) www.nukalert.com/personal-rad-detectors.htm

Preppers.info (various publications and resources in the public domain) www.preppers.info/Free_Downloads.html

Urban Survival Course by David Morris www.secretsofurbansurvival.com or www.surviveinplace.com

"What to do if a Nuclear Disaster is Imminent" by Shane Connor (free 8-page guide with planning tips) www.ki4u.com/guide.htm

When Technology Fails by Matthew Stein www.whentechfails.com

Where There Is No Doctor , *Where There Is No Dentist* and many other free online community health publications by Hesperian Foundation www.hesperian.org/publications_download.php

Find more Links at www.itsadisaster.net and do web searches on civil defense, long term food storage, preparedness products and other key words to get more resources. Hopefully the unthinkable never happens so these materials and skills won't be needed, but learn while you can.

DURING A NUCLEAR ATTACK:

Don't panic... - Try to stay calm and ...

- Do NOT look at flash, blast or fireball - turn away!
- Duck & cover .. and watch out for flying debris or fires. Be aware the 2 shock waves have the force of a tornado and may take 30 seconds to 2 minutes to reach you.
- Take shelter to protect yourself from radioactive fallout. Remember ... **distance, shielding** and **time**!
- Blast could create an EMP and fry electronics like cell phones, computers, cars, pacemakers, radios, TVs, etc.

IF INDOORS - If near blast, stay put if home or building is not damaged. If fires are spreading, cover nose and mouth and find shelter in a basement or building further away. Go as far below ground as possible or in the center of a tall building. The goal is to put as many walls and as much concrete, brick and soil between you and the radioactive material outside. Once inside ...

- Close doors, windows and fireplace damper and turn off air conditioner, ventilation fans, furnace and other intakes since they can pull in air or fallout from outside.
- Go to an underground shelter or make an expedient shelter using as much shielding as possible (like furniture, appliances, books, boxes of dirt, etc.) in your basement or the center of room or building.
- Grab your water, food and supplies and have radiation detection devices ready to monitor radiation levels.
- Keep a battery-operated radio with you to hear updates and stay inside until it is safe to go out.

IF OUTDOORS - Cover mouth and nose with a cloth and take shelter immediately. Get as far below ground as possible or in the center of a tall building. The goal is to put as many walls and as much concrete, brick and soil between you and the radioactive material outside. Remember ... **distance, shielding** and **time.**

IF IN A VEHICLE - Keep windows up, close vents, use "recirculating" air and listen to radio for updates. If possible, drive away from site. If you can't get away and you are near the blast area, immediately seek shelter from deadly fallout and fires.

Things to watch out for:

- **fallout** - can arrive 10-20 minutes after the blast -- looks like gray sand or gritty ash and is very radioactive the first few days so find heavy shielding. Fallout can be carried by winds for hundreds of miles.

- **fires** - gas lines or chemicals may cause them to spread
- **flying & falling objects** - the blast and shock waves can shatter windows and hurl debris or body parts like missiles
- **weak structures, floors or stairs** - be careful since they could have been weakened or damaged by blasts

Listen - Turn on radio or TV (if working) to learn projected paths of fallout or fires. Authorities will give specific instructions for people outside the blast zone -- some may need to evacuate ... others should take shelter.

Stay or go..? - Evacuate if told to do so by local authorities ... and ...

- Grab your **Disaster Supplies Kit**.
- Close doors, windows and fireplace damper.
- Cover your mouth and nose with face mask or cloth.
- Keep listening to radio for evacuation routes & updates.

Pets & livestock - If possible, get them indoors or in shelters, especially milk-producing animals. If fallout has already started, don't even try to save them -- it's not worth the risk.

Take KI..? - If you are near the blast zone or in the projected fallout path, take your KI according to label instructions.

AFTER A NUCLEAR ATTACK:

Reduce exposure - Get out of the area quickly and into nearest building to reduce chances of being exposed to deadly radioactive materials. Remember ... **distance**, **shielding** and **time**.

Things to watch out for:

- **fallout** - looks like gray sand and radiation levels can be deadly the first few days without proper shielding. About 80% of fallout occurs within 24 hours and it can start falling within minutes of a blast.
- **fires** - any size nuke will cause fires due to the intense heat - plus gas lines, chemicals and other objects fuel fires
- **body parts** - there may be a lot of dead bodies or body parts scattered around from the blasts
- **weak structures** - be careful since floors, stairs, roofs or walls might be weakened by the blasts
- **looting, guns & panicked people** - be aware people may

become violent trying to find loved ones, water or food

- **HAZMAT** - watch for areas marked "HAZMAT" or "radiation hazard" and don't go there

Stay put – If near the blast zone or in projected fallout path ...

- Close doors, windows and fireplace damper and turn off air conditioner, ventilation fans, furnace and other intakes since they can pull in air or fallout from outside.

- Go to an underground shelter or make an expedient shelter using as much shielding as possible (like furniture, appliances, books, boxes of earth, food, water, etc.) in your basement or the center of room or building.

- Grab **Disaster Supplies Kit**, have detection devices ready to monitor radiation levels, and take **KI**.

- Keep battery-operated radio with you to hear updates (if working - EMP may knock out communications systems).

- Realize it may take a few days or weeks before radiation levels drop enough for people to move about safely.

What .. no services? - An electromagnetic pulse (EMP) could disrupt or crash systems so you may not have access to TV or radio, phones, the Internet, ATMs, and other devices. It could also impact and hinder Emergency Services' response efforts, electrical and water systems, food distribution, transportation (no traffic lights or navigation tools) and more.

Clean up - If you leave shelter and get exposed to fallout, remove clothes and shoes before re-entering shelter so you don't contaminate others. Rinse body and hair but remember water may be limited. If possible, keep a poncho with a hood just outside the shelter so folks can protect head and clothing while outside. Don't bring poncho inside shelter though.

Weird symptoms - Exposure to radiation may cause an upset stomach, puking or diarrhea, but fear and anxiety cause similar symptoms. A person with radiation sickness is not contagious, but realize severe cases can be lethal. *(see pages 112-114)*

Handling a death in a shelter - If a person (or pet) dies while in a shelter, cover body with a sheet or put it in a bag (or tape several large plastic bags together) and move it outside the shelter. Don't try to bury it if high levels of radiation are still in the area, but do poke several pinholes in bag so gases won't build up.

Claiming a body - Hundreds or thousands of people could be killed at or near ground zero from the blast, fires and deadly radiation. There may be a long delay before bodies can be recovered, and some may never be found.

<u>Water</u> - Until water supplies can be tested, water should be filtered and purified using tips on pages 118 and 152. Make sure everyone has enough water to drink daily, but use it sparingly for cleaning dishes, clothes or personal hygiene.

<u>Food</u> - If you brought perishables into the shelter, use them first (see more tips on page 151). Limit cooking during the first few days in shelter to reduce heat, and make sure you have proper ventilation when you do. Keep in mind, healthy adults can go for weeks with little or no food, so ration out supplies in case you cannot leave the shelter for some time or have trouble finding more. Any food that was exposed to fallout should be washed first.

<u>Milk</u> - Children and infants should drink milk made from dried or canned products until authorities can inspect cows' milk for exposure to fallout.

<u>Sanitation</u> - All shelters should have some form of sanitation like a bucket with disinfectant or existing toilets with trash bags since plumbing may not work. Also realize even mild forms of radiation sickness can cause puking and diarrhea so it could get smelly in the shelter. If possible, keep small bags around for folks to use as barf bags and have wipes or sanitizer handy to reduce the spread of germs. *(see more tips on page 153)*

<u>Recovery</u> - Some emotions people may experience after an attack include shock, fear, disbelief and anger. Everyone handles trauma differently, but adversity can also bring people together. Rebuilding would be a long, slow process, especially if an EMP knocks out communications, utilities and banking systems. Once it is safe to move around outside, many volunteers will be needed to help the area and country rebuild and recover.

Also see TIPS ON RECOVERING FROM A DISASTER for some additional thoughts on recovery, but realize a major nuke or EMP could have devastating consequences and recovery could take years or decades. Many seniors would be a wealth of information since they have knowledge of living during "pre-technology" days.

If more people will learn what to do during a nuclear crisis, there would be less fear and anxiety. Be aware... be prepared ... and have a plan ~ you CAN survive a nuke. Please spread the word...

FOR MORE INFORMATION ABOUT NATIONAL SECURITY

Again, citizens need to remain calm about the threat of terrorist attacks and learn about some of the types, how to prepare for them, and what to expect in some cases. Stay current on news but don't obsess over it ... and be aware of your surroundings as you go about your daily routines and don't hesitate to report something that looks suspicious.

Also consider getting involved with your local community to learn more about preparedness, crime prevention and response. *See pages 222-224*

For more information about National Security, visit the following sites:

Central Intelligence Agency www.cia.gov

Federal Bureau of Investigations www.fbi.gov

INTERPOL www.interpol.int

National Defence and the Canadian Forces www.forces.gc.ca

U.S. Department of Defense www.defense.gov

U.S. Department of Homeland Security www.dhs.gov

What are **YOU** gonna do about...
A THUNDERSTORM?

Thunderstorms are very common... in fact, at any given moment, nearly 2,000 thunderstorms can be in progress over the face of the earth.

Lightning always comes with a thunderstorm since that is what causes the thunder. If you've ever heard someone say lightning never strikes the same place twice... WRONG! Lightning often strikes the same place several times during one storm.

Severe thunderstorms can also bring heavy rains, flooding, hail, strong winds, tornadoes and microbursts (a sudden vertical drop of air).

BEFORE A THUNDERSTORM:

Prepare - Review FLOOD, LIGHTNING, POWER LOSS and WIND MITIGATION at beginning of this Section.

Learn the buzzwords - Learn the terms / words used with thunderstorms...
- **Severe Thunderstorm Watch** - tells you when and where severe thunderstorms are possible
- **Severe Thunderstorm Warning** - severe thunderstorms have been spotted or are occurring

Watch for lightning - If you hear thunder, you're close enough to be struck by lightning - take cover as quickly as possible. Be aware that lightning often strikes miles away from the rainfall or thunderstorm cloud.

Unplug it - Unplug appliances if possible - even ones on a surge protector and it's best to move plugs away from outlets.

DURING A THUNDERSTORM:

Listen - Keep a battery-operated radio handy for local reports on storm (especially severe storms which could cause tornadoes.)

IF INDOORS - Stay inside until the storm passes.
- Don't shower - sounds weird, but wait since water can carry an electrical charge if lightning strikes near home
- Avoid corded objects - corded phones, PCs or a mouse

conduct electricity (could shock you). Cordless and cell phones or wireless devices are usually safe.

IF OUTDOORS - Try to get to safe shelter quickly.

- Move away from tall things (trees, towers, fences or power lines) and metal things (umbrellas, motorcycles or bicycles, wire fences, etc) since they all attract lightning.
- If surrounded by trees, take shelter under the <u>shorter</u> trees.
- Get to a low lying area but watch out for flash floods.
- **Be small** - make yourself a small target by crouching down and put your hands on your knees (and don't lie flat on the ground since that makes you a bigger target!)

IF IN A BOAT - Get to land and to shelter quickly! Water is extremely dangerous when there's lightning.

IF IN A VEHICLE - Keep windows closed and stay out of a convertible, if possible (mainly since you may the highest target if lightning strikes).

<u>Hairy sign</u> - If you feel your hair stand on end and feel tingly (which means lightning is about to strike)... crouch down and bend forward putting hands on your knees (be small), Don't lie flat on ground... makes a bigger target!

<u>If someone is struck by lightning:</u>

- Victim does not carry electrical charge - CAN be touched.
- Call 9-1-1 or local EMS (emergency) telephone number.
- Victim will have 2 wounds - an entrance and an exit burn *(see BURNS [Electrical] in Section 3)*

AFTER A THUNDERSTORM:

<u>Things to avoid:</u>

- **flooded areas** – stay away from flood waters since may be contaminated by oil, gas or raw sewage or electrically charged from underground or downed power lines or lightning – wait for authorities to say it's okay to return
- **moving water** – 6 inches (15 cm) can knock you off your feet and 2 ft (.6 m) can float a car
- **storm-damaged areas**
- **downed power lines**

<u>Recovery tips</u> - Review TIPS ON RECOVERING FROM A DISASTER at end of this Section.

What are YOU gonna do about...
A TORNADO?

The U.S. has more tornadoes than anywhere else in the world (averaging about 1,200 per year), with sightings in all 50 states. Canada is # 2 in volume of tornadoes (averaging about 80 per year) with several high risk areas mostly in central provinces.

Most injuries or deaths caused by tornadoes are from collapsing buildings, flying objects, or trying to outrun a twister in a vehicle. Tornadoes can also produce violent winds, hail, lightning, rain and flooding.

As of 2007, the National Weather Service uses a new scale called the **Enhanced Fujita (EF) scale** that classifies tornadoes based on 28 Damage Indicators to more accurately estimate wind speeds.

Scale	Wind Estimate	Typical Damage *(per NOAA and Wikipedia)*
EF0	65-85 mph 105-137 km/h	**Light**: Peels off some roofs; some damage to gutters or siding; broken branches, etc.
EF1	86-110 mph 138-177 km/h	**Moderate**: Strips surface off roofs; mobile homes overturned; broken windows, etc.
EF2	111-135 mph 178-217 km/h	**Considerable**: Roofs/mobile homes destroyed; trees snap; light-object missiles generated, etc.
EF3	136-165 mph 218-266 km/h	**Severe**: Roofs/walls ripped off sturdy homes; trees debarked; heavy cars lifted & thrown, etc.
EF4	166-200 mph 267-322 km/h	**Devastating**: Well-constructed homes leveled; cars thrown; small missiles generated, etc.
EF5	> 200 mph > 322 km/h	**Incredible**: All homes leveled and swept away; car-sized missiles fly thru air over 100 metres (109 yards); structural damage to high-rises, etc.

BEFORE A TORNADO:

Prepare - Review FLOOD, LIGHTNING, POWER LOSS and WIND MITIGATION at beginning of this Section.

Learn the buzzwords - Learn the terms / words used with tornado threats...
- **Tornado watch** - a tornado is possible - listen for updates
- **Tornado warning** - a tornado has been sighted so take shelter quickly and keep a radio with you for updates

Learn risks - Ask local emergency management office about threats in your area, what the warning signals are, and what to do when you hear them.

Where am I? - Make sure your kids know what county or area you live in and listen for that name on radio or TV updates.

Get tuned in - Keep a battery-operated radio (with spare batteries) handy for weather forecasts and updates. (Environment Canada's Weatheradio and NOAA's Weather Radio have tone-alert features that alert you when a Watch or Warning has been issued.)

Be ready to evacuate - If officials say leave - DO it! *(see EVACUATION)*

Make a plan - Review Section 1 to develop a **Family Emergency Plan** and **Disaster Supplies Kit**.

Learn to shut off - Know where and how to shut off electricity, gas and water at main switches and valves -- ask local utilities for instructions.

Where do I go? - Know locations of shelters where you spend time (schools, nursing homes, office, etc.) The best place is underground (like a basement, a safe room, or storm cellar) or find a hallway, bathroom, or closet in middle of building on the lowest floor.

Do drills - Practice going to shelter with your family and "duck and cover" (use your hands and arms to protect head and stay down low).

Put it on film/chip/drive - Either videotape or take pictures of home and personal belongings and store them off-site with your important papers.

DURING A TORNADO WATCH OR WARNING:

Review above tips and...

Listen - Keep up with local news reports tracking the twister or conditions using a battery-operated radio.

Watch & listen - Some danger signs of a tornado include dark green-ish sky, clouds moving to form a funnel, large hail, or loud roar (like a train).

Be ready to evacuate - Keep listening to authorities - if told to leave, DO it (esp if you live in a mobile home or trailer).

DURING A TORNADO:

Listen - Use a battery-operated radio to hear reports tracking the twister.

Take cover - If you hear or see a tornado coming take cover immediately!

IF IN A TRAILER OR MOBILE HOME – GET OUT!!!
- Get to a stronger shelter... or ...
- Stay low to ground in a ditch and cover head with hands.
- If you hear or see water in the ditch, move quickly to a drier spot (in case lightning strikes nearby).

IF INDOORS - Get to a safe place right away - and avoid windows!!
- In house or small building - Go to basement, storm cellar or middle of building on lowest floor (bathroom, closet or hallway). Get under something sturdy or put mattress or covers over you for protection & stay until danger passes.
- In a school, nursing home, factory or shopping center - Go to designated shelter areas (or interior hallways on lowest floor) -- stay away from open areas.
- In a high-rise building - Go to a small, interior room or hallway on lowest floor possible and avoid windows.

IF OUTDOORS - Try to take shelter in a basement or sturdy building. Or lie in a dry ditch with hands covering your head, but watch and listen for flooding and be aware you're a bigger target for lightning. And if you hear or see water, move since it can carry lightning's electrical charge!

IF IN A VEHICLE - GET OUT and take shelter in a building or lie flat in a ditch with hands covering head (but be aware you're a target for lightning when lying flat & listen for flooding!) DO NOT try to out-drive a tornado! You never know which direction one will go & it moves too fast.

AFTER A TORNADO:

Listen - Use a battery-operated radio to hear reports in case there are more twisters.

Be aware - Watch for broken glass and downed power lines .. and avoid damaged buildings or homes until authorities give the OK to enter.

Injured people - Do not try to move injured people unless they are in danger and call for help immediately. *(see TIPS ON BASIC FIRST AID)*

What to wear - Use sturdy work boots and gloves.

Recovery tips - See TIPS ON RECOVERING FROM A DISASTER

What are YOU gonna do about...
A TSUNAMI?

A tsunami [soo-nah´-mee] is a series of huge, destructive waves caused by an undersea disturbance from an earthquake, volcano, landslide, or even a meteorite. As the waves approach the shallow coastal waters, they appear normal and the speed decreases. Then, as the tsunami nears the coastline, it turns into a gigantic, forceful wall of water that smashes into the shore with speeds exceeding 600 miles per hour (965 km/h)! Usually tsunamis are about 20 feet (6 m) high, but extreme ones can get as high as 100 feet (30 m) or more!

A tsunami is a series of waves and the first wave may <u>not</u> be the largest one, plus the danger can last for many hours after the first wave hits. During the past 100 years, more than 200 tsunamis have been recorded in the Pacific Ocean due to earthquakes and Japan has suffered a majority of them.

The Pacific Ocean tsunami warning system was put in place back in 1949. As of June 2006, the Indian Ocean has a tsunami warning system, and NOAA expanded the Pacific system to include the Caribbean, the Gulf of Mexico and areas of the Atlantic around the U.S. coast as of mid-2007.

Did you know...
> ... a tsunami is <u>not</u> a tidal wave - it has nothing to do with the tide?!
> ... another name used to describe a tsunami is "harbor wave" - "tsu" means harbor and "nami" means wave in Japanese?!
> ... sometimes the ocean floor is exposed near the shore since a tsunami can cause the water to recede or move back before slamming in to shore?!
> ... tsunamis can travel up streams and rivers that lead to the ocean?!

BEFORE A TSUNAMI:

<u>Prepare</u> - Review FLOOD, POWER LOSS and WIND MITIGATION at beginning of this Section.

<u>Learn the buzzwords</u> - Learn words used by both the West Coast / Alaska Tsunami Warning Center (WC/ATWC - for AK, BC, CA, OR, and WA) and the Pacific Tsunami Warning Center (PTWC - for international authorities, HI and all U.S. territories within Pacific basin) for tsunami threats...

- **Advisory** - an earthquake has occurred in the Pacific basin which might generate a tsunami
- **Watch** - a tsunami was or may have been generated, but is at least 2 hours travel time from Watch area
- **Warning** - a tsunami was / may have been generated and could cause damage to Warning area - should evacuate

Learn risks - If new to area, call local emergency management office and ask what the warning signals are and what to do when you hear them. Coastal areas less than 25 feet above sea level and within a mile of shoreline along coasts are at greatest risk. Or visit www.tsunamiready.noaa.gov

Make a plan - Review Section 1 to develop a **Family Emergency Plan** and **Disaster Supplies Kit**.

Listen - Make sure you have a battery-operated radio (with spare batteries) for weather forecasts and updates. (Radios like Environment Canada's Weatheradio and NOAA's Weather Radio have a tone-alert feature that automatically alerts you when a Watch or Warning has been issued.)

Water signs - If near water or shore, watch for a noticeable rise or fall in the normal depth of coastal water - that's advance warning of a tsunami so get to high ground. Also - if water pulls away from shoreline and exposes sea floor - run to higher ground ASAP!!

Feeling shaky...? - If you feel an earthquake in the Pacific Coast area (from Alaska down to Baja), listen to the radio for tsunami warnings.

Is that it...? - Don't be fooled by the size of one wave - more will follow and they could get bigger ... and a small tsunami at one beach can be a giant wave a few miles away!

Be ready to evacuate - Listen to local authorities and leave if you are told to evacuate. *(see EVACUATION)*

DURING A TSUNAMI:

Leave - If you are told to evacuate, DO IT! Remember - a tsunami is a series of waves - the first one may be small but who knows what the rest will bring. Grab your **Disaster Supplies Kit** and GO!

IF ON OR NEAR SHORE - Get off the shore and get to higher ground quickly! Stay away from rivers and streams that lead to the ocean since tsunamis can travel up them too. You cannot outrun a tsunami ... if you see the wave it's too late!

IF ON A BOAT - It depends where you are -- either get to land or go further out to sea ...

- In port - May not have time to get out of port or harbor and out to sea - check with authorities to see what you should do. Smaller boats may want to dock and get passengers and crew to land quickly.
- In open ocean - DO NOT return to port if a tsunami warning has been issued since wave action is barely noticeable in the open ocean! Stay out in open sea or ocean until authorities advise danger has passed.

Don't go there - Do NOT try to go down to the shoreline to watch and don't be fooled by size of one wave - more will follow and they could get bigger so continue listening to radio and TV.

AFTER A TSUNAMI:

Listen - Whether on land or at sea, local authorities will advise when it is safe to return to the area -- keep listening to radio and TV updates.

Watch out - Look for downed power lines, flooded areas and other damage caused by the waves.

Don't go in there - Try to stay out of buildings or homes that are damaged until it is safe to enter and wear sturdy work boots and gloves when working in the rubble.

Strange critters – Be aware that the waves may bring in many critters from the ocean (marine life) so watch out for pinchers and stingers!

RED or GREEN sign in window – After a disaster, Volunteers and Emergency Service personnel may go door-to-door to check on people. By placing a sign in your window that faces the street near the door, you can let them know if you need them to STOP HERE or MOVE ON.

Either use a piece of RED or GREEN construction paper or draw a big RED or GREEN "X" (using a crayon or marker) on a piece of paper and tape it in the window.

- RED means STOP HERE!
- GREEN means EVERYTHING IS OKAY...MOVE ON!
- Nothing in the window would also mean STOP HERE!

Recovery tips - Review TIPS ON RECOVERING FROM A DISASTER at end of this Section.

What are YOU gonna do about...
A VOLCANIC ERUPTION?

A volcano is a mountain that opens downward to a reservoir of molten rock (like a huge pool of melted rocks) below the earth's surface. Unlike mountains, which are pushed up from the earth's crust, volcanoes are formed by their buildup of lava, ash flows, and airborne ash and dust. When pressure from gases and molten rock becomes strong enough to cause an explosion, it erupts and starts to spew gases and rocks through the opening.

Volcanic eruptions can hurl hot rocks (sometimes called **tephra**) for at least 20 miles (32 km) and cause sideways blasts, lava flows, hot ash flows, avalanches, landslides and mudflows (also called **lahars**). They can also cause earthquakes, thunderstorms, flash floods, wildfires, and tsunamis. Sometimes volcanic eruptions can drive people from their homes forever.

Fresh volcanic ash is not like soft ash in a fireplace. Volcanic ash is made of crushed or powdery rocks, crystals from different types of minerals, and glass fragments that are extremely small like dust. But it is hard, gritty, smelly, sometimes corrosive or acidic (means it can wear away or burn things) and does not dissolve in water.

The ash is hot near the volcano but is cool when it falls over great distances. Ashfall is very irritating to skin and eyes and the combination of ash and burning gas can cause lung irritation or damage to small infants, the elderly or people with breathing problems

Did you know...

... there are about 1 million volcanoes on the ocean's floor?!

... volcanic eruptions can impact our global climate since they release ash and gases (like sulfur and carbon dioxide) into the earth's atmosphere and warm the oceans?!

... floods, airborne ash or dangerous fumes can spread 100 miles (160 km) or more?!

... Alaska has had over 40 active volcanoes?!

... Yellowstone National Park actually sits on top of a super-volcano which erupted 3 times in the past 2 million years forming 3 massive calderas (or huge craters)?!

BEFORE A VOLCANIC ERUPTION:

Prepare - Since volcanic eruptions cause many types of disasters, review all

MITIGATION tips at beginning of this Section. Also try to cover and protect machinery, electronic devices, downspouts, etc. from ashfall. Learn more by visiting the USGS Volcano Hazards Program site at http://volcanoes.usgs.gov/ash/

<u>Learn alert levels</u> - Ask emergency management office which volcano warnings or alert levels are used since they vary depending on where you live (can be alert levels, status levels, condition levels or color codes).

<u>Make a plan</u> - Review Section 1 to develop a **Family Emergency Plan** and **Disaster Supplies Kit**. (Note: Put in goggles or safety glasses and dust masks for each family member to protect eyes and lungs from ash.)

<u>Okay to go?</u> - Don't go to active volcano sites unless officials say it's okay.

<u>Be ready to evacuate</u> - Listen to local authorities and leave if you are told to evacuate. *(see EVACUATION)*

DURING A VOLCANIC ERUPTION:

<u>Listen</u> - Do what local authorities say, especially if they tell you to leave!

<u>Leave</u> - If you are told to evacuate, DO IT! Don't think you are safe to stay home … the blast can go for miles and cause wildfires and other hazards!

<u>Watch out</u> - Eruptions cause many other disasters:
- **flying rocks** - hurled for miles at extremely fast speeds
- **mudflows, landslides or lahars** - they move faster than you can walk or run
- **fires** - hot rocks and hot lava will cause buildings and forests to burn
- **lava flows** - burning liquid rock and nothing can stop it
- **gases and ash** - try to stay upwind since winds will carry these -- they are very harmful to your lungs
- **vog** - volcanic smog forms when sulfur dioxide and other pollutants react with oxygen, moisture and sunlight -- can cause headaches, breathing difficulties and lung damage

IF INDOORS - Stay in, but be aware of ash, rocks, mudflows or lava!
- Close all windows, doors, vents and dampers and turn off A/C and fans to keep ash fall out.
- Put damp towels under doorways and drafty windows.
- Bring pets inside (if time, move livestock into shelters).

- Listen for creaking on your rooftop (in case ashfall gets heavy -- could cause it to collapse!)

IF OUTDOORS - Try to get indoors, if not...
- Stay upwind so ash and gases are blown away from you.
- Watch for falling rocks and, if you get caught in rockfall, roll into a ball to protect your head!
- Get to higher ground - avoid low-lying areas since poisonous gases collect there and flash floods could happen.
- Use dust-mask or damp cloth to help breathing, wear long-sleeved shirts and pants, and use goggles.
- Ashfall can block out sunlight and may cause lightning.

IF IN A VEHICLE - Avoid driving unless absolutely required.
- Slow down -- keep speed at 35 mph (56 km/h) or slower, mainly because of thick dust and low visibility.
- Shut off engine and park in garage (driving stirs up ash that can clog motor and damage moving engine parts).
- Look upstream before crossing a bridge in case a mudflow or landslide is coming.

AFTER A VOLCANIC ERUPTION:

Listen - Local authorities will say if and when it's safe to return to area (especially if you had to evacuate) and give other updates when available.

Water - Check with authorities before using water, even if eruption was just ash fall (gases and ash can contaminate water reserves). Don't wash ash into drainpipes, sewers or storm drains since wet ash can wear away metal.

What to wear - If you must be around ash fall, you should wear long sleeve shirts, pants, sturdy boots or shoes, gloves, goggles (or safety glasses) and keep your mouth and nose covered with a dust-mask or damp cloth.

Ash - Dampen ash before sweeping or shoveling buildup so it's easier to remove and won't fly back up in the air as much - but be careful since wet ash is slippery. Wear protective clothing and a dust mask too. Realize ash can disrupt lives of people and critters for months.

Protect - Cover machinery and electronic devices like computers.

Recovery tips - Review TIPS ON RECOVERING FROM A DISASTER at end of this Section. Also visit the USGS Volcano Hazards Program page at http://volcanoes.usgs.gov/

What are _YOU_ gonna do about...
WINTER STORMS & EXTREME COLD?

Winter storms can last for many days and include high winds, freezing rain, sleet or hail, heavy snowfall and extreme cold. These types of winter storms can shut down a city or area mainly due to blocked roads and downed power lines. People can be stranded in their car or trapped at home for hours or days, but there are many other hazards that come with these storms.

The leading cause of death during winter storms is automobile or other transportation accidents and the second leading cause of death is heart attacks. Hypothermia (or freezing to death) is very common with the elderly who sometimes die inside their homes because it is so cold. The best way to protect yourself from a winter disaster is to plan ahead before the cold weather begins. Take advantage of spring sales when winter items are cheaper so you're ready for next winter.

BEFORE A WINTER STORM:

Prepare - Review FLOOD, POWER LOSS, WIND and WINTER STORM MITIGATION at beginning of this Section.

Learn the buzzwords - Learn terms / words used with winter conditions...
- **Freezing rain** - rain that freezes when it hits the ground, creating a coating of ice on roads and walkways
- **Hail** - rain that turns to ice while suspended and tossed in the air from violent updrafts in a thunderstorm
- **Sleet** - rain that turns to ice pellets before reaching ground
- **Winter Weather Advisory** - cold, ice and snow expected
- **Winter Storm Watch** - severe winter weather such as heavy snow or ice is possible within a day or two
- **Winter Storm Warning** - severe winter conditions have begun or are about to begin
- **Blizzard Warning** - heavy snow and strong winds producing blinding snow (near zero visibility) and life-threatening wind chills for 3 hours or longer
- **Frost/Freeze Warning** - below freezing temperatures expected

Be prepared - Review Section 1 to develop a **Family Emergency Plan** and **Disaster Supplies Kit**, and add the following at home for winter storms:

- **calcium chloride** - good for melting ice on walkways (rock salt can blister concrete and kill plants)
- **sand or kitty litter** - to improve traction
- **emergency heating equipment and fuel** - have backup...
  <u>fireplace</u> - gas or wood burning stove or fireplace
  <u>generator</u> – gas or diesel models available and learn how to use it in advance (and never bring it indoors!)
  <u>kerosene heaters</u> – ask Fire Department if they are legal in your community and ask about safety tips in storing fuel
  <u>charcoal</u> - NEVER use charcoal indoors since fumes are deadly in contained room -- fine for outdoor use!!
- **extra wood** - keep a good supply in a dry area
- **extra blankets** – either regular blankets or emergency blankets (about the size of a wallet)

<u>Clean chimney</u> - If you use a wood-burning fireplace often, have it inspected annually and consider having a professional chimney sweep clean it as needed. Learn more in the Chimney Safety Institute of America's FAQs at <u>www.csia.org</u>

DURING A WINTER STORM:

<u>Listen</u> - Get updates from radio and TV weather reports.

<u>What to wear</u> - Dress for the season...
- **layer** - much better to wear several layers of loose-fitting, light-weight, warm clothing than one layer of heavy clothing (outside garment should be waterproof)
- **mittens** - mittens are warmer than gloves
- **hat** - most body heat is lost through the top of your head
- **scarf** - cover your mouth with a scarf or wrap to protect your lungs from cold air

<u>Don't overdo it</u> - Be careful when shoveling snow or working outside since cold can put strain on the heart and cause a heart attack (even in children!)

<u>Carbon monoxide</u> - Learn how to protect your home from winter heating dangers by visiting CDC's Carbon Monoxide site at <u>www.cdc.gov/co/</u>

<u>Watch for signs</u> - playing or working out in the snow can cause exposure so look for signs of...
- **frostbite** - loss of feeling in your fingers, toes, nose or ear lobes or they turn really pale

- **hypothermia** - start shivering a lot, slow speech, stumbling, or feel very tired

If signs of either one ... get inside quickly and get medical help *(see COLD-RELATED ILLNESSES in Section 3)*. Also check out NOAA's Windchill Chart and safety information at www.weather.gov/om/windchill

Power loss – If the power goes off, turn off all tools, appliances and electronic equipment to reduce the load on electrical system once power is restored. It also may protect devices from a power surge that could follow the start-up. (Tip: Leave one light switch on so you know power's back on.)

Leaving? – If you decide to leave home during the winter for some time with the chance of freezing weather hitting while your gone, Canadian officials suggest you ...

- Turn off main breaker or electric switch.
- Turn off water main where it enters house and cover the valve and pump or meter with a blanket or insulating material.
- Drain the water from the plumbing system by turning on water taps and flushing toilets a few times. Add some antifreeze to toilet bowl, sink and bath drains.
- Check draining and frost protection instructions in the manuals for your dishwasher, washing machine, etc.

WINTER DRIVING TIPS

Driving - If you must travel, consider public transportation. Best to travel during the day, don't travel alone, and tell someone where you're going. Stay on main roads and avoid taking back roads.

Winterize car - Make sure you have plenty of antifreeze and snow tires (or chains or cables). Keep gas tank as full as possible during cold weather.

Winter Kit - Carry a "winter" car kit in trunk *(see Section 1)* and throw in...

- **warm things** – mittens, hat, emergency blanket, sweater, waterproof jacket or coat
- **cold weather items** - windshield scraper, road salt, sand
- **emergency items** - bright colored cloth or distress flag, booster cables, emergency flares, tow chain, rope, shovel
- **miscellaneous** - food, water, radio, etc.

Stranded - If you get trapped in your car by a blizzard or break down...

- **get off the road** - if you can, drive car onto shoulder

- **give a sign** - turn on hazard lights and tie a bright cloth or distress flag on antenna, door handle or hang out driver side window (keep above snow so it draws attention)
- **stay in car** - stay inside until help arrives (CAR KIT can provide food, water and comforts if you planned ahead)
- **start your car** - turn on car's engine and heater about 10 minutes each hour (open window slightly for ventilation so you don't get carbon monoxide poisoning)
- **light at night** - turn on inside light so crews or rescuers can see you
- **if you walk** - if you walk away from car, make sure you can see building or shelter (no more than 100 yards/10 m)
- **exercise** - DO NOT overdo it, but light exercises can help keep you warm
- **sleeping** - if others in car, take turns sleeping so someone can watch for rescue crews
- **exhaust pipe** - check exhaust pipe now and then and clear out any snow buildup

AFTER A WINTER STORM:

<u>Check food</u> - If you lost power, check food in both fridge and freezer to ensure it didn't spoil. Foods in a well-filled, well-insulated freezer won't go bad until several days after power goes off. If there are ice crystals in the center of food it's okay to eat or refreeze.

<u>Don't overdo it</u> - Both adults and children need to be careful when playing or working outside in frigid conditions since cold can put strain on the heart and cause a heart attack.

<u>Restock</u> - Stock up on items you used so you're ready for the next one.

<u>Recovery tips</u> - Review TIPS ON RECOVERING FROM A DISASTER starting on next page.

TIPS ON RECOVERING FROM A DISASTER

Unless you've been in a disaster before, it is hard to imagine how you will handle the situation. Coping with the human suffering and confusion of a disaster requires a certain inner strength. Disasters can cause you to lose a loved one, neighbor or friend or cause you to lose your home, property and personal items. The emotional effects of loss and disruption can show up right away or may appear weeks or months later.

We are going to briefly cover "emotional" recovery tips then cover some "general" recovery tips on what to do AFTER a disaster. Remember -- people *can* and *do* recover from all types of disasters, even the most extreme ones, and you <u>can</u> return to a normal life.

EMOTIONAL RECOVERY TIPS – HANDLING EMOTIONS

Since disasters usually happen quickly and without warning, they can be very scary for both adults and children. They also may cause you to leave your home and your daily routine and deal with many different emotions, but realize that a lot of this is normal human behavior. It is very important that you understand no matter what the loss is… there is a natural grieving process and every person will handle that process differently.

SOME NORMAL REACTIONS TO DISASTERS

<u>Right after disaster</u> – shock, fear, disbelief, hard time making decisions, refuses to leave home or area, won't find help or help others

<u>Days, weeks or months after disaster</u> – anger or moodiness, depression, loss of weight or change in appetite, nightmares, trouble sleeping, crying for "no reason", isolation, guilt, anxiety, domestic violence

<u>Additional reactions by children</u> - thumb sucking, bed-wetting, clinging to parent(s) or guardian, won't go to bed or school, tantrums (crying or screaming), problems at school

Please note: If any of your disaster reactions seem to last for quite some time, please consider seeking professional counseling for Post-Traumatic Stress Disorder (PTSD). There is nothing wrong with asking for help!

TIPS FOR ADULTS & KIDS

<u>Death</u> - You may lose loved ones or need to handle bodies during a crisis. Review some tips on pages 155-156.

<u>Deal with it</u> - Recognize your own feelings so you can deal with them properly and responsibly.

<u>Talk or not?</u> - Talking to others can help relieve stress and help you realize you are not alone... other victims are struggling with the same emotions, including your own family. And don't leave out the little ones ... let them talk about their feelings and share your feelings with them. But don't force anyone to talk about their feelings since they might cope better by keeping their thoughts private.

<u>Accept help</u> - Realize that the people who are <u>trying</u> to help you <u>want</u> to help you so please don't shut them out or turn them away.

<u>Time out</u> - Whenever possible, take some time off and do something you enjoy to help relieve stress... and do something fun with the whole family like a hike, a picnic, or play a game.

<u>Rest</u> - Listen to your body and get as much rest as possible. Stress can run you down so take care of yourself and your family members.

<u>Slow down</u> - Don't feel like you have to do everything at once and pace yourself with a <u>realistic</u> schedule.

<u>Stay healthy</u> - Make sure everyone cleans up with soap and <u>clean</u> water after working in debris. Also, drink lots of clean water and eat healthy meals to keep up your strength. If you packed vitamins and herbs in your **Disaster Supplies Kit**, take them.

<u>Work out</u> - Physical activity is good for releasing stress or pent-up energy.

<u>Hug</u> - A hug or a gentle touch (holding a hand or an arm) is very helpful during stressful times.

<u>They're watching you</u> - Kids look to adults during a disaster so your reactions will impact the kids (meaning if you act alarmed or worried – they'll be scared, if you cry – they cry, etc.)

<u>Stick together</u> - Keep the family together as much as possible and include kids in discussions and decisions whenever possible.

<u>Draw a picture</u> - Ask your kids to draw a picture of the disaster to help you understand how he or she views what happened.

<u>Explain</u> - Calmly tell your family what you know about the disaster using facts and words they can understand and tell everyone what will happen next so they know what to expect.

Reassurance - Let your kids and family know that they are safe and repeat this as often as necessary to help them regain their confidence.

Praise - Recognizing good behavior and praise for doing certain things (even the littlest of things) will help boost morale.

Watch your temper - Stress will make tempers rise but don't take out your anger on others, especially kids. Be patient and control your emotions.

Let kids help - Including children in small chores during recovery and clean up processes will help them feel like they are part of the team and give them more confidence.

Let others know - Work with your kids' teachers, day-care staff, babysitters and others who may not understand how the disaster has affected them.

GENERAL RECOVERY TIPS - AFTER A DISASTER

RETURNING TO A DAMAGED HOME:

Listen - Keep a battery-operated radio with you for emergency updates.

Twitter, Facebook, Flickr, etc - Social networking sites allow users to stay current on disaster recovery efforts with messages and pictures. You may not have access to the Internet during or after a crisis, but text messages can sometimes get through when cell and phone systems are down. The Red Cross, FEMA and other relief groups use Twitter to send instant messages (called Tweets) about evacuations and shelter data. And FEMA and DHS partnered with Facebook and MySpace so users can get emergency broadcast warnings and stay updated on friends and families displaced by storms.

What to wear – Use sturdy work boots and gloves.

Check outside first - Before you go inside, walk around outside to check for loose power lines, gas leaks, and structural damage.

Call a professional - If you have any doubts about the safety of your home, contact a professional inspector.

Don't go in there - If your home was damaged by fire, do NOT enter until authorities say it is safe (also don't enter home if flood waters remain around the building).

Use a flashlight - There may be gas or other flammable materials in the area so use a battery-operated flashlight (do not use oil, gas lanterns, candles or torches and don't smoke!)

Watch out - Look for critters, especially snakes (flooding will carry them) and use a stick to poke through debris.

Take & share pics - If you have a camera phone, take shots of the damage to your home or place of business since it may take days before an adjuster gets there. It can also be a way to share updates with neighbors who aren't able to get to the site. The photos could also be uploaded to First Responders and/or media to help prioritize the response efforts.

Things to check - Some things you want to do first...

- Check for cracks in the roof, foundation and chimneys.
- Watch out for loose boards and slippery floors.
- Check for gas leaks (smells like rotten eggs, hear a hissing or blowing sound or see discolored plants or grass) ...
  - Start with the hot water heater then check other appliances.
  - Turn off main valve from outside and call gas company.
- Check electrical system (watch for sparks, broken wires or the smell of hot insulation) ...
  - Turn off electricity at main fuse box or circuit breaker.
  - DO NOT touch fuse box, circuit breaker or wires if in water or if you're wet!
- Check appliances after turning off electricity at main fuse and, if wet, unplug and let them dry out. Call a professional to check them before using.
- Check water and sewage system and, if pipes are damaged, turn off main water valve.
- Clean up any spilled medicines, bleaches, gasoline, etc.
- Open cabinets carefully since things may fall out.
- Look for valuable items (jewelry, etc.) and protect them.
- Try to patch up holes, windows and doors to protect home from further damage.
- If possible, download Iowa Conservation and Preservation Consortium's "Flood Recovery Booklet" to learn how to dry materials like artwork, books, photographs, CD/DVDs, etc. at www.iowaconserveandpreserve.org
- Clean and disinfect everything that got wet (bleach is best) since mud left behind by floodwaters can contain sewage and chemicals. Wear gloves, mask and eye protection when using disinfectants.
- If basement is flooded, pump it out slowly (about 1/3 of the water per day) to avoid damage since walls may collapse if surrounding ground still waterlogged.
- Check with local authorities about water since it could be

contaminated. Wells should be pumped out and the water tested before using, too.

- Throw out food, makeup and medicines that may have been exposed to flood waters and check refrigerated foods to see if they are spoiled. If frozen foods have ice crystals in them then okay to refreeze.

- Throw out moldy items that are porous (like rotten wood, carpet padding, furniture, etc.) if they're too difficult to clean and remove mold. Remove standing water and scrub moldy surfaces with non-ammonia soap or detergent, or a commercial cleaner, rinse with clean water and dry completely. Then use a mixture of 1 part bleach to 10 parts clean water to wipe down surfaces or items, rinse and dry. If possible, visit the EPA web site for tips on cleaning mold at www.epa.gov/iedmold1/cleanupguidelines.html

- Consider having your house tested for mold. *(see AIR QUALITY MITIGATION)*

- Call your insurance agent, take pictures of damage, and keep ALL receipts on cleaning and repairs.

Protect stuff? - Secure valuable items or move them to another location, if possible. Sometimes looting can occur after a disaster, but be smart about protecting your property ... it's not worth getting hurt or shot defending it.

GETTING HELP: DISASTER ASSISTANCE

"The government will save me" - Officials and groups will try to keep basic functions working while helping as many people as possible, but it takes time so expect delays. Local First Responders will be overwhelmed and may not be able to help if you need Police, Fire or EMS services.

Listen - Local TV and radio will announce where to get emergency housing, food, first aid, clothing and financial assistance after a disaster.

Help finding family - The Red Cross maintains a database to help people find family, but don't call office in the disaster area since they'll be swamped.

Agencies that help - The Red Cross is often stationed right at the scene of a disaster to help people with immediate medical, food, and housing needs. Some other sources of help include Salvation Army, church groups and synagogues, and various other Social Service agencies.

President declares a "Major Disaster" (in U.S.) - According to FEMA's Floodsmart.gov web site, less than 10% of all weather emergencies in the

U.S. are declared. In severe disasters, the government (FEMA) steps in and provides people with ...

- Temporary housing (several components available to meet housing needs of victims)
  - Mortgage and Rental Assistance Program (if evicted)
  - Rental Assistance (if dwelling unlivable)
  - Minimal Repair Program
  - Mobile Homes or Other readily fabricated dwellings (may be set up when all other options are exhausted)
- Counseling
- Low interest loans and grants
- Businesses and farms are eligible for aid through FEMA

FEMA's Disaster Recovery Centers - FEMA will set up DRCs at local schools and municipal buildings to manually process applications and where people can meet face-to-face with agencies to ...

- Discuss their disaster-related needs.
- Get information about disaster assistance programs.
- Teleregister for assistance.
- Learn about measures for rebuilding that can eliminate or reduce risk of future loss (mitigation tips).
- Learn how to complete Small Business Administration (SBA) loan application (same form used to qualify all individuals for low cost loans or grants, including repair or replacement of damaged homes & furnishings).
- Request status of their Disaster Housing Application.

Or people can apply for assistance with DRC by calling 1-800-621-FEMA. Also check out FEMA's site at www.DisasterAssistance.gov

Long-term shelter - If your home is damaged or destroyed or you're forced to leave due to on-going threats (like mudslides or flooding), you may need to find temporary or permanent living quarters. This could mean staying in a public shelter or hotel, living with friends or relatives, or renting a home or apartment. During a major disaster, FEMA and the Red Cross offer some assistance but you may be on your own in some cases.

I lost my job (in U.S.) - People who lose their job due to a disaster may apply for weekly benefits using Disaster Unemployment Assistance (DUA). You can call 1-800-621-FEMA (TTY: 1-800-462-7585) or your local unemployment office for registration information.

Legal help (in U.S.) - Local members of the American Bar Association Young Lawyers Division offer free legal counseling to low-income individuals after President declares a major disaster. FEMA can provide more information at DRCs or call 1-800-621-FEMA (TTY: 1-800-462-7585).

<u>Canadian disaster</u> - In the event of a large-scale disaster in Canada, provincial or territorial government would pay out money to individuals and communities in accordance with its provincial disaster assistance program. *(Federal assistance - called DFAA [Disaster Financial Assistance Arrangements] - is paid direct to province or territory.)*

<u>Recovering financially</u> - The American Red Cross and FEMA developed the following list to help you minimize the financial impact of a disaster:

- **First things first** - 1) remove valuables only if residence is safe to enter, 2) try to make temporary repairs to limit further damage, and 3) notify your insurance company immediately!
- **Conduct inventory** - make sure you get paid for items lost
- **Reconstruct lost records** - use catalogs, want ads, Blue Books, court records, old tax forms from IRS, escrow papers, etc. to help determine value of lost possessions
- **Notify creditors and employers** - let people you do business with know what has happened
- **File insurance claim** - get all policy numbers; find out how they are processing claims; identify your property with a sign; file claims promptly, work with adjusters, etc.
- **Obtain loans and grants** - local media will announce options available for emergency financial assistance
- **Avoid contractor rip-offs** - get several estimates; don't rush into anything; ask for proof of licenses, permits and insurance; get contract in writing; never prepay; get signed release of lien; check out contractors with local Better Business Bureau, etc.
- **Reduce your tax bite** - you may be eligible for tax refunds or deductions but realize they can be very complex so you may want to ask an expert for advice

MITIGATION (REDUCING THE IMPACT FOR THE NEXT TIME)

The last thing you want to think about after a disaster is "what if it happens again"?! Before you spend a lot of time and money repairing your home after a disaster, find ways to avoid or reduce the impact of the next one.

FEMA recommends the following mitigation tips AFTER A DISASTER:

- Ask local building department about agencies that purchase property in areas that have been flooded. You may be able to sell your property to a government agency and move to another location.

- Determine how to rebuild your home to handle the shaking of an earthquake or high winds. Ask local government, hardware dealer, or private home inspector for technical advice.

- Consider options for flood-proofing your home. Determine if your home can be elevated to avoid future flood damage.

- Make sure all construction complies with local building codes that pertain to seismic, flood, fire and wind hazards. Make sure roof is firmly secured to the main frame of the house. Make sure contractors know and follow the code and construction is inspected by a local building inspector.

And please review **ALL** Mitigation tips at the beginning of this Section to ensure you're prepared for any future emergencies or disasters.

TIPS ON SHELTER LIVING
DURING OR AFTER AN EMERGENCY

Taking shelter during a disaster could mean you have to be somewhere for several hours, days or weeks .. even months! It could be as simple as going to a basement during a tornado warning or staying home without electricity or water for several days during a major storm.

In many emergencies, the Red Cross and other organizations set up public shelters in schools, city or county buildings and churches. While they often provide water, food, medicine, and basic sanitary facilities, you should plan to have your own supplies - especially water.

Whether your shelter is at home or in a mass care facility use the following tips while staying there during or after an emergency:

Don't leave - Stay in your shelter until local authorities say it's okay to leave. Realize that your stay in shelter can range from a few hours to weeks ... or longer in some cases.

Take it outside - Restrict smoking to well-ventilated areas (outside if it's safe to go out) and make sure smoking materials are disposed of safely!

Behave - Living with many people in a confined space can be difficult and unpleasant but you must cooperate with shelter managers and others.

24-hour watch - Take turns listening to radio updates and keep a 24-hour communications and safety watch going.

Toilet - Bathrooms may not be available so make sure you have a plan for human waste. *(see TIPS ON SANITATION OF HUMAN WASTE)*

Pets - Public shelters may not allow pets (unless it is a service animal assisting a disabled person) so you may have to make arrangements to keep them somewhere else. Try the Humane Society or local Animal Shelter - if they are still functioning after a disaster.

Fallout shelter - Review pages 109-126 for tips on long-term sheltering during a nuclear crisis.

Next we're going to cover some basic things to think about in the event you and your family are without power, running water, and/or functioning toilets during an emergency or disaster. We suggest you read over these topics and think about things you might want to get in advance so you can be prepared for several days or longer.

Tips on Using Household Foods

Cooking in a Disaster Situation

When disaster strikes, you may not have electricity or gas for cooking. For emergency cooking you can use a charcoal grill, hibachi or propane camping unit or stove - but only do this <u>OUTDOORS</u>!

Never use charcoal in an enclosed environment -- it causes deadly fumes!

You can also heat food with candle warmers or a can of sterno.

Canned food can be heated in the can, but remember to remove the paper label and open the can first. And be careful -- don't burn your hand since it may be hot!

Try to limit using salty foods since they can make you thirsty. Also, keep in mind dried foods (like pasta, beans, etc.) require extra water and cooking time so may not be good choices during a disaster situation.

If the electricity goes off, use Food wisely ...

First - Use perishable food and foods from the refrigerator ... and limit opening the fridge (don't stand and stare in it like most of us do!) The refrigerator will keep foods cool for about 4 hours without power if left unopened. Dry ice or a block of ice can be placed inside it too if power is out more than 4 hours.

Second - Use foods from the freezer and, if possible, have a list of items in the freezer taped outside or at least know how things are organized inside to find stuff quickly. (Keeping door shut keeps cold in.) Foods in a well-filled, well-insulated freezer won't go bad until several days after power goes off. Usually there will be ice crystals in the center of food (which means it's still okay to eat or refreeze) for 2-3 days after a power failure. If possible, use block or dry ice to help keep freezer food cold.

Third - Use non-perishable foods and staples in your pantry and cabinets.

Tip For Your Freezer:

Before a disaster strikes, line your freezer with bottled water. The frozen bottles can help keep food cold longer if you lose power, plus you'll have extra water once it melts. This also helps keep freezer as full as possible which makes it more energy efficient, but rotate bottles every 6 months.

TIPS ON WATER PURIFICATION

Water is critical for survival. We can go days, even weeks, without food but we <u>must</u> have water to live. For example, an average man (154 pounds) can lose about 3 quarts/litres of water per day and an average woman (140 pounds) can lose over 2 quarts - and this could increase depending on your weight and size, on the season, and the altitude. Your body loses precious water by sweating and breathing and, of course, by peeing. In fact, you can tell if you are getting dehydrated by the color of your pee. When you drink enough water, your pee will be light-colored or bright yellow, but when dehydrated, it will be dark-colored and you'll pee in smaller amounts.

The average person should drink between 2 and 2 ½ quarts/litres of water per day. Plan on storing about one gallon (4 litres) per day per person for drinking, cooking and personal hygiene - and don't forget water for pets!

Did you know...
... almost 6,000 children die every day from water-related disease?
... about 1.1 <u>billion</u> people don't have access to safe water?

USE ANY OF THE FOLLOWING METHODS TO PURIFY DRINKING WATER:

<u>Boiling</u> - Boil vigorously for 2-10 minutes. Boiling water kills most harmful bacteria and parasites. To improve the taste of boiled water pour it back and forth between two containers to add oxygen back into it.

<u>Bleach</u> - Add 10-20 drops of "regular" household bleach per gallon (about 4 litres) of water, mix well, and let stand for 30 minutes. A slight smell or taste of chlorine indicates water is good to drink. *(NOTE: Do NOT use scented bleaches, colorsafe bleaches, or bleaches with added cleaners!)*

<u>Purifier</u> - Purification tablets are inexpensive and found at sporting goods stores and some drugstores. *(Look for ones that contain 5.25 to 6.0 percent sodium hypochlorite as the only active ingredient.)* Or google MMS (sodium chlorite) since it can be used for purification and long term storage.

<u>Distillation</u> - Involves boiling water and collecting the vapor to remove impurities. *(Check with library or do a web search on distillation.)*

Also, learn how to remove water from other places in your home or office (like the hot water heater, ice cubes, toilet tanks [not the bowl], etc.) And consider purchasing a certified portable water purification device (pitcher filter, faucet filter, etc.) and pack an extra unit in your **Disaster Supplies Kit**. To learn more about water safety visit www.epa.gov/safewater. *Also see tips on filtering water contaminated by fallout on page 118.*

TIPS ON SANITATION OF HUMAN WASTE

In disaster situations, plumbing may not be usable due to broken sewer or water lines, flooding, or freezing of the system. To avoid the spread of disease, it is critical that human waste be handled in a sanitary manner!

Did you know...

... one gram (0.035 oz) of human feces can contain 10 million viruses, 1 million bacteria, 1,000 parasite cysts, and 100 parasite eggs!? [8]

IF TOILET OKAY BUT LINES ARE NOT...

If water or sewer lines are damaged but toilet is still intact, you should line the toilet bowl with a plastic bag to collect waste... but DO NOT flush the toilet!! After use, add a small amount of <u>disinfectant</u> to bag, remove and seal bag (with a twist tie if reusing), and place bag in a tightly covered container away from people to reduce smell.

IF TOILET IS UNUSABLE...

If toilet is destroyed, a plastic bag in a bucket may be substituted. (Some companies make plastic buckets with snap-on lids.) After use, add a small amount of <u>disinfectant</u> to the bag, and seal or cover bucket.

<u>DISINFECTANTS</u> - **easy and effective for home use in Sanitation of Human Waste. Choose one to store with your Disaster Supplies Kit:**

Chlorine Bleach - If water is available, a solution of 1 part liquid household bleach to 10 parts water is best. DO NOT use dry bleach since it can burn you, corrode or dissolve things so not safe for this kind of use.

Calcium hypochlorite - (e.g. HTH, etc.) Available in swimming pool supply or hardware stores and several large discount stores. It can be used in solution by mixing, then storing. Follow directions on the package.

Portable toilet chemicals - These come in both liquid and dry formulas and are available at recreational vehicle (RV) supply stores. Use according to package directions. These chemicals are designed especially for toilets that are not connected to sewer lines.

Powdered, chlorinated lime - Available at some building supply stores. It can be used dry and be sure to get chlorinated lime - *not* quick lime.

There are also several types of portable toilets and sanitation products that range from fairly low dollars to hundreds of dollars. Or get a small shovel so you can at least dig a hole or latrine outside like campers do.

TIPS ON HELPING OTHERS
IN THEIR TIME OF NEED

A disaster really brings out the generosity of many people who want to help the victims. Unfortunately, sometimes this kindness overwhelms agencies that are trying to coordinate relief efforts so please review the following general guidelines defined by FEMA on helping others after a disaster.

- In addition to the people you care for on a daily basis, consider the needs of your neighbors and people with special needs.

- If you want to volunteer your services after a disaster, listen to local news reports for information about where volunteers are needed. Until volunteers are specifically requested, please stay away from disaster areas.

- If you are needed in a disaster area, bring your own food, water and emergency supplies. This is especially important in cases where a large area has been hit since these items may be in short supply.

- Do not drop off food, clothing or items to a government agency or disaster relief organization <u>unless</u> a particular item has been requested. They usually don't have the resources to sort through donations and it is very costly to ship these bulk items.

- If you wish, give check or money order to a recognized disaster relief organization like the Salvation Army or Red Cross. They can process funds, purchase what is needed and get it to the people who need it most. Your entire donation goes towards the disaster relief since these organizations raise money for overhead expenses through separate fund drives.

- If your company wants to donate emergency supplies, donate a quantity of a given item or class of items (such as nonperishable food) rather than a mix of different items. Also, find out where donation is going, how it's going to get there, who's going to unload it and how it will be distributed. Without good planning, much needed supplies will be left unused.

- Donate blood or help organize a blood drive.

DEALING WITH DEATH OR MASS CASUALTIES

Quite often natural or man-made disasters bring not only destruction but death to a community. Sometimes First Responders cannot reach a disaster site for hours, days or weeks so citizens should be prepared to deal with death or the handling of dead bodies.

IF IN A DISASTER SITUATION WITH CASUALTIES AND NO HELP...

- Dead bodies do not cause epidemics after a natural disaster. It's survivors who will most likely spread disease.

- Don't put yourself in danger to recover a body if there is any chemical, biological or radiological contamination in the area or structural damage due to an earthquake, etc.

- People handling bodies should wear gloves and boots and avoid wiping their face or mouth with their hands. (Face masks aren't needed but may be helpful to some handlers.) Wash hands with soap and clean water often, and disinfect tools, clothing, equipment and vehicles used to move the bodies.

- Bodies often leak feces after death so avoid contact with it (and body fluids) to limit exposure to any possible diseases.

- If no First Responders are on scene (and it may be a while before any are), write down any known details about where and when a body was found, name (if known), personal belongings on or with the body, take a photo (if possible) to help with identification later, etc.

IF A LOVED ONE DIES...

In addition to dealing with the sadness and loss, there are several things families may need to think about and plan for if they lose a loved one during a disaster or crisis.

- Realize some bodies may never be recovered or could be contaminated in certain types of disasters so families may not have the body released to them.

- Determine who is Executor of the will (if any) and make 10 to 12 certified copies of death certificate (for probate, insurance benefits, bank accounts, social security, etc.) The certificates are easier to obtain from the mortuary when the funeral arrangements are made.

- File with the probate court within 30 days, if necessary.

- Contact banks/trusts (to change names on accounts), employers (to check on any available benefits), Social Security, etc. If the deceased had a safety deposit box rented in their name only, a court order will be required to open the box.

- Contact credit card companies to ensure accounts are cancelled if the deceased is the only name on the account.

- Check on insurance policies (e.g. life, health, mortgage, auto, etc.), any 401Ks or profit sharing plans, V.A. benefits, etc.

- Consider pets, mail and utilities if the deceased lived alone.

- If the deceased is listed in your will to receive certain property, it'll need to be changed. (And mention this to other family members in case they have left property to the deceased too.)

Section 3

Information
& Tips on
Basic First Aid

What are YOU gonna do about...
AN EMERGENCY?

Everyone should know what to do in an emergency. You should know who to call and what care to provide. Providing care involves giving first aid until professional medical help arrives.

The Emergency Medical Services (EMS) is a network of police, fire and medical personnel, as well as other community resources. People can help EMS by reporting emergencies and helping out victims until EMS can arrive.

During a major disaster, EMS groups will become swamped so if the public is prepared to handle some types of emergencies then we can help some of the victims until EMS arrives.

Your role in the EMS system includes the following things:

BE AWARE...   Realize this is an emergency situation -- you could be putting yourself in danger!

BE PREPARED...   Know how to handle the situation.

HAVE A PLAN!   Check **ABCs...**, call 9-1-1 (or call for an ambulance) and help victim, if possible.

TIPS ON THE ABCs...
AIRWAY, BREATHING & CIRCULATION

In an emergency, you need to check the victim for **ABCs...**

Airway.   Open the airway by tilting the head back, gently lifting the jaw up, and leaving mouth open.

Breathing.   Place your ear over victim's mouth and nose. Look at chest, listen, and feel for breathing for 3 to 5 seconds.

Circulation. Check for a pulse using <u>fingertips</u> (not your thumb) in the soft spot between throat and the muscle on the side of the neck for 5-10 seconds.

*Note: For **heart** emergencies when doing CPR, the steps are now **CAB**!*

TIPS ON MAKING YOUR "EMERGENCY ACTION" PLAN

1. **BE AWARE**... Make sure it's <u>safe</u> to approach area and victim.

   Use your senses...

   Listen for cries for help; screams; moans; explosions; breaking glass; crashing metal; gunshots; high winds; popping, humming or buzzing noises; lots of coughing, etc.

   Look for broken glass; open medicine cabinet, container or bottle near victim; smoke; fire; vapors or mist; downed power lines, etc.

   Watch for signs like trouble breathing; trouble talking; grabbing at throat or chest; pale or blue color in face, lips or ears; lots of people covering mouth or running away, etc.

   Smell smoke or something burning; strong odors or vapors (leave if odor is too strong), etc.

   Feel something burning your eyes, lungs or skin, etc.

2. **BE PREPARED**... The best thing you can do is **STAY CALM...** and <u>THINK</u> before you act!

   Any time there's an emergency or disaster, most people are scared or confused and many don't know what to do. Take a few seconds and breathe in through your nose and out through your mouth to help slow your heartbeat and calm down. <u>Always</u> ask if you can help... either ask the victim or people around who may be helping.

3. **HAVE A PLAN!** Check **ABCs**, call 9-1-1 and help victim, if possible.

   ... Check victims' **ABCs... Airway, Breathing, & Circulation** *(Note: For **heart** emergencies, the steps are now CAB!)*

   ... call 9-1-1, 0 for Operator or local emergency number for an ambulance *(see tips on next page)*

   ... help the victim, if possible -- and STAY until help arrives.

   Before giving first aid, you must have the victim's permission. Tell them who you are, how much training you've had, and how you plan to help. Do <u>not</u> give care to someone who refuses it - unless they are unable to respond.

TIPS ON CALLING 9-1-1 FOR AN AMBULANCE

Whenever there is an emergency, use the following tips to help decide if you should call 9-1-1 (or local emergency number) for an ambulance.

Call if victim...

... is trapped

... is not responding or is passed out

... is bleeding badly or bleeding cannot be stopped

... has a cut or wound so bad and deep that you can see bone or muscles

... has a body part missing or is torn away

... has pain below the rib cage that does not go away

... is peeing, pooping or puking blood (called passing blood)

... is breathing weird or having trouble breathing

... seems to have hurt their head, neck or back

... is jerking uncontrollably (called having a seizure)

... has broken bones and cannot be moved carefully

... acts like they had a heart attack (chest pain or pressure)

If you call 9-1-1 there may be a recording or delay while your call is being processed. DO NOT HANG UP -- wait for a 9-1-1 dispatcher.

When you talk to 9-1-1 or the emergency number...

... try to stay CALM and describe what happened and what is wrong with the victim

... give the location of the emergency, your name and the phone number you are calling from

... follow their instructions in case they tell you what to do for the victim

... do NOT hang up until the 9-1-1 operator tells you to.

Tips On Reducing the Spread of Germs Or Diseases

Whenever you perform first aid on anyone, there is always a chance of spreading germs or diseases between yourself and the victim. These steps should be followed no matter what kind of first aid is being done -- from very minor scrapes to major emergencies -- to reduce the risk of infection.

BE AWARE...

> ... Try to avoid body fluids like blood or urine (pee).
>
> ... Cover any open cuts or wounds you have on your body since they are doorways for germs!

BE PREPARED...

> ... Wash your hands with soap <u>and</u> water <u>before</u> and <u>after</u> giving first aid.
>
> ... Have a first aid kit handy, if possible.
>
> ... Put something between yourself and victim's body fluids, if possible ...
>
>> <u>blood or urine</u> - wear disposable gloves or use a clean dry cloth
>>
>> <u>saliva or spittle</u> – use a disposable Face Shield during Rescue Breathing
>
> ... Clean up area with household bleach to kill germs.

... and... HAVE A PLAN!

> ... *see TIPS ON MAKING <u>YOUR</u> "EMERGENCY ACTION" PLAN two pages back.*

Tips On Good Samaritan Laws

The definition of a "Samaritan" is a charitable or helpful person. Most states have Good Samaritan laws that were designed to protect citizens who try to help injured victims with emergency care. If a citizen uses "logical" or "rational" actions while making wise or careful decisions during an emergency situation then they can be protected from being sued.

To learn more about your state's Good Samaritan laws, check with your local library, search the web or contact an attorney.

What are YOU gonna do about...
BITES & STINGS?

ANIMAL & HUMAN BITES

Americans and Canadians report approximately 5 million bites each year (mostly from dogs). Both humans and animals carry bacteria and viruses in their mouths, however, human bites are more dangerous and infection-prone because people seem to have more reactions to the human bacteria.

Things to watch for...

> **Puncture or bite marks**
> **Bleeding**
> **Infection** - Pain / tenderness, redness, heat, swelling, pus,
> red streaks (also read about MRSA on pages 198-199)
> **Allergic Reaction** - Feeling ill, dizzy or trouble breathing

What to do...

- Wash the bite as soon as possible to remove saliva and dirt from bite wound - use running water and soap or rinse area with hydrogen peroxide.
- Control bleeding using direct pressure with cloth or gauze.
- Pat dry and cover with sterile bandage, gauze, or cloth - don't put cream or gel on wound -- may prevent drainage.
- May want to raise bitten area to reduce swelling or use a cold pack, bag of frozen peas, or cloth with ice cube in it.
- Call local emergency number or call Animal Control
- Watch for allergic reactions or infection for a few days.

...also...

- Get to a doctor or hospital if bleeding is really bad, if you think animal could have rabies, or if stitches are required.

INSECT BITES & STINGS

Covering first aid for bites & stings in general, then West Nile Virus.

Things to watch for...

> **Stinger** (Note: honeybees leave a stinger and venom sac)
> **Puncture or bite mark**
> **Burning pain or Swelling**
> **Allergic Reaction** - Pain, itching, hives, redness or
> discoloration at site, trouble breathing, signs of shock
> (pale, cold, drowsy, etc.)

What to do...

- Run away from area if there's a swarm or nest nearby.
- Remove stinger by scraping it away with credit card, long fingernail or using tweezers. Don't try to squeeze it out since this causes more venom to get in the victim.
- Wash wound with soap and water or rinse with hydrogen peroxide.
- Cover with a bandage or clean cloth and apply ice pack.
- Watch for allergic reactions for a few days (see above).
- Call Fire Department or bee removal expert if needed.

(See WEST NILE VIRUS on next page. TICKS covered on pages 167-168.)

To relieve pain from an insect bite or sting:

Activated charcoal - Make a paste using 2-3 capsules and a small amount of warm water. Dab paste on sting site and cover with gauze or plastic to keep it moist. This will help draw out venom so it collects on your skin. Note, powder makes a black mess but easily wiped off with a towel. *(see FIRST AID KITS in Section 1)*

Baking Soda - Make a paste of 3 parts baking soda + 1 part warm water and apply to the sting site for 15-20 minutes.

Clay mudpack - If in the wilderness, put a mudpack over injury and cover with bandage or cloth. The mudpack must be a mix of clay-containing soil since clay is the key element but don't use if any skin is cracked or broken.

Meat tenderizer - Mixing meat tenderizer (check ingredient list for "papain") with warm water and applying to the sting will help break down insect venom. (Papain is a natural enzyme derived from papaya.)

Urine (Pee) - Another remedy useful in the wilderness sounds totally gross (but has a history of medical applications in a number of cultures) is urine (pee) which reduces the stinging pain. (Unless you have a urinary tract infection, the pee will be sterile and at the least won't do any harm!)

Some potential pain-relieving and anti-inflammatory remedies:

fresh aloe - break open a leaf or use 96-100% pure aloe gel

lemon juice - from a fresh lemon

vitamin E - oil from a bottle or break open a few gel capsules

store brands - if over-the-counter methods preferred, use calamine cream or lotion and aspirin or acetaminophen

WEST NILE VIRUS

West Nile virus (WNV) is primarily spread by mosquitoes that feed on infected birds. But realize, out of 700+ species of mosquitoes in the U.S. (and 74 species in Canada), very few - less than 1% - become infected with WNV. And out of all the people bitten by an infected mosquito, less than 1% will become severely ill so chances are pretty slim you'd ever get it.

The virus usually causes fever, aches and general discomfort. Severe cases can cause inflammation of the lining of the brain or spinal cord (meningitis), inflammation of the brain itself (encephalitis) or a polio-like syndrome that can result in loss of function of one or more limbs (WN poliomyelitis or acute flaccid paralysis). These conditions can be life-altering or fatal. People of all ages could develop serious health effects, but seniors and folks with weakened immune systems are at greatest risk.

Things to watch for...
>   *(Most symptoms appear 2 to 15 days after being bitten)*
>   **Mild flu-like symptoms** - fever, headache & body aches
>   **Mild skin rash and swollen lymph glands**
>   **Severe symptoms** - severe headache, high fever, neck stiffness, confusion, shakes, coma, convulsions, muscle weakness, paralysis, meningitis or encephalitis

What to do...
- There is no "cure" other than a body fighting off the virus naturally - mainly just watch symptoms.
- Consider boosting immune system to help fight virus (like taking astragalus, Vitamin C, garlic, mushrooms, zinc, good multiple vitamin + mineral supplement, etc. - but check with doctor if taking prescription medications).
- If **mild** symptoms appear, keep watching person for a few weeks in case symptoms get worse.
- If **severe** symptoms appear, get medical attention quickly since it could become deadly.

Things to do to avoid mosquito bites ...
- Stay indoors at dawn, dusk, and early evenings when mosquitoes are most active.
- Wear long-sleeved shirts and long pants when outdoors.
- Spray clothing and exposed skin with repellent containing **DEET** (N,N-diethyl-meta-toluamide) -- the higher % of DEET, the longer you're protected from bites (6.65% lasts almost 2 hours; 20% lasts about 4 hours, etc.) Two other repellents are **picaridin** or oil of **lemon eucalyptus**.

- Don't put repellent on small children's hands since it may irritate their mouths or eyes.
- Get rid of "standing water" sources around yard and home since they are breeding grounds for mosquitoes.
- The CDC says Vitamin B and "ultrasonic" devices are NOT effective in preventing mosquito bites!

There is a growing concern about mosquitoes and other vectors spreading diseases or being used as "bioterrorism", but we're only listing West Nile Virus for now due to space. Always listen to health officials for information on mosquito-borne and other types of infections.

For more information visit CDC's Division of Vector-Borne Diseases at www.cdc.gov/ncezid/dvbd/ ..or.. Public Health Agency of Canada's Infectious Diseases at www.phac-aspc.gc.ca/id-mi/

SEA CRITTER (MARINE LIFE) STINGS

There are just too many types of sea critters in our oceans and seas so we can't cover all the various kinds of stings and bites that could happen, but a few common stings are shown here. To learn about specific types of sea critters (marine life), check with your local library or on the Internet.

Things to watch for...
> **Puncture marks or tentacles on the skin**
> **Pain or burning**
> **Swelling or red marks**
> **Possible Allergic Reaction** - Pain, itching, hives, redness or discoloration at site, trouble breathing, signs of shock (pale, cold, drowsy, etc.)

What to do...
- Rinse skin - use seawater, vinegar, ammonia, or alcohol (in whatever form is handy - rubbing alcohol or booze.) Fresh water might make it hurt worse.
- DO NOT rub skin - it could make it worse!
- Try to remove any tentacles attached to skin, if possible... but DO NOT use bare hands... use a towel or tweezers.
- Soak sting or make a paste (below) to help relieve pain:
  tropical jellyfish - soak area in vinegar
  stingray or stonefish - soak area in hot water
- Cover sting with sterile bandage or gauze, or clean cloth.
- Call local emergency number, if necessary.

To relieve pain from a sea critter sting:

Baking Soda Paste - Make a paste of 3 parts baking soda + 1 part warm water and apply to sting site until it dries. Scrape off paste with a knife or credit card to help remove some of the skin. (Note: two other easy pastes are sand and seawater <u>or</u> flour and seawater. Scrape off as above.)

Urine (Pee) – Again, we know this sounds weird... but pee has a history of medical applications and can reduce stinging pain. (Unless you have a urinary tract infection, it will be sterile and at least won't do any harm!)

SNAKE BITES

According to the FDA and the National Institutes of Health, about 8,000 people in the U.S. are treated for poisonous snake bites each year. Poisonous snakes have triangular heads, slit-like pupils, and two long fangs which make puncture wounds at end of each row of teeth. Non-poisonous snake bites leave two rows of teeth marks but no puncture wounds, but don't use bite mark to determine type since swelling may hide wounds.

Things to watch for...
> **Puncture and/or bite marks**
> **Pain and Swelling**
> **Nausea and puking**
> **Difficulty breathing or swallowing**
> **Possible Allergic reaction** – Weakness or dizziness; redness or discoloration at bite; trouble breathing; signs of shock (pale, cold, drowsy, etc.)

What to do...
- If possible, try to identify type or color of snake but don't put yourself in danger!
- Wash bite wound with soap and water.
- Keep bitten body part <u>below</u> heart level, if possible.
- Call emergency number or animal control, if necessary.

If bite is from a <u>Poisonous</u> snake, also do this...
- Remove constrictive items (like rings or watches) since swelling may occur.
- DO NOT apply tourniquet or ice.
- Monitor breathing and make sure airway is open.
- Keep victim still to slow down circulation of venom.
- DO NOT let victim eat or drink anything or take medication since it could interfere with emergency treatment.

- If possible and safe, remove venom - esp. if help is hours away. (Most snakebite kits have proper venom extractors in them.)
- DO NOT use "cut and suck" method!
- Get to a doctor or hospital to receive antivenin.

The worst effects may not be felt for hours after a bite from most poisonous North American snakes, but it is best if antivenin is given as quickly as possible (or at least within 12-24 hours of the bite).

SPIDER BITES, SCORPION STINGS, & TICKS

There are only a dozen or so spiders that can actually cause symptoms or side effects to humans with a bite -- the most serious are black widows and brown recluses. Tarantulas are also a little serious but do not cause extreme reactions and rarely will kill a human.

Scorpions will sting anything that touches them. Their sting feels like a small electrical shock (almost like a hot needle). Scorpions whip their tails over their body and zap their enemy many times, but it happens so quick it may only feel like one sting.

You may think ticks are insects but they're actually bloodsucking arachnids. Adult ticks have eight legs and two body segments just like spiders, mites and chiggers. Ticks grab onto a host (animals or people walking through brush) and sink their harpoon-like barbed mouth and head into the host's skin to dine until they're full of blood. Then they drop off and wait for the next meal to pass by. Since ticks feast on one spot for days, they can spread bacteria and diseases from host to host (like from animals to humans) - even by touching them.

The main threat of both spiders and scorpions is the allergic reaction humans have to their bite or sting so symptoms need to be watched carefully. Obviously the main threat of ticks is the risk of illness or disease (like lyme disease, Rocky Mountain spotted fever or tick paralysis).

Things to watch for...

Bite or sting mark or ticks
Pain or burning feeling
Redness or Swelling or Rash
Stomach pain or puking
Flu-like symptoms - fever, dizziness, weakness, headache, body aches, swollen lymph nodes, etc.
Change in skin color or bruising or rash (may look kind of like a bulls-eye)

Possible Allergic reactions - trouble breathing or swallowing, signs of shock (pale, cold, etc.)

What to do for SPIDERS and SCORPIONS...

- Try to identify the type of spider or scorpion, but don't put yourself in danger!
- Wash bite wound with soap and water or rubbing alcohol.
- Apply a cold pack (a baggie or cloth with ice will work).
- Get to a doctor or hospital to get antivenin (if a poisonous spider / scorpion) or call emergency number, if necessary.
- Watch for allergic reactions or infections for several days.

What to do for TICKS...

Key things are to find a tick before it feasts for days and to remove a tick slowly with head intact so it doesn't spew bacteria into the blood stream.

- DO NOT use petroleum jelly, liquid soap, nail polish or heat - they don't work!
- Use tweezers or commercial tick remover (or at least cover fingers with a tissue).
- Grasp tick close to skin where head is buried - don't squeeze it!
- Slowly pull tick straight up until skin puckers (may take several seconds but tick will loosen it's barbs and let go).
- DO NOT throw tick away - may need it tested! Put it in zippered baggie with moist paper towel, date it, and put in refrigerator.
- Wash bite wound and tweezers with soap and water.
- Call local health department or vet to ask if tick needs to be identified or tested. If not, throw away baggie.
- Watch for rash, infection or symptoms for a week or so.

Things to do to avoid ticks ...

- Wear light-colored pants & long-sleeve shirt (to see ticks), a hat (to keep out of hair) and tuck in (pants in socks + shirt in pants).
- Do full body checks couple times a day during tick season.
- Use tick repellent with DEET.

For more information about ticks, lyme disease and other illnesses visit www.cdc.gov/ticks or www.cdc.gov/lyme or www.cdc.gov/ncezid/dvbd .. or .. the Public Health Agency of Canada's Infectious Diseases site at www.phac-aspc.gc.ca/id-mi/

What are YOU gonna do about...
BLEEDING?

CONTROLLING BLEEDING

Things to watch for...
> **Source of bleeding**
> **Pain and/or Swelling**
> **Object sticking out or stuck in wound** (like a piece of metal or glass or a bullet)
> **Shock** (pale, cold or clammy, drowsy, weak or rapid pulse, etc.)

What to do...
- Be aware of your surroundings and be prepared to call for help. (*see TIPS ON CALLING 9-1-1 FOR AMBULANCE*)

If there IS object sticking out of wound (or possibly deep inside):
- Put thick soft pads around the object (or around wound).
- Gently try to apply pressure to help stop the bleeding.
- DO NOT try to remove or press on the object!
- Carefully wrap with a roller bandage to hold thick pads around the object.
- Get medical attention immediately!

If there is NO object sticking out of the wound:
- Be careful since there might be something inside wound.
- Cover wound with a clean cloth or sterile gauze pad and press firmly against the wound... and follow above steps if victim has an object <u>inside</u> the wound.
- If cloth or gauze becomes soaked with blood, DO NOT remove it! Keep adding new dressings on top of old ones.
- Carefully elevate injured body part above the level of victim's heart but be aware...there may be broken bones.
- Keep applying pressure on dressings until bleeding stops.
- Use firm roller bandage to cover gauze or cloth dressings.

If bleeding won't stop:
- Put pressure on nearby artery to help slow blood flow
  <u>Arm</u> – press inside upper arm, between shoulder & elbow
  <u>Leg</u> – press area where leg joins front of the hip (groin)

INTERNAL BLEEDING

Minor internal bleeding is like a bruise - a vein, artery or capillary can break or rupture spewing blood under the skin. A more serious form of internal bleeding can be caused by a major fall, crushing accident or a blow to the head. It's very hard to tell if a person is suffering from internal bleeding since there may not be blood outside the body. Symptoms don't always appear right away but can be life-threatening so get medical help quickly.

Things to watch for...
>**Abdominal pain or tenderness**
>**Pain and/or Swelling in abdomen** (around belly button)
>**Shock** (pale, cold or clammy, drowsy, weak or rapid pulse, etc.)
>**Either a fast or slow pulse**
>**Coughing up bright, foamy blood** (if dark red means been bleeding inside for a while)
>**Blood shows up in victim's pee, poop or puke**

What to do...
- Be aware of surroundings and call for an ambulance.
- Don't move victim if injuries to head, neck or spine.
- Check **ABCs... Airway, Breathing & Circulation**.
- Stay with victim until help arrives

(Please review HEAD, NECK & SPINE INJURIES and SHOCK too)

NOSEBLEEDS

What to do...
- Have the person sit down, lean forward and pinch the soft part of the nose for about 10 minutes.
- Put an icepack or cold compress on the bridge of the nose.

SLASHED OR SEVERED BODY PARTS/AMPUTATION

What to do...
- Keep direct pressure on the stump to stop the bleeding.
- Find body part, if possible, and wrap in gauze or clean cloth.
- Put body part in an airtight plastic bag, put bag in ice water and take it to the hospital with the victim.

What are YOU gonna do about...
BREATHING PROBLEMS?

ASTHMA ATTACK

Things to watch for...
> **Noisy breathing or wheezing**
> **Difficulty in breathing or speaking**
> **Blueness of skin, lips and fingertips or nails**

What to do...
- Make sure victim has nothing in mouth (open airway).
- Have victim sit up straight to make breathing easier.
- If victim has medication, or an inhaler, have them take it.
- Try to keep victim and yourself calm.
- If attack is severe, call for ambulance or emergency help.

Some tips that could possibly help slow down an asthma attack:
(Note: These tips are NOT to be used as a replacement for medical attention but could be helpful in the early stages of an asthma attack.)

Pursed lip breathing - At the first sign of an attack, breathe in deeply through nose and out through mouth with lips pursed (like blowing up a balloon). It will help relax the body and may get rid of stale air in lungs.

Drink a warm liquid or caffeine - Drinking one or two cups of coffee or tea that have caffeine could help relax the bronchial tubes. If you decide to drink a soda, do not use ice since cold could possibly trigger an attack - the warmer the better.

For more information about Asthma visit the CDC NCEH's Air Pollution and Respiratory web site at www.cdc.gov/asthma/

RESCUE BREATHING (NOT BREATHING)
Rescue breathing (or mouth-to-mouth resuscitation) should only be done when the victim is not breathing on his or her own. Make sure the victim is not choking on anything like vomit, blood or food *(if so, see CHOKING)* and check them using the **ABCs... Airway, Breathing**, and **Circulation**!

Continued on next page ...

Things to watch for...
> Grabbing at throat
> Can't feel, see or hear any breaths
> Trouble breathing or talking
> Bluish color of skin, lips, fingertips/nails, and earlobes

What to do...

- BE AWARE... make sure there's no head or neck injury first!
- Carefully move victim so they are flat on their back.
- If possible, grab a disposable mouth-to-mouth or CPR face shield.
- Tilt adult's head all the way back and lift chin. (Be careful with child's or infant's head... just tilt it a little bit!)
- Watch chest, listen, and feel for breathing for 5 seconds.

If victim is NOT breathing begin Rescue Breathing...

- Pinch victim's nose shut.
- Open your mouth wide to make a tight seal around the victim's mouth. *(Note: For infant, cover both mouth and nose with your mouth.)*
- Give victim 2 slow breaths to make their chest rise.
- Check for pulse using your fingers in soft spot between throat and the muscle on side of neck for 5-10 seconds.
- Continue Rescue Breathing if victim has a pulse but is not breathing...
  Adult - give 1 breath every 5 seconds.
  Child or Infant - give 1 breath every 3 seconds.
- Check pulse and breathing every minute until victim is breathing on their own.

...also...

- If victim pukes... turn them gently on their side, wipe mouth clean, turn them back and continue Rescue Breathing until they are breathing on their own.

NOTE: If victim NOT breathing and DOES <u>NOT</u> have pulse, see HEART EMERGENCIES for tips on Giving CPR (see page 189)!

What are YOU gonna do about...
BROKEN OR FRACTURED BONES?

A fracture is the same as a break and can range from a small chip to a bone that breaks through the skin. If you suspect a fracture, use a splint to keep the victim from moving too much and get professional help... and let the trained medical experts decide what is wrong! Also review HEAD, NECK OR SPINE INJURIES, if needed.

Things to watch for...
> **Pain, bruising or swelling**
> **Bleeding**
> **Limb or area moves strange or looks strange**
> **Shock** (pale, cold or clammy, weak or rapid pulse, etc.)

What to do...
- DO NOT move bone or try to straighten limb if bone breaks through skin!
- Try not to move the victim unless they are in danger.
- Have victim sit or lie down to rest the injured part.
- If possible, raise or elevate the injured part.
- Put a cold compress or ice pack on injury to reduce swelling.
- If help is delayed or you need to move victim, splint injury the same way it was found.
- Be prepared to call an ambulance, if necessary.

TIPS ON SPLINTING
A splint can be made using magazines, newspapers, a pillow, wood, etc.

Some basic tips on splinting include...
> ... always splint an injury the same way it was found
> ... make sure item being used is longer than the broken bone
> ... use cloth strips, neck ties, thin rope, etc. for ties
> ... put something soft between the splint and the bone
> ... tie splint <u>above</u> and <u>below</u> the break... but not too tight!
> ... touch area below the splint and ask victim if they can feel it -- if not, loosen ties.
> ... keep the victim warm with a blanket or whatever is available.

What are _you_ gonna do about...
BURNS?

Depending on how bad a burn is will determine what it is called:

First degree burns - hurts only top layer of skin; turns pink or red; some pain and swelling; no blisters (usually from sun, chemicals, or touching something hot)

Second degree burns - hurts the two upper layers of skin; very painful and causes swelling that lasts several days; blisters and possibly scars (usually from deep sunburn, chemicals, fire or hot liquid spills)

Third degree burns - hurts all skin layers and possibly tissue; charred, raw or oozing areas; destroys cells that form new skin; nerve cells are destroyed and can take months to heal (usually from being exposed to fire or electrical shock for a long time). Can cause severe loss of fluids, shock and death.

BURNS FROM FIRE OR HOT LIQUIDS

Things to watch for...
> **Skin is red and swollen**
> **Blisters may open and ooze clear or yellowish fluid**
> **Minor to Severe Pain**

What to do...
- BE AWARE... and don't put yourself in danger!
- Stop the burning by putting out flames and move victim from source of the burn. (If victim is on fire, tell them to STOP, DROP and ROLL!)
- Cool burn by using large amounts of <u>running</u> cool water for about 10 minutes. For hard to reach areas, wet a cloth, towel or sheet and carefully keep adding water.
- Try to remove clothing, rings or jewelry in case of swelling. (DO NOT remove items stuck to burned areas!)
- Cover burn with a sterile bandage or clean cloth. (Try to keep fingers and toes separated with bandage or cloth.)
- Seek medical attention, if necessary.

Things you should NOT do...
- DO NOT break any blisters!
- DO NOT remove any item that sticks to skin!

- DO NOT apply any creams, oils or lotions to the burns - wait for the medical experts!

CHEMICAL BURNS

Also see TERRORISM (in Section 2) for information, signs & symptoms, and treatment for several chemical agents in liquid, solid or aerosol forms that may cause chemical burns.

Things to watch for...
> **Rash or blisters**
> **Trouble breathing**
> **Dizziness or headache**
> **Name of the chemical**

What to do...
- Rinse area with cool running water at least 15 minutes.
- Remove any clothing, rings or jewelry that may have the chemical on it.
- Make note of chemical name for medical staff or hospital.

ELECTRICAL BURNS

Things to watch for...
> **Electrical appliances or wires**
> **Downed power lines**
> **Sparks and/or crackling noises**
> **Victim may have muscle spasms or trembling**
> **Lightning during a storm**

What to do...
- BE AWARE... don't put yourself in danger! If power line is down, wait for Fire Department or Power Company.
- DO NOT go near victim until power is OFF! Pull plug at wall outlet or shut off breaker. Once off, okay to touch victim.
- If victim struck by lightning, they <u>can</u> be touched safely!
- Check **ABCs ... Airway, Breathing, & Circulation** if victim is passed out - you may need to do Rescue Breathing or CPR. *(see BREATHING PROBLEMS and HEART PROBLEMS)*

Continued on next page ...

- Don't move victim unless they are in danger.
- There should be 2 wounds - usually have enter and exit burns.
- DO NOT try to cool the burn with anything.
- Cover burn with a dry sterile bandage or clean cloth.
- Seek medical attention, if necessary.

SUNBURN

Sunblocks and lotions should be applied at least 20 minutes <u>BEFORE</u> going in the sun so it can be absorbed into skin layers, especially on your little ones! Use one with SPF 30 or higher and 3 or 4 star UVA protection.

Remember… dark colors absorb heat so best to wear light or white colors to reflect sunlight. And you can get sunburned on cloudy days just as easily as sunny days - if you can see a shadow, you're still catching some rays.

Things to watch out for…
> **Blisters or bubbles on the skin**
> **Swelling or pain**

What to do…
- Cool the burn by using cool cloths or pure aloe vera gel.
- Get out of sun or cover up to avoid further damage.
- Take care of blisters by loosely covering them and don't pick at them!

To help relieve the pain from a sunburn if NO blisters exist:

Aloe vera - Break open a fresh leaf or use 96-100% pure aloe gel.

Baking soda - Add 1/2 cup baking soda to a warm bath and soak for half an hour.

Vinegar - Put some regular or cider vinegar on a cloth and apply to sunburned area.

Whole milk - Apply a cool compress soaked in whole milk to the area.

What are YOU gonna do about...
CHOKING?

Things to watch for...
> **Trouble breathing**
> **Coughing or choking for several minutes**
> **Gripping the throat with one or both hands**
> **High-pitched wheezing**
> **Bluish color of skin, lips, fingertips/nails, and earlobes**

ATTENTION: There are TWO separate "**What to do...**" parts here... one for <u>ADULTS & CHILDREN</u> (below) and one for <u>INFANTS</u> (see next page)!

What to do... for <u>ADULTS & CHILDREN</u> *(Children over age 1)*

- Tell victim to try and cough it out. Ask "are you choking?" If victim nods yes, tell him/her you are going to help.

- Stand behind victim, wrap your arms around him/her and place your fist (thumb side in) just above victim's belly button well below the breastbone.

- Grab the fist with your other hand and give quick, upward thrusts into their abdomen.

- Continue giving thrusts until the object is coughed out and victim can breathe, cough or talk or until he/she stops responding or passes out.

If <u>ADULT or CHILD</u> stops responding or passes out:

- Yell for help, check breathing, and position victim on a flat surface so you can begin CPR (30 compressions and 2 breaths) - or do Hands-only CPR - to help force object out.

- Find hand position in center of chest over breastbone
  FOR <u>ADULTS</u> – see illustration 3-1 on page 190
  FOR <u>CHILDREN</u> – see illustration 3-2 on page 191

- Begin chest compressions:
  <u>ADULTS</u> – Using **both** hands, compress chest 30 times.
  <u>CHILDREN</u> – Using **one** hand, compress chest 30 times.

- Check mouth for object after every set of 30 compressions then give 2 rescue breaths (if doing). After 5 sets, call 911.

- Continue doing 30:2 sets until victim moves, coughs or talks or help arrives.

What to do... for <u>INFANTS</u> *(Newborn to age 1)*

- If infant stops breathing, have someone call an ambulance.
- Turn infant face down on your forearm and support its head with that hand -- hold at angle so it's head is lower than chest. (May want to brace arm holding infant against your thigh.)
- Give 5 back blows between infants' shoulder blades with the heel of your other hand.
- If no object comes out, turn infant over so it is facing up on your forearm (still at an angle so head lower than chest) -- use your **first two fingers** to find the center of the breastbone on infant's chest.
- Give 5 thrusts to infant's chest using <u>only</u> **2 fingers**! (Each thrust should be 1½ inches [3.81 cm] deep!)
- Repeat steps until infant can breath, cough, or cry or until he/she stops responding or passes out.

If <u>INFANT</u> stops responding or passes out:

- Place infant on a firm, flat surface above ground (like on a table or counter) so you can begin Infant CPR.
- Yell for help and check infant's breathing.
- Find finger position in center of chest over breastbone *[see illustration 3-3 on page 192]*
- Using **2 fingers only**, compress chest 30 times.
- Open the airway and check mouth for object(s). If you see it, take it out.
- Give 2 breaths ... and remember, cover both mouth and nose on Infants!
- Repeat giving sets of 30 compressions and 2 rescue breaths, checking the mouth for objects. After 5 sets, call 911 (if they haven't already been called).
- Continue doing 30:2 sets until infant starts to respond or help arrives.

What are YOU gonna do about...
COLD-RELATED ILLNESSES?

FROSTBITE

Frostbite (or frostnip which is the early stages of frostbite) is when certain parts of your body are exposed to severe or extreme cold - mainly your fingers, toes, ears, cheeks and nose. Freezing temperatures can form ice crystals in the fluids in and around cells in your body. This damages and dries out cell tissues and membranes, and extreme cases can impact deep nerves, muscles or even bones... or even lead to the loss of a limb.

Things to watch for...
> **Skin appears white and waxy**
> **Numbness or no feeling in that area**
> **Possible blisters**

What to do...

- Handle area gently; DO NOT rub it!
- Remove tight or constrictive clothing (gloves, boots, socks, etc.) and any jewelry.
- Warm gently using body heat or soaking area in warm water (between 100-105 degrees Fahrenheit / between 38-41 degrees Celsius) until area is red and feels warm. *(Person may feel a burning sensation or pain as the area warms back up.)*
- Loosely bandage area with dry, sterile dressing or cloth.
- If fingers or toes are frostbitten, separate them with sterile gauze or clean cloth.
- Try not to break any blisters.

Things you should NOT do...

- DO NOT rub or massage the area since this may cause damage to cells!
- DO NOT rub snow on the area!
- DO NOT try to warm with dry radiant heat (meaning don't warm with a blow-dryer or hold in front of fire or hot stove). Using warm water is best.
- DO NOT try to thaw a frostbitten body part if it has a chance of re-freezing (if you are stuck in the wilderness) since this could cause more damage.

HYPOTHERMIA

Hypothermia starts setting in when your body core (the vital organs - heart, lungs, and kidneys) drops below 95 degrees Fahrenheit (35 degrees Celsius). When exposed to extreme cold for a long time, your brain begins to shut down certain bodily functions to save internal heat for the core.

Things to watch for...
>   **Shivering and numbness**
>   **Confusion or dizziness**
>   **Stumbling and weakness**
>   **Slow or slurred speech**
>   **Shock** (pale, cold or clammy, weak or rapid pulse, etc.)

What to do...
- Gently move victim to a warm place.
- Check breathing and pulse (**ABCs... Airway, Breathing, & Circulation**).
- Handle victim gently and DO NOT rub body or limbs.
- Remove any wet clothing and replace with dry clothing and/or blankets.
- If possible, place victim in a sleeping bag, especially if in the wilderness. (Note: Your body heat can help heat victim... so cuddle up - if victim says it's okay!)
- Cover the head and neck with a hat or part of a blanket (75% of the body's heat is lost through top of the head).
- DO NOT WARM VICTIM TOO QUICKLY, such as putting them in warm water! (If the body warms too fast, it can dump cold blood into the heart and body core causing a possible heart attack or drop in body temperature.)
- If hot water bottles or hot packs are used, wrap in a towel or blanket first then place on side of the chest or on groin (hip) area. (If heat is put on arms or legs then blood could be drawn away from body core - keep heat on the core!)
- Let victim sip a warm, sweet, nonalcoholic drink.
- Keep watching victim's **ABCs...**

Things you should NOT do...
- DO NOT rub or massage the victims limbs!
- DO NOT put victim in a hot bath! It will warm him/her TOO quickly.
- DO NOT put hot packs on arms or legs... put them against the body (chest or groin area).

What are _YOU_ gonna do about...
CONVULSIONS & SEIZURES?

Convulsions are usually brought on by a high fever, poisoning or injury and is basically a violent seizure _(see "Things to watch for...")_.

Seizures are usually related to epilepsy (also known as seizure disorder since seizures occur repeatedly during person's life), and about 2 million Americans and 300,000 Canadians suffer from epilepsy. There are many types and forms of seizures that range from a short episode of blank staring to convulsions -- and most seizures only last from 1-3 minutes or less.

Things to watch for...

> **Victim falls to floor and shakes or twitches in the arms, legs or body for a minute or longer**
>
> **Blank staring or vacant expression and minor twitching of the face or jerking of the hand** (usually a mild epileptic seizure)
>
> **Loss of body fluids or functions** (drooling, may pee or poop)
>
> **No memory of what happened, confusion**

What to do...

- Have someone call for an ambulance, esp. if victim was poisoned or injured or if seizure lasts over 3-5 minutes.
- Stay calm... you can't stop the convulsion or seizure.
- DO NOT put anything between teeth or in mouth!
- Move things that could hurt or fall on victim.
- Put something soft under victim's head, if possible.
- When convulsion or seizure is over, help roll victim on to their side to keep an open airway.
- Look for any other injuries and keep checking **ABCs... Airway, Breathing & Circulation**.
- Stay with victim until help arrives and try to calm them.

If victim is epileptic:

Ask if the victim takes any medications for seizures and help him/her take them according to the instructions.

Also may want to review TERRORISM (in Section 2) for information, signs & symptoms, and treatment for several chemical agents that may cause convulsions.

What are YOU gonna do about...
DIZZINESS & FAINTING?

DIZZINESS

Dizziness is a symptom, usually combined with feeling sick to the stomach, sweating, and feeling some kind of movement that really isn't there.

Things to watch for...

> **If dizzy feeling does not pass quickly or is really bad**
> **Fainting or passing out**
> **Vapors, mist or strange smells**

What to do...

- Have victim sit or lie down and close their eyes or focus on a nearby object that is not moving.
- Tell victim to try to keep their head still.

FAINTING

Fainting is a temporary loss of consciousness (passes out) and may indicate a more serious condition. It's usually caused due to a lack of oxygenated blood to the brain. Be aware several types of injuries could cause fainting.

Things to watch for...

> **Visible injuries like bleeding from the ears or a bite or sting**
> **Pupils are enlarged or very small** (if different sizes, it could be a stroke)
> **Vapors, mist or strange smells**
> **Bluish color of skin, lips, fingertips or nails** (may not be getting air - *see BREATHING PROBLEMS*)

What to do...

- If victim is still passed out, put victim on their side to keep an open airway.
- Once victim is awake, gently roll them onto their back.
- Prop feet and the lower part of legs up with pillows or something (only if victim is not hurt).
- Loosen any tight clothing, esp. around neck and waist.
- Check **ABCs... Airway, Breathing & Circulation**.
- Make sure victim rests before trying to get up.
- If necessary, contact doctor if symptoms persist.

What are YOU gonna do about...
DROWNING?

Things to watch for...
> **Signs of breathing**
> **Bluish color of skin, lips, fingertips or nails** (may not be getting air)
> **Pulse**

What to do...

- Have someone call for an ambulance.
- Once victim is out of the water, check **ABCs... Airway, Breathing & Circulation**.
- Check to see if there are any injuries or objects in mouth.
- If victim is not breathing or has no pulse, begin Rescue Breathing and/or CPR. *(see BREATHING PROBLEMS for Rescue Breathing and HEART PROBLEMS for CPR)*
- Once victim starts breathing on their own, cover with a blanket or dry towels to keep warm and have them lay on their side for a while.
- Stay with victim at all times until medical help arrives.

What are YOU gonna do about...
EAR INJURIES?

FOREIGN OBJECT IN EAR

If something crawls in or gets stuck in the ear...

- Keep victim calm and have them sit down with head tilted sideways.
- Use a flashlight to try to see object in ear...

  if a bug - turn ear up toward sun or flashlight - most bugs are drawn to light so it might crawl out on it's own

  if a loose item - tilt head and try to shake it out

  if still in but see it - IF you see item, gently try to remove with tweezers, but DO NOT do this if victim is squirming or item is deep in ear - you could damage the eardrum!
- Get medical help if not successful or can't visually locate object (doctors have special tools for ears).

NOISE-INDUCED HEARING LOSS (NIHL)

Millions of people are exposed to hazardous sound levels daily. Loud impulse noise (like an explosion) or loud continuous noise at work or play damage the delicate hair cells of the inner ear and the hearing nerve.

Sometimes damage can be temporary - like after a concert when your ears ring for a bit then go back to normal. But repeated loud noise or a massive impulse noise could lead to permanent damage - damage that cannot be reversed. Be aware certain types of disasters like tornadoes, a terrorist's bomb, or even hurricanes can cause a form of hearing loss.

Things to watch for...

Bombs, tornadoes, power tools, loud music, jet ski, etc.
Having to shout to be heard over noise (too loud)
Ringing or buzzing in ears

What to do...

- Avoid loud situations or at least wear ear plugs or muffs.
- Have hearing tested annually (esp. if you work around loud noises)
- Protect children's ears. (Note: using cotton isn't enough.)

To learn more about NIHL, visit National Institute on Deafness and Other Communication Disorders' site at www.nidcd.nih.gov

What are YOU gonna do about...
EYE INJURIES?

Things to watch for...
> **Severe or constant pain or burning**
> **Object stuck in the eye** (like a piece of metal or glass)
> **Redness and swelling**
> **Blurry vision, trouble keeping eye open, light sensitive**
> **Vapors or fumes in the air**
> **If injury is from a chemical, make a note of the name for Poison Control if possible**

What to do...
- Avoid rubbing eye since this can cause more damage.
- Have victim sit down with their head tilted backwards.
- Wash hands before touching eye area.

If the injury is a <u>loose</u> foreign object:
- Gently separate eyelids to see if you can locate a foreign object - can try removing it by wiping gently with damp tissue.
- Ask victim if he/she wears contact lenses, and if so, ask him or her to remove them.
- Have victim lean over sink or lie on back, hold eye open, and gently flush eye with lukewarm water or a saline solution.
- Get medical help if you are not successful.

If there is an object sticking out of the eye:
- Put thick soft pads around the object that is sticking out.
- DO NOT try to remove or press on the object!
- Carefully wrap with a roller bandage to hold thick pads around the object.
- Get medical attention immediately!

If injury is from a blow to the eye:
- Apply an icepack to reduce pain and swelling.
- Seek medical attention if damage to eye or blurred vision.

Continued on next page...

If the injury is from a chemical:

- Call your local Poison Control Center (or 1-800-222-1222 in the U.S.) and have name of chemical handy, if possible.

- If victim is wearing contact lenses, <u>ask Poison Control if they should be removed and whether to keep or dispose of them</u>! If okay and able to take out, ask victim to remove lenses.

- Have victim lean over sink, lie down, or get in shower - hold eye(s) open, and gently flush with lukewarm water for at least 15 minutes. (If only one eye has chemical in it, make sure head is turned so it doesn't pour into the other eye.)

- Tell victim to roll eyeball(s) around while flushing to wash entire eye.

- DO NOT press or rub the eyes!

- May want to cover eyes with clean dressing & bandages but ask Poison Control or check label on bottle. For example, if chemical is mustard gas (sulfur mustard) you should <u>not</u> cover eyes ... but wear shades to protect them.

- Get medical attention immediately!

Things you should NOT do...

- DO NOT try to remove an object that is stuck into the eye!

- DO NOT try to remove their contacts (if any)... let the victim do it!

- DO NOT try to move the eyeball if it comes out of the socket!

Things you SHOULD do...

- Protect your eyes with safety glasses or goggles when playing sports or working with tools or chemicals ... and wear shades during the day (to help reduce UV exposure).

- When an eye injury occurs, have an ophthalmologist (an eye physician <u>and</u> surgeon) examine it as soon as possible. You may not be realize how serious an injury is at first.

Also may want to review TERRORISM (in Section 2) for information, signs & symptoms, and treatment on several chemical and biological agents that may cause eye injuries or discomfort.

What are YOU gonna do about...
HEAD, NECK OR SPINE INJURIES?

Things to watch for...
> **Convulsions or seizures**
> **Intense pain in the head, neck or back**
> **Bleeding from the head, ears or nose**
> **Blurry vision**
> **Tingling or loss of feeling in the hands, fingers, feet or toes**
> **Weird bumps on the head or down the spine**
> **Shock** (pale, cold or clammy, drowsy, weak or rapid pulse, etc.)

What to do...

- Do not try to move victim unless they are in extreme danger and support victim's head and neck during movement.

- Have someone call an ambulance immediately!

- Check to see if victim is alert and check **ABCs... Airway, Breathing & Circulation** ... and if you need to give them Rescue Breathing or CPR... DO <u>NOT</u> tilt their head back! *(see BREATHING PROBLEMS for Rescue Breathing and HEART PROBLEMS for CPR)*

- Try to control any bleeding using direct pressure. *(see BLEEDING)*

- If victim is passed out, hold their head gently between your hands while waiting for help to arrive. This will keep them from moving suddenly when/if they wake up.

What are YOU gonna do about...
HEART PROBLEMS?

Heart attacks can kill and most victims die within 2 hours of the first few symptoms. Most people deny they are having a heart attack - even if they have chest pains and shortness of breath... but DON'T take any chances! A heart attack can lead to <u>Cardiac Arrest</u>.

Cardiac arrest means that the heart stops beating and causes victim to pass out followed by no sign of breathing and no pulse.

Cardiopulmonary resuscitation (CPR) is used to help pump oxygenated blood through the body to the brain until the medical experts arrive.

- **Conventional CPR** - combines chest compressions and Rescue Breathing using **C-A-B**
- **Hands-only CPR** - hard and fast chest compressions (100 per minute ~ do it to the beat of that song "Staying Alive" by the Bee Gees)

Hands-only CPR should only be used on an adult that suddenly collapses. It should not be used on children and infants or on adults whose cardiac arrest is from respiratory causes (like near-drowning or a drug overdose). Those victims all benefit from combined CPR and Rescue Breathing.

Please note: CPR is now **C-A-B** .. **C**ompressions - **A**irway - **B**reathing!

HEART ATTACK

Things to watch for...
> **Chest pain that can spread to shoulder, arm, or jaw**
> **Shortness of breath or trouble breathing**
> **Strange pulse** (faster or slower than normal or sporadic)
> **Pale or bluish skin color**

What to do...
- Tell victim to STOP what they're doing, sit down and rest.
- Call for an ambulance immediately!
- Loosen any tight clothing, esp. around neck and waist.
- Ask victim if they are taking any prescribed medicines for their heart... and if they do, have them take it!
- Take a couple of pure aspirin, if available.
- Watch victim's breathing and be prepared to give CPR.

CARDIAC ARREST (GIVING CPR)

Main thing is do compressions to keep blood moving until help arrives!

Things to watch for...
> **Not responding or passed out**
> **Not breathing and no pulse**
> **Broken bones or chest, head, neck or spine injuries**

What to do...
- Yell for help. Send someone to call **9-1-1** and get an AED
- Take about 5-10 seconds to check for pulse and breathing.

If no pulse or normal breathing is detected, begin CPR:

Note: CPR steps are now **C-A-B** = **C**ompressions-**A**irway-**B**reathing

Circulation; Perform Chest Compressions
- Find hand position in center of chest over breastbone – see illustrations on next 3 pages...

  FOR <u>ADULTS</u> – *[see illustration 3-1 on page 190]*
  FOR <u>CHILDREN</u> – *[see illustration 3-2 on page 191]*
  FOR <u>INFANTS</u> – *[see illustration 3-3 on page 192]*

- Begin chest compressions (at least 100 compressions per minute) using the following guidelines:

  <u>ADULTS</u> – Using **both** hands, compress chest 30 times.
  <u>CHILDREN</u> – Using **one** hand, compress chest 30 times.
  <u>INFANTS</u> – Using **2 fingers**, compress chest 30 times.

- Allow chest to recoil completely after each compression.

Airway; Open Airway
- Tilt head all the way back and lift chin. (Be careful with child's or infant's head... just tilt a little bit!)
- Maintain airway

Breathing; Breaths
- Give victim 2 breaths (1 second each). If not comfortable giving rescue breaths or have trouble making chest rise within 10 seconds, keep doing compressions. Push hard & push fast to keep blood moving through victim!

- Repeat 30 chest compressions (and 2 breaths, if doing) until an AED or medical help arrives or victim recovers.

- If victim recovers (starts breathing or pukes and pulse resumes), turn victim onto their side to keep airway open.

CPR Position for Adults (9 years & older)

Illustration 3-1

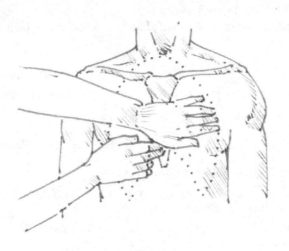

1. Find hand position

2. Position shoulders over hands. Push hard and fast at least 2 inches deep for 30 compressions, give 2 rescue breaths (if doing), and repeat 30:2 until help arrives/victim recovers.
(Hands-only CPR: keep doing 100 compressions a minute!)

CPR POSITION FOR CHILDREN (1 - 8 YEARS)

Illustration 3-2

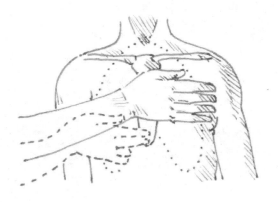

1. Find hand position

2. Position shoulder over hand. Push hard and fast about 2 inches deep for 30 compressions, give 2 rescue breaths (if doing), and repeat 30:2 until help arrives/victim recovers.

CPR Position for Infants (under 1 year)

Illustration 3-3

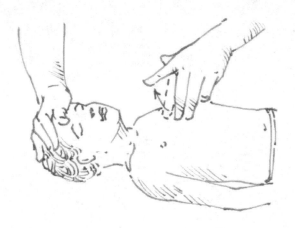

1. Find finger position

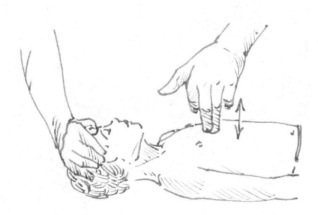

2. Position hand over fingers. Push hard and fast about 1½ inches deep for 30 compressions, give 2 rescue breaths (if doing), and repeat 30:2 until help arrives/victim recovers.

What are YOU gonna do about...
HEAT-RELATED ILLNESSES?

There are two major types of heat illness – **HEAT EXHAUSTION** and **HEAT STROKE**. If heat exhaustion is left untreated it can lead to heat stroke. Both conditions are serious, however, **heat stroke** is a <u>major</u> medical emergency and getting victim's body temperature cooled down is more critical than getting fluids in their body. Heat stroke can lead to death.

Things to watch for...

> Heat Cramps
> **Muscle pains and spasms (usually first sign that body's having trouble with the heat)**

> Heat Exhaustion
> **Cool, clammy, or pale skin**
> **Light-headed or dizzy and weak**
> **Racing heart**
> **Sick to the stomach (nausea)**
> **Very thirsty or heavy sweating (sometimes)**

> Heat Stroke (also called Sunstroke)
> **Very hot and dry skin**
> **Light-headed or dizzy**
> **Confusion, drowsiness or fainting**
> **Rapid breathing and rapid heartbeat**
> **Convulsions, passes out or slips into a coma**

What to do...

- Get victim to a cool or shady place and rest.
- Lightly stretch or massage muscles to relieve cramps.
- Loosen clothing around waist and neck to improve circulation and remove sweaty clothes.
- Cool down victim's body - put wet cloths on victim's face, neck and skin and keep adding cool water to cloth... or if outdoors, use hose or stream. Also, fan the victim or get inside air-conditioned place.
- Have victim sip <u>cool water</u> (NO alcohol – it dehydrates!)

If victim refuses water, pukes or starts to pass out:

- Call for an ambulance or call 9-1-1.

Continued on next page...

- Put victim on their side to keep airway open.
- Keep cooling down their body by placing ice or cold cloths on wrists, neck, armpits, and groin area (where leg meets the hip) or keep adding water to cloths. Also fan the victim.
- Check victim's **ABCs... Airway, Breathing, & Circulation**.
- Stay with victim until medical help arrives.

Remember, **HEAT STROKE** (also known as sunstroke) is a medical emergency and can cause the victim to slip into a coma -- getting a victim's body temperature cooled down is more important than getting fluids in their body!

What are YOU gonna do about...
INFECTION?

It is important to be very careful and protect yourself against the spread of disease or infection when caring for an open wound or a wound that is bleeding. *(Review TIPS ON REDUCING THE SPREAD OF GERMS OR DISEASES at beginning of this section)*

INFECTION

Germs are the main cause of an infection so whenever you perform first aid on anyone (including yourself), there is always a chance of spreading germs or diseases. All injuries - from tiny cuts to massive wounds - <u>must</u> be cleaned immediately to reduce the chances of infection! And keep cleaning a wound until it is completely healed.

Things to watch for...
    Sore or wound is red and swollen or has red streaks
    Sore or wound is warm or painful
    Wound may open and ooze clear or yellowish fluid
    Fever or muscle aches or stiffness in the neck

What to do...

- ALWAYS wash your hands before <u>and</u> after caring for a wound... even if it's your own!

- Immediately wash minor wounds with soap and water or rinse with hydrogen peroxide.

- Cover wound with sterile bandage or gauze -- best to clean and change bandage daily. An open wound is a doorway for germs and infection to get inside the body.

- Use an antibiotic cream or gel to help disinfect the wound and kill germs. *(Note: don't use cream or gel if wound is from a bite since it might seal wound and keep it from draining.)*

- Boost your immune system to help fight infection (like taking astragalus, Vitamin C, garlic, mushrooms, zinc, and a good multiple vitamin + mineral supplement, etc. - but check with your doctor first if taking any prescription medications).

- If infection gets worse, you may want to see a doctor.

Also may want to review INFECTIOUS DISEASES on next page.

What are YOU gonna do about...
INFECTIOUS DISEASES?

The immune system is a complex network of cells, tissues, and organs that work together to defend the body against attacks by foreign invaders such as bacteria, viruses, parasites and fungi. Because the human body provides an ideal environment for many microbes, they try to break in. It is the immune system's job to keep them out or, failing that, to seek out and destroy them.[9] But if a person's immune system is weak or damaged, germs and infection can settle in, leading to illness or possibly death.

According to the Centers for Disease Control and Prevention, infectious diseases are the leading cause of death worldwide. And with air travel and international trade, infectious microbes are carried across borders every day by humans, animals, insects and contaminated foods.

Some "old" diseases like malaria and measles are found in certain parts of the world, but "new" diseases like HIV/AIDS and West Nile are spreading around the globe. Plus every year there's some form of influenza and the common cold that spreads and affects people.

There are many infectious diseases -- too many to cover -- so we're only covering a common one (flu) and some emerging ones (avian flu, C. diff and staph). First, we describe each illness followed by "Things to watch for", then summarize "How they spread" and "What to do" for all of them at the end. Educate yourself about threats of emerging diseases and listen to officials for advice on how to protect yourself and your loved ones.

Influenza (flu) is a respiratory illness caused by the influenza virus that affects millions of people each year. Flu causes about 250,000 - 500,000 deaths worldwide every year, and a major outbreak (called a pandemic) could increase the death toll dramatically. The best way to prevent the flu is to boost your immune system and get vaccinated, esp people with weakened immune systems. There are several antivirals approved for treatment.

There are 3 types of flu viruses: A, B, and C. Influenza A viruses can infect humans and mammals (including pigs, horses and seals) but wild birds are the natural host. Typically, wild birds don't get sick but A viruses can be deadly to domestic chickens and turkeys. Influenza B viruses are normally found only in humans and generally don't cause severe widespread illness, while Influenza C viruses cause mild illness in humans.

Since strains can mutate or cross over to other species, it could lead to widespread illness and death. The worst influenza A outbreak on record was the

Spanish flu pandemic of 1918-1919 which may have killed up to 50 million people worldwide.

Things to watch for (flu)...
> **Possible symptoms** - fever (usually high), headache, sore throat, cough, runny nose, body aches, weakness, diarrhea or puking (more common in children)
> **Possible complications** - bacterial pneumonia (lung inflammation), shortness of breath, hospitalization

Avian flu (bird flu) is an influenza A virus subtype that occurs mainly in birds, is highly contagious among birds, and can be deadly to them. According to the CDC there are many different subtypes but one of them is the H5N1 virus. H5N1 does not usually infect people, but infections have occurred. To date, most human cases caught this flu from domestic chickens or ducks and over 50% of those patients died.

The recent H1N1 (swine flu) scare demonstrated how quickly virulent flu strains can spread globally, and that strain will continue to spread for years to come, like a regular seasonal influenza virus.

According to a recent worst-case scenario outlined by the World Bank, a flu pandemic of avian or other origin could kill more than 70 million people worldwide and lead to a "major global recession" costing more than $3 trillion.[10] Several vaccines are currently in development for avian and swine flu plus there are some antiviral drugs available for treatment.

Things to watch for (avian, H1N1 or other variants)...
> **Flu-like symptoms** - fever, headache, sore throat, cough, runny nose, body aches, fatigue, puking or diarrhea
> **Possible complications** - eye infections (avian flu), pneumonia, severe breathing problems or death

C. diff (Clostridium difficile or C. difficile) is a toxin-producing bacterium that causes diarrhea and more serious conditions like colitis (inflammation of the colon). There are many different strains and most make only two toxins that cause minor symptoms that are easily treated. However, a mutated strain called NAP1 (or the 027 or BI strain) makes about 20 times more toxins so symptoms are much more severe. And now NAP1 is starting to show signs of becoming drug-resistant.

Experts estimate C. diff sickens about 500,000 Americans a year and the rate of infection grows by about 10% each year. C. diff is fairly common among older adults in hospitals or in long-term care facilities and typically occurs after using antibiotics. One out of five people who get the infection will get it again, and recurrences can be more severe or even deadly.

Unfortunately C. diff spores can survive on most surfaces for months, and most hospital cleaners won't kill it, but a solution of bleach and water could. Also, alcohol-based hand sanitizers used in many health facilities do not work so staff, patients and visitors must wash hands with soap and water frequently to reduce spreading the infection.

Things to watch for (C. diff)...
> **Mild symptoms** - watery diarrhea (at least three times a day for 2 or more days with no blood in your poop), possible cramping or minor abdominal pain or tenderness
> **Severe symptoms** - watery diarrhea 10 to 15 times a day, abdominal cramping and pain, fever, blood or pus in poop, nausea / pukey, dehydration, loss of appetite, weight loss

Note: Not all cases of diarrhea are C. diff, but if you have it several times a day for 2 or more days, see your doctor immediately.

Staph (staphylococcus aureus) are bacteria about a third of the population carries on their skin or in their nose. Bacteria can enter the body through a cut, bite or wound and may cause infection. Some strains of staph have become drug resistant (called methicillin-resistant Staphylococcus aureus or **MRSA**). According to the CDC, staph bacteria are one of the most common causes of skin infections in the U.S. Most infections are minor (like a pimple, bump or boil) and can be treated with antibiotics. However, it can quickly turn into deep, painful abscesses that require surgical draining. Sometimes the bacteria remain confined to the skin, but they can also penetrate into the body, causing potentially life-threatening infections in bones, joints, surgical wounds, the bloodstream, heart valves and lungs.

Staph infections, including MRSA, occur most often in hospitals, nursing homes and facilities where people have weakened immune systems. MRSA also threatens police, firefighters and EMS workers, school kids and the community in general. In fact, the CDC reports MRSA is now killing more Americans each year than AIDS.

Things to watch for (staph / MRSA)...
> **Possible symptoms** - skin infection that may look like a pimple or boil and can be red, swollen, painful, or have pus or other drainage
> **Severe** - pneumonia, bloodstream or wound infections

How infectious diseases spread...
Most infectious diseases are spread by close person-to-person contact

primarily by touching people or things contaminated with bodily fluids (like pee, poop, sweat, droplets from sneezing, etc) -- then touching your eyes, nose, or mouth. Other diseases (like MRSA) can be spread by sharing personal items like towels or razors or by medical staff using contaminated items like stethoscopes or blood pressure cuffs. Keep in mind some bacteria or viruses can survive on objects for days, weeks or months.

What to do to reduce the spread of infectious diseases...

- Wash hands often using soap and water or use hand sanitizer (with at least 60% alcohol in it) to reduce the spread of germs. But keep in mind sanitizers don't work against some bugs so it's best to wash up.

- Tell healthcare workers and visitors to wash their hands before they touch you or your stuff -- don't be timid!

- If you have a fever, stay home! And wait 24 hours after fever breaks before you return to work or school.

- Use antibiotics only when absolutely necessary. Consider boosting your immune system to help fight infections.

- Sick people should cover mouth and nose with tissue or sleeve when coughing or sneezing, wash hands often, and wear a face mask around others (if very ill).

- Keep cuts and scrapes clean and covered until healed.

- Clean counters, doorknobs, fixtures, phones, remotes, nurse call buttons, linens, etc. often with a bleach solution.

- Don't share silverware, razors, clothing, towels, or bedding and wash objects with soap and hot water.

- Follow doctor's instructions and limit activities outside home until fever and symptoms have gone away.

For more information, visit the following web sites ...

Influenza / Flu: www.cdc.gov/flu/   www.phac-aspc.gc.ca/influenza/
  (all kinds)   www.flu.gov   www.who.int/topics/influenza/en/

C. diff: www.cdc.gov/HAI/organisms/cdiff/Cdiff_infect.html
        www.phac-aspc.gc.ca/id-mi/cdiff-eng.php
        www.mayoclinic.com/health/c-difficile/DS00736

Staph: www.cdc.gov/mrsa
        www.mayoclinic.com/health/mrsa/DS00735

Or call CDC Hotline at 1-800-CDC-INFO. See more tips on pages 231-232

What are YOU gonna do about...
POISONING?

Please make sure you have the local **Poison Control Center** phone number near a telephone since many poisonings can be cared for without the help of ambulance personnel. The people who staff Poison Control Centers (PCCs) have access to information on most poisonous substances and can tell you what care to give to counteract the poison.

POISON CONTROL CENTER # 1-800-222-1222 (U.S. only)

If outside U.S., write in local **Poison Control Centre** phone # below:

_____

POISON - ABSORBED THROUGH THE SKIN

Review TERRORISM (in Section 2) for information, signs & symptoms, and treatment on several poisonous chemical and biological agents that could be absorbed through skin.

Things to watch for...
> **Reddened skin or burns**
> **Poison on skin, clothing or in the area**
> **Bites or marks from insect or animal** *(see BITES & STINGS)*
> **Possible Allergic Reaction -** Pain, discoloration or redness at site, trouble breathing, signs of shock (pale, cold, drowsy, weak or rapid pulse, etc.)

What to do...
- Be aware - make sure it's safe, then ask what happened.
- Move victim to safety (away from poison), if necessary.
- Find the container (if any) or name of the poison and call local Poison Control Center or an ambulance.
- Remove clothing that may have poison on it - don't pull over head - cut it off. (Seal clothing in a bag then seal that bag in a bag - ask officials how to dispose of it later.)
- Flush skin with running water for 10 minutes.
- Wash area gently with soap and water. *(Note: some chemical agents don't suggest using soap so may want to ask.)*
- Monitor breathing and watch for any allergic reactions.

POISON - INHALED BY BREATHING

Review TERRORISM (in Section 2) for information, signs & symptoms, and treatment on several poisonous chemical and biological agents that could be inhaled from humans' or critters' wet or dried body fluids, from soil, or from powders, gas, mist, or vapors.

Things to watch for...
> **Strong odors or fumes**
> **Find the source of odor or fumes** (be aware of threat)
> **Difficulty in breathing or dizzy**

What to do...
- Be aware - make sure it's safe...then ask what happened.
- Get victim out to fresh air.
- Avoid breathing fumes - open windows & doors (if safe).
- Call Poison Control Center or an ambulance.
- If victim isn't breathing consider doing Rescue Breathing - but ONLY if sure poison cannot be spread person to person. *(see TERRORISM then BREATHING PROBLEMS)*

POISON - POISONOUS PLANTS (IVY, OAK, & SUMAC)

Three common poisonous plants found in Canada and the U.S. include:

<u>Poison ivy</u> - can grow as a shrub or vine and is found across most of Canada and U.S. It has white or cream-colored berries (or flowers in Spring) and leaves are usually three leaflets to a stem but vary in color, size, shape and texture around the world. *[see illustration 3-4 on page 203]*

<u>Poison oak</u> - can grow as a shrub or vine and found throughout the West and Southwest (very common in Oregon and California). It also varies widely in shapes and colors but usually has distinctive shape of an oak leaf and red fuzzy berries. The leaves usually come in leaflets of three to a stem but can be in groups of five or more. It is best to learn what it looks like where you live. *[see illustration 3-5 on page 203]*

<u>Poison sumac</u> - is a tall shrub or small tree and mostly lives in standing water (like swamps and peat bogs). It has whitish green berries and bright green, pointy leaves that grow 6 to 12 leaves in pairs along both sides of each stem plus one leaf on each tip. *[see illustration 3-6 on page 204]*

All 3 of these plants have a sap called **urushiol** [oo-roo-she-ol] which is a sticky, colorless oil that stains things black when exposed to air. This sap is in the leaves, berries, stems and roots of all 3 types and can stick around a long time if the sap stays dry (which is why you need to rinse off whatever gets exposed - yourself, pets, clothing, shoes and laces, tools or camping stuff.) Never burn these plants since smoke can carry the oil and irritate skin, nose or lungs.

The rash is caused by your body's reaction to this oil and can show up as quickly as a few hours or take several days ... or never, in some cases, since some people don't have reactions to urushiol. It can irritate pets' skin too.

Note: the rash itself is <u>not</u> contagious but the OIL (urushiol) is what is transferred by hands, fingers, clothing or fur!! Make sure you wash your hands after touching the rash to avoid spreading any urushiol.

Things to watch for...
> **Inflamed red rash**
> **Extremely itchy skin or burning feeling**
> **Blisters**
> **Swelling or fever**
> **Allergic reactions** (weakness, dizziness, swelling in mouth or lips, trouble breathing or swallowing)

What to do...
- It is CRITICAL to wash affected area with soap and running water then apply rubbing alcohol using cotton balls on area to remove any excess oil as quickly as possible.
- Immediately and carefully remove and wash any clothing and/or shoes that got exposed to the poison. *(Remember to wash pets, tools or anything else exposed to oil too.)*
- If a rash or sores develop, use calamine lotion or baking soda paste several times a day on area.
- Take an antihistamine to reduce reaction (read label first).
- If condition gets worse or spreads onto large areas of body, eyes or face, see a doctor.

To relieve pain from poison ivy, oak, or sumac:

Baking soda - Make a paste using 3 parts baking soda with 1 part water and apply on rash.

Jewelweed - Studies indicate a plant that grows near poison ivy called jewelweed (has tiny, orange-yellow, horn-shaped flowers with reddish or white spots) can be used directly on area that brushed against ivy. Crush juicy stems in your hands and apply to the area - even if there's no rash yet since it may help reduce inflammation. *[see illustration 3-7 on page 204]*

Illustration 3-4
Poison Ivy

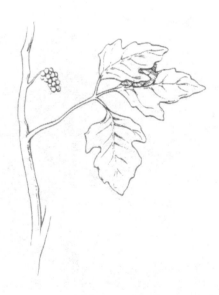

Illustration 3-5
Poison Oak

Illustration 3-6
Poison Sumac

Illustration 3-7
Jewelweed

POISON - SWALLOWED

See TERRORISM (in Section 2) for information, signs & symptoms, and treatment on several poisonous chemical and biological agents that could be swallowed from eating or drinking something contaminated.

Things to watch for...
> **Burns on the mouth, tongue and lips**
> **Stomach pains**
> **Open medicine cabinet; spilled or open containers**
> **Difficulty breathing**
> **Convulsions or seizures**
> **Weakness or dizziness**
> **Passed out**

What to do...
- Stay calm and find out exactly what, how much, and how long ago it was swallowed.
- Call Poison Control Center (1-800-222-1222 in the U.S.) or an ambulance and have bottle or container handy (if possible).
- NEVER give victim anything to eat or drink unless told to do so by Poison Control Center or a Medical professional!!
- If victim pukes, lay them on their side to keep airway open. Save a sample of the vomit IF the poison is unknown so the hospital can try to identify it.
- If victim isn't breathing consider doing Rescue Breathing - but ONLY if sure poison cannot be spread person to person. *(Check with Poison Control Center. Also review TERRORISM then BREATHING PROBLEMS)*

The American Academy of Pediatrics recommends parents no longer use syrup of ipecac (pronounced ip'- î - kak) as a poison treatment intervention in the home. Immediately contact local Poison Control Center for help.

If you decide to keep a few 1 ounce bottles in your First Aid Kit ... <u>use ONLY on the advice of a Medical professional or the Poison Control Center</u>! Syrup of ipecac is sold by most pharmacies without a prescription and used to induce vomiting (makes you puke) -- again, use only if instructed to do so.

What are <u>YOU</u> gonna do about...
SHOCK?

According to the Mayo Clinic, shock may result from trauma, heatstroke, blood loss, an allergic reaction, severe infection, poisoning, severe burns or other causes. When a person is in shock, his or her organs aren't getting enough blood or oxygen, which if untreated, can lead to permanent organ damage or death.

Things to watch for...
> **Pale, cold, and clammy skin**
> **Rapid heartbeat but weak pulse**
> **Quick and shallow breathing**
> **Dizziness or confusion**
> **Bluish color on lips and fingertips or nails**
> **Sick to their stomach or puking**
> **Intense thirst**

What to do...
- Call for an ambulance.
- Look for injuries and watch **ABCs... Airway, Breathing & Circulation**.
- Position victim using the following tips:
  <u>alert and awake</u> - place victim flat on their back with legs raised slightly
  <u>passed out or puking</u> - place victim on side to keep airway open
- Loosen any tight or restrictive clothing.
- Cover victim with a blanket or towel.
- Talk calmly to victim until help arrives (whether they are alert or not).

What are <u>YOU</u> gonna do about...
A STROKE?

According to the American Stroke Association, about 700,000 Americans suffer strokes each year and almost 1/4 of those victims die making stroke the #3 killer in the U.S. Canada reports about 40,000-50,000 new strokes annually killing about 16,000 Canadians making it the 4th leading cause of death according to the Heart and Stroke Foundation of Canada.

A stroke (or "brain attack") occurs when oxygen and vital nutrients carried by blood are cut off causing brain cells to die. It's cut off because...

> ...a blood vessel is blocked in the neck or brain (by a blood clot or narrowing of an artery) -- called an **ischemic** [is-KEM-ik] stroke *(causes about 83% of strokes)*

... **or** ...

> ...a blood vessel bursts or leaks -- called **hemorrhagic** [hem-o-RAJ-ik] stroke or bleeder *(causes 17% of strokes)*

NOTE: You only have 2 - 6 hours maximum to stop permanent brain damage from a stroke - so get to a hospital as quickly as possible (within 3 hours is best!)

Things to watch for...
> **Sudden confusion, trouble speaking or understanding**
> **Loss of muscle control on one side of the body**
> **Loss of balance, stumbling, dizziness or fainting**
> **Different sized pupils** (one pupil small / one enlarged)
> **Severe headache**
> **Blurred or double-vision in one or both eyes**
> **Shock** (pale, cold or clammy, weak or rapid pulse, etc.)
> **Transient ischemic attack (TIA / mini-stroke)** - a minor or warning stroke - risk of major stroke is high

What to do...
- Call 9-1-1 for an ambulance.
- Get victim to lie back with head raised (put pillows or blankets under head and shoulders so partially sitting up).
- Loosen any tight or restrictive clothing.
- See if there are any other injuries.
- If victim is drooling or having problems swallowing, place them on their side to keep the airway open.
- Stay with victim until medical help arrives.

What are YOU gonna do about...
TOOTH INJURIES?

Millions of tooth injuries happen every year - many from sports injuries or accidents, but also from chomping down on hard objects.

Things to watch for...
> **Tooth or teeth (or pieces if chipped)**
> **Object caught between teeth or stuck in gum**
> **Redness, swelling or bleeding**

What to do...
- Get to a dentist as quickly as possible.

If a permanent tooth is knocked out:
- Hold tooth by the crown or sides (not the root) and, if dirty, gently rinse with milk or water (but don't scrub it).
- If possible, gently insert tooth back into socket then hold in place or carefully bite down on gauze or cloth. If you can't get tooth back in socket, put it in milk (or water).
- Get medical attention immediately since many permanent teeth can be saved if replaced within 15-30 minutes!

If tooth is chipped, cracked or broken:
- Rinse damaged area with warm water.
- Apply a cold compress on area to reduce swelling.
- Call your dentist as soon as possible.

Things you should NOT do...
- DO NOT touch, scrub or hold the root or ligaments.
- DO NOT use teeth to open bottles or tear things and avoid chewing hard candy, ice, etc.
- DO NOT leave a knocked out tooth exposed to air or it will dry out - put it in milk (or water as a last resort!)

Things you SHOULD do...
- Wear a mouth guard and protective gear when playing sports and always wear your seat belt when in a vehicle.
- When a tooth injury occurs, go see a dentist.
- Practice good dental habits - brush & floss daily and rinse toothbrush with hydrogen peroxide weekly to kill germs.

Section 4

Emergency Contact Names & Numbers

ABOUT THE RED CROSS

The Red Cross disaster relief gives assistance to people affected by disaster. They also feed emergency workers, handle inquiries from family outside the disaster area, provide blood and blood products to victims, and helps those affected by disaster to access other available resources.

American Red Cross
2025 E Street, NW
Washington, DC 20006
Phone: (202) 303-5000
www.redcross.org

Canadian Red Cross
170 Metcalfe Street, Suite 300
Ottawa, Ontario K2P 2P2
Phone: 613.740.1900 Fax: 613.740.1911
To Donate by Phone: 1-800-418-1111
www.redcross.ca

Mexican Red Cross
Calle Luis Vives 200
Colonia Polanco
México D.F. 11510
Phone: (5255) 1084 4510 / 1084 4511
www.cruzrojamexicana.org.mx

International Federation of Red Cross and Red Crescent Societies
P. O. Box 372
CH-1211 Geneva 19
Switzerland
Telephone: (+41 22) 730 42 22
www.ifrc.org

The IFRC online Directory has an alphabetic listing by country of all the Red Cross and Red Crescent Societies worldwide.

ABOUT THE SALVATION ARMY

The Salvation Army gives hope and support to vulnerable people in 117 countries around the world. They offer practical assistance for children and families, often tending to the basic necessities of life and brings relief to people around the world through its emergency and disaster services.

The Salvation Army National Headquarters (USA)
P.O. Box 269
Alexandria, VA 22313
To Donate by Phone: 1-800-SAL-ARMY
www.salvationarmyusa.org

The Salvation Army Canada and Bermuda Territorial Headquarters
2 Overlea Boulevard
Toronto, Ontario M4H 1P4
Phone: 416 425 2111
www.salvationarmy.ca

The Salvation Army Mexico Territorial Headquarters
San Borja #1456, Colonia Vértiz Narvarte,
Delegación Benito Juárez
México 03600, DF
Phone: [55] 5575-1042; 5559-5244 / 9625
www.ejercitodesalvacionmx.org

The Salvation Army International Headquarters
101 Queen Victoria St
London EC4P 4EP
England
Telephone: (+44 20) 7332 0101
www.salvationarmy.org

Click on the world map or use the drop down menu to find your country's web site. Or click on the "Contact" menu item for more information.

About the Federal Emergency Management Agency (FEMA)

FEMA's continuing mission within DHS is to lead the effort to prepare the nation for all hazards and effectively manage federal response and recovery efforts following any national incident. FEMA also initiates proactive mitigation activities, trains first responders, and manages the National Flood Insurance Program.

FEMA Partners:

Emergency management is not the result of one government agency alone. FEMA works with many government, non-profit and private sector agencies to assist the public in preparing for, responding to, and recovering from disasters. These players make up the emergency response "team."

- Local Emergency Management Agencies
- State & Territory Emergency Management Offices
- National Emergency Management Organizations
- Federal-level Partners
- Partnerships with the Private Sector

• Local Emergency Management Agencies

Even the largest, most widespread disasters require a local response. Local emergency management programs are the heart of the nation's emergency management system. FEMA supports them by offering training courses for emergency managers and firefighters, with DHS funding for emergency planning and equipment, by conducting exercises for localities to practice response, and by promoting ways to minimize disasters' effects. FEMA also builds partnerships with mayors, county boards, Tribal governments and officials who share responsibility for emergency management.

Visit your City/County web site to see if there's a link to your Emergency Management, Emergency Services or Homeland Security Office or check the Blue Government pages in your city or county phone book.

• State & Territory Emergency Management Agencies

Just like local EMAs above, every state emergency management agency is an integral part of the emergency management system. State and Territory offices coordinate federal, state, and local resources for mitigation, preparedness, response and recovery operations for citizens with support from FEMA and it's partners. *The next several pages list all State and U.S. Territory Emergency Management offices and agencies in alphabetical order.*

Alabama Emergency Management Agency
P. O. Drawer 2160
Clanton, AL 35046-2160
(205) 280-2200
http://ema.alabama.gov

Alaska Division of Homeland Security and
Emergency Management
P. O. Box 5750
Fort Richardson, AK 99505-5750
(907) 428-7000
www.ak-prepared.com

American Samoa Territorial Emergency
Management Coordination (TEMCO)
American Samoa Government
P. O. Box 1086
Pago Pago, AS 96799
011 (684) 699-6415

Arizona Div of Emergency Management
5636 East McDowell Road
Phoenix, AZ 85008
(602) 244-0504
Tollfree 1-800-411-ADEM
www.dem.azdema.gov

Arkansas Dept of Emergency Management
Bldg. # 9501, Camp Joseph T. Robinson
North Little Rock, AR 72199
(501) 683-6700
www.adem.arkansas.gov

California Emergency Management Agency
3650 Schriever Avenue
Mather, CA 95655
(916) 845-8510
www.calema.ca.gov

Colorado Div of Emergency Management
9195 East Mineral Avenue, Suite 200
Centennial, CO 80112
(720) 852-6600
http://dola.colorado.gov/dem/index.html

Connecticut Department of Emergency
Management & Homeland Security
25 Sigourney Street, 6th Floor
Hartford, CT 06106
(860) 256-0800
Tollfree 1-800-397-8876
www.ct.gov/demhs

Delaware Emergency Management Agency
165 Brick Store Landing Road
Smyrna, DE 19977
(302) 659-3362
Tollfree 1-877-SAY-DEMA
www.dema.delaware.gov

District of Columbia Homeland Security &
Emergency Management Agency
2720 Martin Luther King Jr. Avenue, SE
Washington, DC 20032
(202) 727-6161
http://hsema.dc.gov

Florida Division of Emergency
Management
2555 Shumard Oak Blvd.
Tallahassee, FL 32399
(850) 413-9969
www.floridadisaster.org

Georgia Emergency Management Agency
P. O. Box 18055
Atlanta, GA 30316
(404) 635-7000
www.gema.state.ga.us

Guam Homeland Security / Office of Civil
Defense
221B Chalan Palasyo
Agana Heights, Guam 96910
011 (671) 475-9600
www.guamhs.org

Hawaii State Civil Defense
3949 Diamond Head Road
Honolulu, HI 96816
(808) 733-4300
www.scd.hawaii.gov

Idaho Bureau of Homeland Security
4040 Guard Street, Building 600
Boise, ID 83705
(208) 422-3040
www.bhs.idaho.gov

Illinois Emergency Management Agency
2200 South Dirksen Parkway
Springfield, IL 62703
(217) 782-7860
Tollfree 1-800-782-7860
www.state.il.us/iema

Indiana Department of Homeland Security
Room E208
302 W. Washington Street
Indianapolis, IN 46204
(317) 232-3980
www.in.gov/dhs

Iowa Homeland Security & Emergency
Management
7105 N.W. 70th Avenue
Camp Dodge, Building W-4
Johnston, IA 50131
(515) 725-3231
www.iowahomelandsecurity.org

Kansas Div of Emergency Management
2800 S.W. Topeka Boulevard
Topeka, KS 66611-1287
(785) 296-3176
www.kansas.gov/kdem

Kentucky Emergency Management
EOC Building
100 Minuteman Parkway
Frankfort, KY 40601
(502) 607-1638 or (502) 607-1600
Tollfree 1-800-255-2587
http://kyem.ky.gov

Louisiana Homeland Security &
Emergency Preparedness
7667 Independence Boulevard
Baton Rouge, LA 70806
(225) 925-7500
www.ohsep.louisiana.gov

Maine Emergency Management Agency
72 State House Station
Augusta, ME 04333
(207) 624-4400
www.state.me.us/mema

Commonweath of the Northern **Mariana
Islands** Emergency Management Office
Office of the Director
P. O. Box 10007
Saipan, MP 96950
(670) 322-9529
www.cnmiemo.gov.mp

National Disaster Management Office
Office of the Chief Secretary
P. O. Box 15
Majuro, Republic of the **Marshall Islands**
96960
011 (692) 625-5181

Maryland Emergency Management Agency
Camp Fretterd Military Reservation
5401 Rue Saint Lo Drive
Reistertown, MD 21136
(410) 517-3600
Tollfree 1-877-MEMA-USA
www.mema.state.md.us

Massachusetts Emergency Management
Agency
400 Worcester Road
Framingham, MA 01702-5399
(508) 820-2000
www.state.ma.us/mema

Michigan Emergency Management &
Homeland Security Division
4000 Collins Road
Lansing, MI 48910
(517) 336-6198
www.michigan.gov/emhsd

National Disaster Control Officer
Federated States of **Micronesia**
P. O. Box PS-53
Kolonia, Pohnpei - Micronesia 96941
011 (691) 320-8815

Minnesota Homeland Security and
Emergency Management (HSEM)
Department of Public Safety
444 Cedar Street, Suite 223
St. Paul, MN 55101-6223
(651) 201-7400
www.hsem.state.mn.us

Mississippi Emergency Management
Agency
P. O. Box 5644
Pearl, MS 39288-5644
(601) 933-6362
Tollfree 1-800-222-MEMA (6362)
www.msema.org

Missouri State Emergency Management
Agency
P. O. Box 116
Jefferson City, MO 65102
(573) 526-9100
http://sema.dps.mo.gov

Montana Disaster and Emergency Services
P. O. Box 4789
Fort Harrison, MT 59639-4789
(406) 324-4777
http://dma.mt.gov/DES/

Nebraska Emergency Management Agency
1300 Military Road
Lincoln, NE 68508
(402) 471-7421
www.nema.ne.gov

Nevada Division of Emergency
Management
2478 Fairview Drive
Carson City, NV 89701
(775) 687-0300
http://dem.state.nv.us

New Hampshire Department of Safety
Bureau of Emergency Management
Homeland Security and Emergency
Management
33 Hazen Drive
Concord, NH 03305
(603) 271-2231
www.nh.gov/safety/divisions/hsem/

New Jersey Office of Emergency
Management
P. O. Box 7068
West Trenton, NJ 08628-0068
(609) 963-6900
www.nj.gov/njoem

New Mexico Dept of Homeland Security
and Emergency Management
P. O. Box 27111
Santa Fe, NM 87502
(505) 476-9600
www.nmdhsem.org

New York State Emergency Management
Office
Building 22, Suite 101
1220 Washington Avenue
Albany, NY 12226
(518) 292-2200
www.dhses.ny.gov

North Carolina Emergency Management
4713 Mail Service Center
Raleigh, NC 27699-4713
(919) 733-3825
www.ncem.org

North Dakota Department of Emergency
Services
P. O. Box 5511
Bismarck, ND 58506-5511
(701) 328-8100
www.nd.gov/des

Ohio Emergency Management Agency
2855 West Dublin-Granville Road
Columbus, OH 43235-2206
(614) 889-7150
www.ema.ohio.gov

Oklahoma Department of Emergency
Management
2401 Lincoln Blvd, Suite C51
Oklahoma City, OK 73105
(405) 521-2481
www.ok.gov/OEM

Oregon Emergency Management
P. O. Box 14370
Salem, OR 97309-5062
(503) 378-2911
www.oregon.gov/OMD/OEM/

Palau NEMO Coordinator
Office of the President
P. O. Box 100
Koror, Republic of Paulau 96940
011 (680) 488-2422

Pennsylvania Emergency Management
Agency
2605 Interstate Drive
Harrisburg, PA 17110
(717) 651-2001
www.pema.state.pa.us

Puerto Rico Emergency Management
P. O. Box 9066597
San Juan, PR 00906-6597
(787) 724-0124
www.gobierno.pr/AEMEAD/Inicio

Rhode Island Emergency Management
Agency
645 New London Avenue
Cranston, RI 02920
(401) 946-9996
www.riema.ri.gov

South Carolina Emergency Management
2779 Fish Hatchery Road
West Columbia, SC 29172
(803) 737-8500
www.scemd.org

South Dakota Office of Emergency
Management
118 West Capitol Avenue
Pierre, SD 57501
(605) 773-3231
www.dps.sd.gov/emergency_services/
emergency_management/

Tennessee Emergency Management Agency
3041 Sidco Drive
Nashville, TN 37204
(615) 741-0001
www.tnema.org

Texas Department of Public Safety
Division of Emergency Management
P. O. Box 4087
Austin, TX 78773-0220
(512) 424-2138
www.txdps.state.tx.us/dem/

Utah Division of Homeland Security
1110 State Office Building
Salt Lake City, UT 84114
(801) 538-3400
http://publicsafety.utah.gov/
    emergencymanagement/

Vermont Emergency Management
103 South Main Street
Waterbury, VT 05671-2101
(802) 244-8721
www.dps.state.vt.us/vem

Virgin Islands Territorial Emergency
  Management Agency-VITEMA
102 Estate, Hermon Hill
Christiansted, St. Croix, VI 00820
(340) 774-2244

Virginia Dept of Emergency Management
10501 Trade Court
Richmond, VA 23236-3713
(804) 897-6500
www.vaemergency.com

Washington State Military Department
Emergency Management Division
Building 20, M/S: TA-20
Camp Murray, WA 98430
(253) 512-7000
www.emd.wa.gov

West Virginia Div of Homeland Security
  & Emergency Management
Building 1, Room EB-80
1900 Kanawha Blvd. East
Charleston, WV 25305
(304) 558-5380
www.dhsem.wv.gov

Wisconsin Emergency Management
P. O. Box 7865
Madison, WI 53707-7865
(608) 242-3232
http://emergencymanagement.wi.gov

Wyoming Office of Homeland Security
122 West 25th Street
Herschler Bldg, 1st Floor East
Cheyenne, WY 82002
(307) 777-4663
http://wyohomelandsecurity.state.wy.us

As of 15-Jun-2011 (per FEMA web site)
Fedhealth verified info & links:14-Aug-2011

• NATIONAL EMERGENCY MANAGEMENT ORGANIZATIONS

National Emergency Management Association (NEMA) - membership includes State EM Directors.   www.nemaweb.org

International Association of Emergency Managers (IAEM) - membership includes local emergency managers.   www.iaem.com

• FEMA'S FEDERAL-LEVEL PARTNERS

Numerous federal agencies and departments are partners in the nation's emergency management system. Before a disaster, they participate in training exercises and conduct a variety of activities to help the nation prepare for disasters. For example, the Federal Communications Commission and the Commerce Department's National Weather Service provide on-going warning and disaster tracking services. During a catastrophic disaster, FEMA coordinates the federal response, working with 28 federal partners and the American Red Cross to provide emergency food and water, medical supplies and services, search and rescue operations, transportation assistance, environmental assessment, and more. The National Disaster Medical System is a partnership set up to provide emergency medical services in a disaster, involving FEMA, Department of Health and Human Services, Department of Defense, the Veterans Administration, as well as public and private hospitals across the country.

• **FEMA PARTNERSHIPS WITH THE PRIVATE SECTOR**

FEMA encourages all sectors of society -- from business and industry to volunteer organizations -- to work together in disaster preparation, response and recovery. (*Please review APPENDIX A and B.*)

NATIONAL RESPONSE FRAMEWORK

The National Response Framework is a guide that details how the Nation conducts all-hazards response – from the smallest incident to the largest catastrophe. This document establishes a comprehensive, national, all-hazards approach to domestic incident response.

The NRF identifies the key response principles, as well as the roles and structures that organize national response. It describes how communities, States, the Federal Government and private-sector and nongovernmental partners apply these principles for a coordinated, effective national response. In addition, it describes special circumstances where the Federal Government exercises a larger role, including incidents where Federal interests are involved and catastrophic incidents where a State would require significant support. It lays the groundwork for first responders, decision-makers and supporting entities to provide a unified national response.

The NRF retains the same core principles of the **National Incident Management System (NIMS)** in which first responders from different jurisdictions and disciplines can work together more closely to effectively respond to natural disasters and emergencies, including acts of terrorism.

To learn more about the National Response Framework (NRF), visit www.fema.gov/nrf

To learn more about the National Incident Management System (NIMS) visit www.fema.gov/emergency/nims/

ABOUT PUBLIC SAFETY CANADA

As Canada's lead department for public safety, Public Safety Canada (PS) works with five agencies and three review bodies. They are united in a single portfolio and report to the same minister. The result is better integration among federal organizations dealing with national security, emergency management, law enforcement, corrections, crime prevention and borders.

PS AGENCIES:

Canada Border Services Agency (CBSA) - facilitates legitimate cross-border traffic and supports economic development while stopping people and goods that pose a potential threat to Canada.

Canadian Security Intelligence Service (CSIS) - investigates and reports on activities that may pose a threat to the security of Canada. CSIS also provides security assessments.

Correctional Service Canada (CSC) - is responsible for managing offenders sentenced to two years or more in federal correctional institutions and under community supervision.

National Parole Board (NPB) - is an independent decision making body that grants, denies or revokes parole for inmates in federal prisons. NPB helps protect society by facilitating the timely reintegration of offenders into society as law-abiding citizens.

Royal Canadian Mounted Police (RCMP) - enforces Canadian laws, prevents crime and maintains peace, order and security.

PS MANDATE:

To keep Canadians safe from a range of risks such as natural disasters, crime and terrorism. To do this, Public Safety Canada coordinates and supports the efforts of federal organizations ensuring national security and the safety of Canadians. PS also work with other levels of government, first responders, community groups, the private sector and other nations.

PS PROGRAMS:

• EMERGENCY MANAGEMENT

PS is responsible for developing and implementing federal policies for emergency management. The all-hazards and multidisciplinary approach creates a unified, federal system for managing emergencies of a national magnitude. Some areas of responsibilities include: Critical infrastructure protection, Cyber security, Disaster mitigation, Emergency preparedness, Response and Recovery.

• NATIONAL SECURITY

PS runs the Government Operations Centre, which monitors potential threats to the national interest around-the-clock. The Centre can also provide coordination and support in the event of a national emergency.

• LAW ENFORCEMENT

PS helps law enforcement agencies put in place the necessary policies and technology for better data and intelligence sharing and contributes funds for policing services in over 300 First Nations and Inuit communities in partnership with provincial and territorial governments.

• CORRECTIONS

PS leads the development of federal policy and legislation for Canada's correctional system in order to safely reintegrate offenders into the community.

• CRIME PREVENTION

PS works with volunteer groups, governments and businesses to support local solutions to crime and victimization.

EMERGENCY PREPAREDNESS IN CANADA:

• CRITICAL INFRASTRUCTURE PROTECTION

Critical infrastructure consists of physical and information technology facilities, networks, services and assets that are critical to the well-being, operations and continuity of our country. PS funds research and work with private sector partners to protect national critical infrastructure.

The Canadian Cyber Incident Response Centre (CCIRC) is responsible for monitoring threats and coordinating the national response to any cyber security incident. Its focus is the protection of national critical infrastructure against cyber incidents.

• FINANCIAL ASSISTANCE PROGRAMS

PS administers the Joint Emergency Preparedness Program (JEPP) and the Disaster Financial Assistance Arrangements (DFAA). JEPP funding ensures communities have response skills and equipment in place to deal with emergency situations of any type. DFAA shares the costs of responding to and recovering from disasters when the costs of doing so exceed the fiscal capacity of provincial and territorial governments.

• TRAINING AND EDUCATION

The Canadian Emergency Management College in Ontario provides training and educational resources for emergency managers. And the National Exercise Program (NEP) consists of training courses and operation centre exercises that hone the National Emergency Response System.

• PUBLIC INFORMATION

Public awareness campaigns provide Canadians with information needed to become better prepared for an emergency. Public Safety Canada manages Emergency Preparedness Week every May and offers various guides and publications online for individuals, educators and businesses.

• PARTNERS

During a major disaster or emergency, PS works closely with various Government of Canada departments, agencies and Provincial and Territorial Emergency Management Organizations (listed below in alphabetical order).

PROVINCIAL & TERRITORIAL
EMERGENCY MANAGEMENT ORGANIZATIONS (EMOs)

Alberta
Alberta Emergency Management Agency
Alberta Municipal Affairs
18th Floor, Commerce Place
10155 - 102 Street
Edmonton, AB   T5J 4L4
Tel: (780) 422-9000
Tollfree 310-0000 (in Alberta)
www.aema.alberta.ca

British Columbia
Provincial Emergency Program
Headquarters
P. O. Box 9201 Station Prov. Govt.
Victoria, BC V8W 9J1
Tel: (250) 952-4913
www.pep.bc.ca

PEP Central Region
1255 - D Dalhousie Drive
Kamloops, BC V2C 5Z5
(250) 371-5240

PEP North East Region
3235 Westwood Drive
Prince George, BC V2N 1S4
(250) 612-4172

PEP North West Region
Suite 1B - 3215 Eby Street
Terrace, BC V8G 2X8
(250) 615-4800

PEP South East Region
403 Vernon Street
Nelson, BC V1L 4E6
(250) 354-5904

PEP South West Region
14275 - 96th Avenue
Surrey, BC V3V 7Z2
(604) 586-4390

PEP Vancouver Island Region
2261 Keating Cross Rd, Block A-Ste 200
Saanichton, BC V8M 2A5
(250) 952-5848

Manitoba
Manitoba Emergency Measures
 Organization
1525 - 405 Broadway Avenue
Winnipeg, MB R3C 3L6
Tel: (204) 945-4772
Tollfree 1-888-267-8298
www.ManitobaEMO.ca

New Brunswick
New Brunswick Emergency Measures
  Organization
Department of Public Safety
P. O. Box 6000
Fredericton, NB E3B 5H1
Tel: (506) 453-2133
www.gnb.ca/cnb/emo-omu/index-e.asp

Newfoundland and Labrador
Emergency Management
Dept of Municipal and Provincial Affairs
P. O. Box 8700
St. John's, NL A1B 4J6
Tel: (709) 729-3703
www.mpa.gov.nl.ca/ma/fes/emo

Northwest Territories
Emergency Management
Municipal and Community Affairs
Government of Northwest Territories
P. O. Box 1320
Yellowknife, NT X1A 2L9
Tel: (867) 873-7554
www.maca.gov.nt.ca/emergency_
  management/index.htm

Nova Scotia
Nova Scotia Emergency Management
P. O. Box 2581
Halifax, NS B3J 3N5
Tel: (902) 424-5620
www.gov.ns.ca/emo

Nunavut
Nunavut Emergency Management
Department of Community & Government
  Services
P. O. Box 1000, Station 700
Iqaluit, NU X0A 0H0
Tel: (867) 979-6262
http://cgs.gov.nu.ca/en/nunavut-emergency-
management

Ontario
Emergency Management Ontario
Ministry of Community Safety and
  Correctional Services
77 Wellesley St. West, Box 222
Toronto, ON M7A 1N3
Tel: (877) 314-3723
www.emergencymanagementontario.ca

Prince Edward Island
Emergency Measures Organization
134 Kent Street, Suite 600
Charlottetown, PE C1A 7N8
Tel: (902) 894-0385
www.gov.pe.ca/jps/index.php3?number=
  1030226&lang=E

Québec
Direction générale de la Sécurité civile et
  de la sécurité incendie
Ministère de la Sécurité publique
2525, boul. Laurier, 5e étage
Sainte-Foy, QC G1V 2L2
Tel: (866) 644-6826
www.securitepublique.gouv.qc.ca/

Saskatchewan
Saskatchewan Emergency Management
  Organization (SaskEMO)
100 - 1855 Victoria Avenue
Regina, SK S4P 3T2
Tel: (306) 787-9563
www.cps.gov.sk.ca/SaskEMO

Yukon Territory
Yukon Emergency Measures Organization
Department of Community Services
P. O. Box 2703, EMO
Whitehorse, YK Y1A 2C6
Tel: (867) 667-5220
www.community.gov.yk.ca/emo/

Fedhealth verified info & links:14-Aug-2011

To learn more about Public Safety Canada, visit www.publicsafety.gc.ca or
call their General enquiries line at 613-944-4875 or 1-800-830-3118.

A few other interesting links for Canadians are PS's Family Preparedness
site at www.getprepared.ca and the Public Health Agency of Canada site
at www.phac-aspc.gc.ca

APPENDIX A
Citizen Corps / CERT
(Volunteer Programs for Americans & Canadians)

WHAT IS CITIZEN CORPS?

Citizen Corps was created to help coordinate volunteer activities that make the nation's communities safer, stronger, and better prepared to respond to any emergency situation. Citizen Corps is managed at local levels by Citizen Corps Councils, which bring together existing crime prevention, disaster preparedness, and public health response networks with the volunteer community and other groups.

CITIZEN CORPS PROGRAMS & PARTNERS

Community Emergency Response Teams (CERTs) educate people about disaster preparedness and trains them in basic disaster response skills, such as fire safety, light search and rescue, and disaster medical operations. Using their training, CERT members can assist others in their neighborhood or workplace following an event and can take a more active role in preparing their community. The program is administered by DHS. Learn more at www.citizencorps.gov/cert

Fire Corps promotes the use of citizen advocates to enhance the capacity of resource-constrained fire and rescue departments at all levels: volunteer, combination, and career. Citizen advocates can assist local fire departments in a range of activities including fire safety outreach, youth programs, and administrative support. Fire Corps provides resources to assist fire and rescue departments in creating opportunities for citizen advocates and promotes citizen participation. Fire Corps is funded through DHS and is managed and implemented through a partnership between the National Volunteer Fire Council, the International Association of Fire Fighters, and the International Association of Fire Chiefs. Visit www.firecorps.org

Medical Reserve Corps (MRC) strengthens communities by helping medical, public health and other volunteers offer their expertise throughout the year as well as during local emergencies and other times of community need. MRC volunteers work in coordination with existing local emergency response programs and also supplement existing community public health initiatives, such as outreach and prevention, immunization programs, blood drives, case management, care planning, and other efforts. The MRC program is administered by the Department of Health & Human Services. Check out www.medicalreservecorps.gov

Neighborhood Watch incorporates terrorism awareness education into its existing crime prevention mission, while also serving as a way to bring residents together to focus on emergency preparedness and emergency response training. Funded by Department of Justice, Neighborhood Watch is administered by the National Sheriffs' Association. Learn more at www.usaonwatch.org

Volunteers in Police Service (VIPS) works to enhance the capacity of state and local law enforcement to utilize volunteers. VIPS serves as a gateway to resources and information for and about law enforcement volunteer programs. Funded by DOJ, VIPS is managed and implemented by the International Association of Chiefs of Police. To learn more visit www.policevolunteers.org

Citizen Corps **Affiliate Programs & Organizations** offer communities resources for public education, outreach, and training; represent volunteers interested in helping to make their community safer; or offer volunteer service opportunities to support first responders, disaster relief activities, and community safety efforts. Some Affiliates include:

The **American Radio Relay League** (ARRL) represents the interests of the more than 650,000 U.S. Radio Amateurs (or "HAMS"). Many amateurs have organized themselves under a formal structure to better provide public service and emergency communications like the Amateur Radio Emergency Service (ARES) and Radio Amateur Civil Emergency Service (RACES). Learn more by visiting www.arrl.org or contact your local Emergency Management office.

Civil Air Patrol is a congressionally chartered, non-profit corporation and is the civilian auxiliary of the U.S. Air Force. CAP supports Homeland Security efforts by providing coastal patrol, air/ground observation, radio communications and relay, aerial reconnaissance, air-to-ground photography, radiological monitoring, and disaster and damage assessment assets. Learn more by visiting www.gocivilairpatrol.com

National Association for Search and Rescue is a non-profit membership association comprised of thousands of paid and non-paid professionals interested in all aspects of search and rescue throughout the United States and around the world. NASAR has trained over 30,000 responders since 1989 utilizing its internationally respected SARTECH© Certification Program. NASAR is dedicated to ensuring that volunteers (non-paid professionals) in search and rescue are as prepared as the career public safety personnel (fire, law and emergency medical services) with whom they work on a daily basis. Learn more at www.nasar.org.

Some other Affiliates include The American Legion, Home Safety Council, National Safety Council, National Voluntary Organizations Active in

Disaster (NVOAD) and many others. To learn more about **Citizen Corps** or to check if there's a local council in your community, please visit www.citizencorps.gov.

MORE ABOUT **CERT**

In the United States and Canada, the **Community Emergency Response Team (CERT)** program helps train volunteers to assist first responders in emergency situations in their communities. CERT members give critical support to first responders in emergencies, provide immediate assistance to victims, organize spontaneous volunteers at a disaster site, and collect disaster intelligence to support first responder efforts.

The CERT course is taught in the community by a trained team of first responders who have completed a CERT Train-the-Trainer course conducted by their state training office for emergency management, or FEMA's Emergency Management Institute (EMI), located in Emmitsburg, Maryland. CERT training includes disaster preparedness, disaster fire suppression, basic disaster medical operations, and light search and rescue operations and is usually delivered in 2-1/2 hour sessions, one evening a week over a 7 week period.

FEMA's online "Introduction to Community Emergency Response Teams", IS 317, is an independent study course that serves as an introduction to CERT for those wanting to complete training or as a refresher for current team members. It has six modules with topics that include an Introduction to CERT, Fire Safety, Hazardous Material and Terrorist Incidents, Disaster Medical Operations, and Search and Rescue. It takes between six and eight hours to complete the course. The IS 317 can be taken by anyone interested in CERT. However, to become a CERT volunteer, one must complete classroom training offered by a local government agency such as the emergency management agency, fire or police department. To learn more, visit www.citizencorps.gov/cert/IS317/

For more information about CERT programs or to check if a CERT is in your community, please visit   www.citizencorps.gov/cert/   ... or visit www.cert-la.com (click on "Other CERT Program Links") ... or call your local, state, provincial, or territorial Emergency Management Office to ask about volunteer opportunities.

Or visit your local or state / provincial web site to learn about other types of volunteer groups in your area and get involved!

APPENDIX B
Business Continuity
(Plan for the Unexpected)

WHAT IS BUSINESS CONTINUITY?

Basically the concept we're focusing on means how quickly your business could reopen and function following a flood, fire, terrorist attack or even pandemic flu. By planning in advance with managers and employees, the odds of a company surviving and recovering from a disaster increase dramatically.

According to the Department of Homeland Security's *Ready Business* site, America's businesses form the backbone of the nation's economy; small businesses alone account for over 99% of all companies with employees, employ 50% of all private sector workers and provide nearly 45% of the nation's payroll. However, according to the Insurance Information Institute, up to 40% of small businesses do not reopen after a major disaster.

A commitment to planning today will help support employees, customers, the community, the local economy and even the country.

TIPS ON DEVELOPING YOUR BUSINESS PLAN

No matter what size your business is you should plan in advance to manage any type of emergency. Obviously, a large company's plan will be much more complex than a small home office or a Mom & Pop shop, but the following tips may help you get started.

Please note, we are only covering some key issues here extracted from DHS' *Ready Business* site then listing some resources and links at the end, but realize there are many resources available to business owners including consultants who can develop a business continuity plan for your company.

Learn risks - Ask your local emergency management office what types of disasters are common in the places where you have offices or buildings and review those topics in this book.

Learn about NTAS Alerts - Review the U.S. Department of Homeland Security's **National Terrorism Advisory System** to learn about NTAS Alerts and resources available for businesses and citizens. *(see pages 80-81)*

<u>Travel</u> - Stay current on travel updates and restrictions by visiting www.cdc.gov/travel or www.state.gov/travel

<u>Make a plan</u> - Visit www.ready.gov/business to download Sample Plans, Checklists, Forms, etc. Also ...

- Find out which staff, materials, procedures and equipment are needed to keep your business operating.
- Create a list of suppliers, shippers, and key contacts you use daily.
- Decide where you would go if your building, office or store is not useable. (Known as a continuity of operations plan or COOP.)
- Plan for payroll continuity.
- Define who will help develop your company's emergency plan.
- Make sure everyone involved knows what to do and have backup staff trained and ready to fill in, if needed.
- Share your plans with others in your building or complex and talk to local First Responders, vendors and others to exchange ideas, experience and knowledge.
- Update and review plans at least once a year if not more often.

<u>Keep employees in mind</u> - A good plan includes your most important asset.

- Keep lines of communication open both ways with newsletters, alert systems through email or voicemail, Q & A sessions with management and key personnel involved with planning, etc.
- Ensure you have plans for disabled employees and assign "buddies" to help during an emergency. Visit www.nod.org for tips.
- Update employee emergency contact data often and keep a current copy with other important papers off-site or in Grab & Go kits.
- Practice, practice, practice -- make sure all employees do drills and know what to do and where to go during and after a disaster.

<u>Make or get Grab & Go kits</u> - Review Section 1 for tips on assembling a **Disaster Supplies Kit** for your people. Share ideas with employees too since they may want to make their own small "Office Kit" with personal items. Many companies sell pre-stocked or customized Corporate Kits based on number of employees and days needed - check online vendors like www.thecuresafety.com or call your local Red Cross.

<u>Stay or go..?</u> - Plan in advance how staff should **shelter-in-place** versus **evacuate** the building. *(see THINK ABOUT SHELTER in Section 1 and EVACUATION topic in Section 2)*

Things to plan for if instructed to "Shelter-in-place":

- Listen to local authorities and tune in radio or TV for updates.

- If possible, know who's in the building if there is an emergency.
- Set up a warning system (and remember folks with hearing or vision disabilities or non-English speaking workers).
- Determine which room or area will be used for shelter for each type of disaster <u>in advance</u> (i.e. some emergencies require staying above ground - others may be best underground or in a sealed room - review Section 2 for tips on sheltering). Discuss ideas with others in your building or complex or with First Responders.
- Calculate air requirements for sealed room. *(see HAZARDOUS MATERIALS or TERRORISM topic)*
- Consider installing a safe room. *(see MITIGATION TIPS)*
- Assign certain people to grab Kits, take headcounts, seal off room, etc. and have backups lined up in case someone's off or injured.
- Take a headcount or have a checklist of people in shelter.
- Practice, practice, practice -- make sure employees know shelter-in-place plans and be ready to explain procedures to newbies not familiar with your plans (like customers or suppliers who might be at your building when an event occurs).

Things to plan for when making an "Evacuation plan":
- If possible, know who's in the building if there is an emergency.
- Decide in advance who in your staff and your building has the authority to order an evacuation. And if local authorities tell you to leave - DO it!
- Determine who is in charge of shutting down critical operations and systems and locking doors (if possible) during evacuation.
- Draw a map of your shop or building and mark locations of exits, disaster and first aid kits, fire extinguishers and utility shut-off points. Plan at least two escape routes from different sections of facility. Post copies of maps so employees can find them easily and share copies with local First Responders.
- Set up a warning system (and remember folks with hearing or vision disabilities or non-English speaking workers).
- Have flashlights handy or install emergency lighting to help staff exit safely. (Note: <u>never</u> use lighters since there may be gas leaks.)
- Pick two meeting places (assembly sites) in advance for staff to go - one near the facility and one further away. Also discuss how employees should notify someone if they need to leave the site or aren't able to reach one.
- Take a headcount or have a checklist of people at assembly site.
- Practice, practice, practice -- make sure employees know evacuation plans and be ready to explain procedures to newbies not familiar with your plans (like customers or suppliers who might be

at your building when an event occurs). Practice drills with other tenants or businesses in your complex and share plans and ideas.

Practice fire drills - Fire is the most common of all business disasters.
- Contact local Fire Marshal and request an inspection of your shop or building.
- Install **smoke detectors** and fire extinguishers and test them often!
- Set up a warning system (and remember folks with hearing or vision disabilities or non-English speaking workers).
- Do fire drills and make sure people know how to stay below the smoke, how to test doors to see if they are hot, etc. *(see tips in FIRES & WILDFIRES topic)*

Be prepared for medical emergencies - Provide first aid and CPR training to your staff and keep first aid kits stocked and accessible. *(see Section 3 for TIPS ON BASIC FIRST AID)*

Get involved - Join or form a CERT with your local EM. *(see page 224)*

Practice & fine tune - Take notes on things that should be modified during drills and get feedback from employees so your plan is continually improving. Let everyone know about changes to plans and practice drills often. And don't forget your new hires - include plan in Training Programs.

Encourage preparedness - Provide customized copies of this book to all your employees (and customers) so they can develop their own personal family plans and kits at home. Send preparedness reminder tips in emails or newsletters.

Have a communications plan - Write a crisis communications plan in advance so you are prepared to communicate with employees, customers and others during and after a disaster.
- **Employees** - Be prepared to tell workers when, if and how to report to work after an emergency (either through voicemail, email or manual call system). Explain how the incident may affect jobs.
- **Management** - Give executives as much information as possible to protect employees, customers, vendors and nearby facilities.
- **Public** - You may need to update the media and general public about the safety or status of employees or buildings and that plans are in place for recovery.
- **Customers** - Stay in touch with clients so they know when products or services are back in stock or online.
- **Government** - Let officials know what your company can do to help in recovery efforts and ask for help, if needed.

- **Other Businesses/Immediate Neighbors** - Be prepared to give neighboring companies or competitors updates on the nature of the situation in case they need to make plans for their own safety.

Help employees recover - Support your workers as they cope with the stress of recovering from a disaster. See TIPS ON RECOVERING FROM A DISASTER ... and ...
- Provide time off so workers can get their home life in order.
- Offer care or professional counselors on-site.
- Get folks back into work routines once possible.

TIPS ON PROTECTING YOUR BUSINESS

Ready Business suggests in addition to emergency planning, the following steps be taken to safeguard your company and secure your physical assets.

Review insurance - Meet with your agent or provider to review policies.
- Ask if current coverage includes physical losses, flood coverage and business interruption. Also visit www.floodsmart.gov for tips.
- Plan how you would pay creditors, employees and yourself.
- Find out what records your provider would need after a disaster and store those papers in a safe place.
- Download Insurance Discussion Form and Computer Inventory Form off the *Ready Business* site at www.ready.gov/business.

Utilities - Think about what your company would do if there's no power, gas, telecommunications, sewer and other utilities.
- Talk to providers and ask about alternative and backup options during disruptions of service.
- Ask how and when to turn off utilities and never try to turn gas back on - call the gas company!
- Consider getting portable generators but <u>never</u> use them inside since they produce deadly carbon monoxide gas.
- Get wireless phones, walkie-talkies or other devices that don't rely on electricity so you can stay in touch with employees and customers. Keep extra batteries on-hand too.
- Have backup providers lined up in case your telephone or Internet services are down locally.
- Make sure **Disaster Supplies Kit** includes sanitation items in case sewer lines are damaged. *(see TIPS ON SANITATION OF HUMAN WASTE near end of Section 2)*

Protect assets - There are some things you can do in advance to protect your building and equipment ...

- Install smoke and carbon monoxide detectors and fire extinguishers and test them often.
- Draw a map of your building and mark locations of exits, fire extinguishers and utility shut-off points. Post copies so employees can find them easily and share copies with local First Responders.
- Consider installing extra security measures like alarm systems, automatic sprinklers, closed circuit TV, keypad or card access systems, or security guards.
- Think about all the ways people and deliveries enter and leave your building and the potential risks associated with them. *(See TERRORISM topic which covers specific things businesses should be aware of about NTAS alerts and tips on handling bomb threats and suspicious packages.)*
- Learn about FEMA's Pre-Disaster Mitigation (PDM) loans and other cost-saving mitigation tips for structures and property by visiting www.fema.gov.
- Plan how you would replace machinery, computers or equipment quickly if it's damaged or destroyed and keep extra supplies on-hand.
- Decide where you could run the business if your shop's not usable.
- Ensure any backup location complies with local, state and federal codes and other safety regulations and ask your insurance agent if operating at another facility impacts your policy.

Secure equipment - Use straps or L-braces to batten down cabinets or machinery, move heavy items to lower shelves and raise electrical equipment off the floor. *(see MITIGATION TIPS at beginning of Section 2)*

Airborne threats - Several types of disasters can impact the air quality of a building from mold due to flooding, airborne particles from a biological attack or dirty bomb, or smoke from a wildfire. Ask if there are options to improve air quality and protection in the Heating, Ventilating and Air-Conditioning (HVAC) system.

- Make sure unit is in good, working condition.
- Practice shut-down procedures for the HVAC system.
- Secure outdoor air intakes but never seal them. Ask if they can be relocated to an area with limited access (especially intakes that are close to or underground.)
- Consider upgrading the filtration system with High Efficiency Particulate Arrester (HEPA) filter fans or get portable HEPA filters to help remove dander, dust, molds, smoke and other contaminants. *(see AIR QUALITY MITIGATION)*

<u>Cyber threats</u> - Computer crime and hactivism cost businesses billions of dollars every year. Whether you use one computer or a massive network, it is critical to keep your system protected from viruses and attacks.

- Make sure computers <u>and</u> wireless devices have current anti-virus software and firewalls .. schedule them to scan daily or weekly and update virus patterns often. Encourage employees to protect their personal home devices too.

- Set security preferences as high as possible on Internet browsers and virus packages.

- Do NOT open emails or attachments from unknown sources.

- Use long passwords (best to use both numbers and letters), change them often and don't share them with others.

- Backup data often and keep a daily or weekly backup off-site.

- Make sure someone knows how to download patches or fixes in case a computer or system gets infected.

- If your business is hacked, file a complaint with the **Internet Crime Complaint Center** at www.ic3.gov (The IC3 is a partnership between the Federal Bureau of Investigation [FBI] and the National White Collar Crime Center [NW3C]. According to the FBI's Cyber Division, agents have been closely trained to be discreet, to protect your public image and your intellectual property, and to not disrupt your operations.)

- Stay current on cyber threats by joining DHS National Cyber Security Division's **US-CERT** www.us-cert.gov or the FBI's **InfraGard** www.infragard.net or visit Public Safety Canada's Cyber site at www.publicsafety.gc.ca for advisories. Or check out National Cyber Security Alliance at www.staysafeonline.org

- Find tools and guides on the Institute for Business and Home Safety's **Open for Business**® site at www.disastersafety.org

- Review ABOUT CYBER ATTACKS in TERRORISM topic.

<u>Pandemic planning</u> - According to the U.S. Chamber of Commerce, each year the flu kills 36,000-40,000 Americans, hospitalizes over 200,000 and costs the U.S. economy over $10 billion in lost productivity and direct medical expenses. Health experts warn a pandemic flu could kill over half a million Americans, hospitalize 2 million more, and cost the [U.S.] economy an estimated $160 - $675 billion.[11] Another scenario predicted by the World Bank estimates a pandemic could kill more than 70 million people worldwide and create havoc in global markets.

If a global pandemic occurs, it could change our way of life dramatically. Schools, work, transportation and other services may close for long periods of time. (For instance, the 1918 flu pandemic lasted 18 months while other pandemics weaken for a while then recur.) Supplies will be scarce, medical facilities will be overwhelmed and travel will be very difficult. Planning for a crisis of this magnitude may seem overwhelming, but an informed and prepared staff and public will know how to protect themselves and decrease their risk during a pandemic.

- Talk with local public health officials and health care providers to get their input and recommendations on pandemic planning and stay current on health alerts and advisories.
- Get travel updates and restrictions by visiting www.cdc.gov/travel or www.state.gov/travel or www.who.int/ith/en/
- Adopt business practices that encourage sick employees to stay home (like using Skype or instant messaging) and anticipate how to function with a smaller workforce for weeks or months at a time.
- Think about how your business would function if suppliers, banks, transportation and delivery services are limited or shut down. And encourage staff to keep at least a few weeks supplies at home.
- Remind employees to reduce the spread of infections by washing hands or using alcohol-based sanitizers often, covering coughs and sneezes with a tissue or shirt sleeve, and wiping down work stations, phones and keyboards with disinfectant or bleach.
- Visit www.flu.gov *(more flu links on page 199)*

ADDITIONAL BUSINESS CONTINUITY RESOURCES

There are many books, groups and sites focusing on business continuity, as well as consultants who develop a plan for your business. The following links are just a sampling of the thousands of resources so spend some time researching to see which ones fit your needs. Also ask local emergency management office for any suggested business continuity plans or data.

DHS *Ready Business* - A more in-depth overview of business continuity, forms, checklists and brochures are available on the U.S. Department of Homeland Security's *Ready Business* site at www.ready.gov/business

NFPA 1600 - The National Fire Protection Association's 300 codes and standards influence every building, process, service, design, and installation in the United States. **NFPA 1600 Standard on Disaster/Emergency Management and Business Continuity Programs** is not a handbook or "how-to" guide with instructions on building a comprehensive program, but it outlines the management and elements that organizations should use to develop a program for mitigation, preparedness, response, and recovery. Businesses can download a copy of NFPA 1600 at www.nfpa.org.

FEMA Business & Industry Guide - An excellent resource for businesses produced by FEMA is the **Emergency Management Guide for Business**

& Industry. It is a step-by-step approach to emergency planning, response and recovery for companies of all sizes and available on FEMA's web site at www.fema.gov.

Red Cross - Both the American and Canadian Red Cross have courses and programs designed specifically for the workplace. The American Red Cross also has a **Guide to Business Continuity Planning CD-ROM**. To learn more about their CD visit www.redcross.org or call your local Chapter.

IBHS Toolkit - The Insurance Institute for Business & Home Safety created **Open for Business®**, a comprehensive disaster planning online or print toolkit, and **OFB-EZ** for very small business owners. Learn more at www.disastersafety.org

Web links - The following list includes some agencies, companies and non-profit groups providing products, services, free e-newsletters and resources about business continuity, planning and workplace safety (in alphabetical order).

American Institute for Preventive Medicine www.healthylife.com

Association of Contingency Planners www.acp-international.com

Business Roundtable Partnership for DR www.businessroundtable.org

Centers for Disease Control and Prevention www.cdc.gov/workplace

Continuity Central www.continuitycentral.com

CPM Online www.contingencyplanning.com

Depiction www.depiction.com

DERA International www.disasters.org

Disaster Recovery Journal www.drj.com

Disaster Resource Guide www.disaster-resource.com

IBHS www.disastersafety.org

Institute for Business Continuity Training www.ibct.com

National Institute for Occupational Safety & Health www.cdc.gov/niosh

Preparis www.preparis.com

PS-Prep www.fema.gov/privatesector/preparedness/

Public Safety Canada www.publicsafety.gc.ca

Public Risk Management Association www.primacentral.org

The ICOR www.theicor.org

US Chamber of Commerce www.uschamber.com

US Small Business Administration www.sba.gov

APPENDIX C
School Safety Resources
(Tools for Educators, Officials & Parents)

According to the U.S. Department of Education, every day more than 50 million students attend schools that continue to be havens of safety. In fact, crime in schools has been decreasing since 1992. The CDC reports the number of children and youth homicides that are school-related make up only 1% of the total number of child and youth homicides in the U.S. However, recent events have sparked an interest in school safety.

Parents / guardians need to be proactive and work with school officials to find out what the procedures and plans are in the event of a disaster, lockdown or evacuation. Get involved by attending school safety planning meetings, working with local PTAs or volunteering your time at the school. And keep the lines of communication open with your children starting at a very early age so kids feel comfortable coming to you with questions or problems they may face at school.

Due to limited space, we are providing a sampling of the many agencies, companies and nonprofits providing products, services and resources about School safety and planning (in alphabetical order). Please spend some time researching these links to see which ones fit your school's specific needs. Also check out **Additional Resources & Web Sites** on page 244.

American Psychological Association (offers books, videos, articles and news on topics like bullying, natural disasters, trauma, violence, etc.) www.apa.org/topics/violence

American Red Cross (offer Youth Programs like Masters of Disaster, Be Ready 1-2-3, etc.) www.redcross.org

American School Counselor Association (offers resources and publications for Counselors & Members, Administrators and Parents & Public) www.schoolcounselor.org

CDC Healthy Schools Healthy Youth! (offers data on health topics like Crisis Preparedness & Response, Injury & Violence, etc.) www.cdc.gov/HealthyYouth

Center for Safe Schools (provides physical and online resources for the prevention of school violence and recovery after traumatic events, list of State School Safety Centers, etc.) www.safeschools.info

Jane's (company offers comprehensive School Safety and planning guides for education and security professionals) www.janes.com

KidsPeace (resources to help kids deal with crisis) www.kidspeace.org

National Association of School Psychologists (offers resources for Students, Families and Educators) www.nasponline.org

National School Safety and Security Services (company specializing in school security, training, assessments and consulting for K-12 schools - site has lots of resources, free newsletter, etc.) www.schoolsecurity.org

National School Safety Center (offers solutions, products and free resources for schools and communities) www.schoolsafety.us

PTA (offers resources on safety [search school safety]) www.pta.org

Ripple Effects (company provides software tools for teachers and kids including some free resources) www.rippleeffects.com

U.S. Department of Education Office of Safe and Drug-Free Schools Emergency Planning (offers plans, guides, grant programs, examples, links and resources for school leaders) www.ed.gov/emergencyplan

U.S. Department of Health & Human Services Pandemic Flu site (offers checklists, tools and guides for schools) www.flu.gov

U.S. Department of Homeland Security Ready.gov site (tips for families and kids on how to prepare for emergencies & disasters) www.ready.gov

U.S. Secret Service Safe School Initiative (provides threat assessment resources on school shootings) www.secretservice.gov/ntac.shtml

More resources for K-12 educators, parents and students available on our Schools/Youth Links page at www.itsadisaster.net

END NOTES

[1] U. S. Department of Commerce, NOAA, Pacific Marine Environmental Laboratory, Tropical Atmosphere Ocean, "Frequently Asked Questions about El Niño and La Niña", (www.pmel.noaa.gov/tao/elnino/faq.html), 2004.

[2] NOAA News Online (Story 2317), "NOAA Announces the Return of El Niño", (www.noaanews.noaa.gov/stories2004/s2317.htm), September 10, 2004.

[3] NOAA "Answers to La Niña frequently asked questions", (www.elnino.noaa.gov/lanina_new_faq.html), May 3, 2001.

[4] Katherine McIntire Peters, "Congress questions Homeland Security's approach to nuclear detection", Government Executive.com, (www.govexec.com/story_page_pf.cfm?articleid=41058), September 25, 2008.

[5] Adam Entous, "Bush Signs Measure Boosting U.S. Bioterror Defenses" (Reuters online, June 12, 2002).

[6] John Markoff, "Before the Gunfire, Cyberattacks", The New York Times, (www.nytimes.com/2008/08/13/technology/13cyber.html), August 13, 2008.

[7] Centers for Disease Control Public Health Emergency Preparedness & Response, Agents, Diseases, & Threats, Radiation Emergencies, Information for the Public, "Dirty Bombs", (www.bt.cdc.gov/radiation/dirtybombs.asp), July 28, 2003.

[8] Water Supply and Sanitation Collaborative Council, "WASH Facts and Figures", (www.wsscc.org), Geneva, Switzerland, 2002.

[9] National Institutes of Health, National Institute of Allergy and Infectious Diseases, "NIAID Overview: Immune System Research", (www.niaid.nih.gov/facts/overview.htm), June 23, 2004.

[10] Michelle Fay Cortez and Jason Gale, "Baxter Sent Bird Flu Virus to European Labs by Error (Update 2), Bloomberg.com (www.bloomberg.com/apps/news?pid=20601202&sid=aTo3LbhcA75I), February 24, 2009.

[11] U.S. Chamber of Commerce, Issues Center, Homeland Security & Defense, Pandemic Planning, (www.uschamber.com/issues/index/defense/pandemic_influenza.htm), 2006.

RESOURCES

About.com. "Top 50 Emergency Uses for Your Camera Phone" by Paul Purcell, (Excerpted from www.disasterprep101.com), August 2008.

American Dental Association. Manage Your Oral Health, "Dental Emergencies & Injuries", www.ada.org/public/manage/emergencies.asp, 03/14/05.

American Heart Association. *2005 Guidelines for Cardiopulmonary Resuscitation and Emergency Cardiovascular Care, Currents Winter 2005-2006*, November 2005.

American Heart Association. *Hands-Only CPR simplifies saving lives for bystanders*, April 2008.

American Heart Association. *Heartsaver CPR AED Student Workbook*, March 2011.

American Medical Association. Journals of the AMA, JAMA Consensus Statement, *Tularemia as a Biological Weapon Medical and Public Health Management*, Chicago, IL, 2001.

American Red Cross. *American Red Cross Standard First Aid*, Washington, D.C.: The American National Red Cross, 1988.

American Red Cross. *Community First Aid & Safety*, Washington, D.C.: The American National Red Cross, 1998.

American Red Cross. *Coping With Disaster – Emotional Health Issues for Victims*, Washington, D.C.: The American National Red Cross, 1991.

American Red Cross. *Disaster Preparedness for Seniors by Seniors*, Washington, D.C.: The American National Red Cross and the Rochester-Monroe County Chapter of the American Red Cross, 1995.

American Red Cross. *First Aid Fast*, Washington, D.C.:The American National Red Cross, 1995.

American Red Cross and California Community Foundation. *Disaster Preparedness for Disabled & Elderly People*, Washington, DC: The American National Red Cross, 1985.

American Red Cross, Los Angeles Chapter. *The Emergency Survival Handbook*, Los Angeles, CA: Los Angeles Chapter, American Red Cross, 1985.

American Red Cross, Los Angeles Chapter. *Safety and Survival in an Earthquake - Third Edition*, Los Angeles, CA: L. A. Chapter, American Red Cross, 1986.

Aviation Week. "E-Bombs Could Go Mainstream" by David Hambling, (www.aviationweek.com /aw/generic/story_generic.jsp?channel=dti&id=news/EBOMB031109.xml), March 11, 2009.

BBC News. "Cybercrime threat rising sharply" by Tim Weber, (www.bbc.co.uk), 31-Jan-2009.

BBC News. "MRSA risk from dog and cat bites", http://news.bbc.co.uk/2/hi/health/8109314.stm, 21-Jun-2009

Bottom Line Secrets. "A New Hospital Epidemic: C. Difficile Bacteria'", Daily Health News, 2/5/2009.

Bottom Line Secrets. "New Sunscreen Labels Tell the 'Truth'", Daily Health News, 3/31/2008.

Bottom Line Secrets. "When Silence Beats Talk Therapy", Daily Health News, 2/23/2009.

California Department of Health Services. Indoor Air Quality Info Sheet, *Mold in My Home: What Do I Do?*, Richmond, CA, June 2006.

Centers for Disease Control and Prevention. Influenza, Avian flu, *General Information on Avian Influenza (Bird Flu), (all 6 topics)*, Atlanta, GA, 11/10/2004.

Centers for Disease Control and Prevention. Influenza, H1N1 (swine) flu, *General Information (all topics)*, Atlanta, GA, April 29 - May 8, 2009.

Centers for Disease Control and Prevention. Influenza, *Influenza (the Flu): Questions & Answers*, Atlanta, GA, 11/10/2004.

Centers for Disease Control and Prevention. Influenza, *Key Facts About the Flu: How to Prevent the Flu and What To Do If You Get Sick*, Atlanta, GA, 11/10/2004.

Centers for Disease Control and Prevention. Mass Casualties, *Preparing for a Terrorist Bombing: A Common Sense Approach*, Atlanta, GA, 7/19/2005.

Centers for Disease Control and Prevention Division of Healthcare Quality Promotion.

Antimicrobial Resistance, *CA-MRSA Information for the Public*, Atlanta, GA, 02/03/2005.

Centers for Disease Control and Prevention Emergency Preparedness and Response. Bioterrorism Agents, *Anthrax: What You Need to Know*, Atlanta, GA, 07/31/2003.

Centers for Disease Control and Prevention Emergency Preparedness and Response. Bioterrorism Agents, *Children and Anthrax: A Fact Sheet for Parents*, Atlanta, GA, 11/07/2001.

Centers for Disease Control and Prevention Emergency Preparedness and Response. Bioterrorism Agents, *Facts about Botulism*, Atlanta, GA, 10/14/2001.

Centers for Disease Control and Prevention Emergency Preparedness and Response. Bioterrorism Agents, *Facts about Pneumonic Plague*, Atlanta, GA, 10/14/2001.

Centers for Disease Control and Prevention Emergency Preparedness and Response. Bioterrorism Agents, *Facts about Ricin*, Atlanta, GA, 02/05/2004.

Centers for Disease Control and Prevention Emergency Preparedness and Response. Bioterrorism Agents, *Frequently Asked Questions (FAQs) about Plague*, Atlanta, GA, 10/3/2002.

Centers for Disease Control and Prevention Emergency Preparedness and Response. Bioterrorism Agents, *Frequently Asked Questions (FAQs) about Smallpox*, Atlanta, GA, 12/29/2004.

Centers for Disease Control and Prevention Emergency Preparedness and Response. Bioterrorism Agents, *Key Facts about Tularemia*, Atlanta, GA, 10/07/2003.

Centers for Disease Control and Prevention Emergency Preparedness and Response. Bioterrorism Agents, *Smallpox Disease Overview*, Atlanta, GA, 12/30/2004.

Centers for Disease Control and Prevention Emergency Preparedness and Response. Chemical Emergencies, *Facts about Chlorine*, Atlanta, GA, 03/18/2003.

Centers for Disease Control and Prevention Emergency Preparedness and Response. Chemical Emergencies, *Facts about Cyanide*, Atlanta, GA, 01/27/2004.

Centers for Disease Control and Prevention Emergency Preparedness and Response. Chemical Emergencies, *Facts about Ricin*, Atlanta, GA, 02/05/2004.

Centers for Disease Control and Prevention Emergency Preparedness and Response. Chemical Emergencies, *Facts about Sarin*, Atlanta, GA, 03/07/2003.

Centers for Disease Control and Prevention Emergency Preparedness and Response. Chemical Emergencies, *Facts about Sulfur Mustard*, Atlanta, GA, 03/12/2003.

Centers for Disease Control and Prevention Emergency Preparedness and Response. Chemical Emergencies, *Facts about VX*, Atlanta, GA, 03/12/2003.

Centers for Disease Control and Prevention Emergency Preparedness and Response. *Other Frequently Asked Questions (FAQs) about Preparedness and Response and Water Safety*, Atlanta, GA, 10/25/2001.

Centers for Disease Control and Prevention Emergency Preparedness and Response. Mass Casualty Event Preparedness and Response, *Coping With a Traumatic Event: Information for the Public*, Atlanta, GA, 09/24/2003.

Centers for Disease Control and Prevention Emergency Preparedness and Response. Preparation & Planning, *Chemical Agents: Facts About Sheltering in Place*, Atlanta, GA, 11/08/2004.

Centers for Disease Control and Prevention Emergency Preparedness and Response. Preparation & Planning, *Sheltering in Place During a Radiation Emergency*, Atlanta, GA, 05/20/2005.

Centers for Disease Control and Prevention Emergency Preparedness and Response. Radiation Emergencies, *Acute Radiation Syndrome*, Atlanta, GA, 05/20/2005.

Centers for Disease Control and Prevention Emergency Preparedness and Response. Radiation

Emergencies, *Dirty Bombs*, Atlanta, GA, 04/07/2003.

Centers for Disease Control and Prevention Emergency Preparedness and Response. Radiation Emergencies, *Frequently Asked Questions (FAQ) about a Nuclear Blast*, Atlanta, GA, 12/26/2003.

Centers for Disease Control and Prevention Emergency Preparedness and Response. Radiation Emergencies, *Nuclear Terrorism & Health Effects*, Atlanta, GA, 04/07/2003.

Centers for Disease Control and Prevention National Center for Environmental Health. Air Pollution & Respiratory Health, *Asthma*, Atlanta, GA, 03/04/2003.

Centers for Disease Control and Prevention National Center for Environmental Health. Air Pollution & Respiratory Health, *Carbon Monoxide*, Atlanta, GA, 06/06/2002.

Center for Disease Control and Prevention National Center for Infectious Diseases. *General Information about Clostridium difficile Infections,* At;amta. GA. 07/22/2005.

Center for Disease Control and Prevention National Center for Infectious Diseases. *Protecting the Nation's Health in an Era of Globalization: CDC's Global infectious Disease Strategy (Executive Summary)*, Atlanta, GA, 2002.

Center for Disease Control and Prevention National Center for Infectious Diseases, Division of Vector-Borne Infectious Diseases. *West Nile Virus - Questions and Answers (various topics)*, Atlanta, GA, 09/09/2004.

Center for Disease Control and Prevention National Center for Infectious Diseases, Special Pathogens Branch. Disease Information, *Viral Hemorrhagic Fevers*, Atlanta, GA, 01/29/2002.

City of Surprise Crisis Response Team. *Steps to Consider When A Loved One Dies*, Surprise, AZ, 2007.

Connor, Shane, CEO, KI4U, Inc. *Fallout Shelters & Nuclear Civil Defense FAQ*, www.radshelters4u.com, Updated 01/16/2005.

Connor, Shane, CEO, KI4U, Inc. *Nuclear Blast & Fallout Shelters FAQ - Parts II and III*, www.radshelters4u.com/index2.htm and /index3.htm, Updated 01/16/2005.

Connor, Shane, CEO, KI4U, Inc. *What To Do if a Nuclear Disaster is Imminent!*, www.ki4u.com/guide.htm, Updated 09/16/2006.

De Blij, H. J. *Nature on the Rampage*, Smithsonian Institute, Washington D.C.: Smithsonian Books, 1994.

Discover Magazine. "Caught in a National Disaster? Twitter May Save Your Life." by Melissa Lafsky, September 3, 2008.

Emergency Preparedness Canada, British Columbia Provincial Emergency Program, Canadian Mortgage and Housing Corporation, Health Canada, Geological Survey of Canada, Insurance Bureau of Canada. *Earthquakes in Canada?*, Her Majesty the Queen in Right of Canada, Department of Natural Resources Canada, 1996.

Emergency Preparedness Canada, Canadian Geographic, Environment Canada, Geological Survey of Canada, Insurance Bureau of Canada, Natural Resources Canada, Statistics Canada, The Weather network. *Natural Hazards - a National Atlas of Canada*, Canadian Services Canada, 1997.

Environment Canada. The Green Lane™, *Winter Power Failure*, Gatineau, Quebec, 2005-09-29.

Federal Emergency Management Agency. *Are You Ready? A Guide to Citizen Preparedness,*Washington, D.C., December 2002 (+ updated version February 2005).

Federal Emergency Management Agency. *Home Fallout Shelter modified ceiling shelter-basement location plan a*, H-12-A, Washington, D.C., April 1980.

Federal Emergency Management Agency. *The Humane Society of the United States Offers Disaster Planning Tips for Pets, Livestock and Wildlife*, Washington, D.C., 1997.

Federal Emergency Management Agency. *Information for Pet Owners,* Washington, D.C., 27-Nov-2007.

Federal Emergency Management Agency. *Preparedness Planning for a Nuclear Crisis A Citizen's Guide to Civil Defense and Self-Protection*, Washington, D.C., 1987.

Federal Emergency Management Agency. *Returning Home After the Disaster – An Information Pamphlet for FEMA Disaster Workers*, Washington, D.C., 1987.

Federal Emergency Management Agency. *Terrorism Fact Sheet & Backgrounder*, Washington, D.C., 11-Feb-2003.

Federal Emergency Management Agency. *Volcanoes Fact Sheet & Backgrounder*, Washington, D.C., 1998.

Federal Emergency Management Agency and the American Red Cross. *Emergency Preparedness Checklist*, Washington D.C., 1993.

Federal Emergency Management Agency and the American Red Cross. *Food and Water in an Emergency*, Washington D.C., 1994.

Federal Emergency Management Agency and the American Red Cross. *Helping Children Cope with Disaster*, Washington D.C., 1993.

Federal Emergency Management Agency and the American Red Cross. *Preparing for Emergencies - A Checklist for People with Mobility Problems*, Washington D.C., 1995.

Federal Emergency Management Agency and the American Red Cross. *Your Family Disaster Supplies Kit,* Washington D.C., 1992.

Federal Emergency Management Agency, American Red Cross, Home Depot, National Association of Home Builders, Georgia Emergency Management Agency. *Against the Wind - Protecting Your Home from Hurricane Wind Damage,* Washington D.C., 1993.

Federal Emergency Management Agency and the Wind Engineering Research Center at Texas Tech University. *Taking Shelter From the Storm Building a Safe Room Inside Your House, Second Edition,* Washington D.C., August 1999.

Fleetwood, Richard, Founder, SurvivalRing. *The Ultimate Civil Defense Digital Library CD Volume One,* www.survivalring.org or www.survivalcd.com, Feb-2005.

Harvard Center for Risk Analysis. *Using Decision Science to Empower Informed Choices About Risks to Health, Safety, and the Environment*, Boston, MA, 2003.

Health Canada. Emergency Preparedness and Response, *Tularemia (Rabbit fever)*, Ottawa, Ontario, Canada, 2004-01-09.

Information on avalanches obtained from the Internet online information page, "Avalanche Awareness", (http://nsidc.org/snow/avalanche/) maintained by the National Snow and Ice Data Center, University of Colorado Cooperative Institute for Research in Environmental Sciences, Boulder, November 2000. *(Revised URL 2003)*

Jane's Information Group. *Jane's Citizen's Safety Guide*, Surrey, UK, 2004.

Kearny, Cresson H. *Nuclear War Survival Skills,* Updated and Expanded 1987 Edition, (Original Edition Published September 1979 by Oak Ridge National Laboratory, a Facility of the U.S. Department of Energy), Oregon: Oregon Institute of Science and Medicine. (Electronic Editions were prepared and published by Arnold Jagt, www.oism.org/nwss, 2003).

Kozaryn, Linda D. "Defending Against Invisible Killers - Biological Agents", American Forces Press Service, March 1999, Department of Defense.

LiveScience.com. "Caribbean to Get Tsunami Warning System as Scientists Fret" by Bjorn Carey, 14-January-2005.

Mayell, Mark and the Editors of *Natural Health* Magazine. *The Natural Health First-Aid Guide: the definitive handbook of natural remedies for treating minor emergencies,* New York: Pocket Books, 1994.

Mayo Clinic, Infectious Disease. *C. difficile,* www.mayoclinic.com, December 3, 2008.

MSNBC.com. "A bad germ gets worse 'C. diff' rivals MRSA as the next deadly bacteria threat, experts say" by JoNel Aleccia, Health Writer, MSNBC, May 2, 2008.

MSNBC.com. "New tornado scale factors more damage" by The Associated Press, www.msnbc.msn.com/id/11148978/, 02/02/2007.

National Institutes of Health, National Institute on Deafness and Other Communication Disorders. Health Information, Hearing, Ear Infections, and Deafness, *Noise-Induced Hearing Loss,* Bethesda, MD, September 2002.

National Oceanic and Atmospheric Administration. NOAA News Online (Story 2359) "NOAA Reports Record Number of Tornadoes in 2004", 12/30/2004.

National Oceanic and Atmospheric Administration, National Weather Service, National Hurricane Center. *Saffir-Simpson Hurricane Wind Scale Summary Table,* 21-May-2010.

National Oceanic and Atmospheric Administration, National Weather Service, Storm Prediction Center. *The Ehanced Fujita Scale (EF Scale,* 02/02/2007.

National Oceanic and Atmospheric Administration, National Weather Service, West Coast & Alaska Tsunami Warning Center. *Physics of Tsunamis,* 02/20/2003.

National Oceanic and Atmospheric Administration, National Weather Service, West Coast & Alaska Tsunami Warning Center. *Tsunami Safety Rules,* 02/20/2003.

Nelson, T.J., Research Biochemist and Radiation Safety Officer. *Duck and Cover,* http://brneurosci.org/duckandcover.html, 10/18/2003.

Nova Scotia Museum. An Illustrated Guide to Common Nova Scotian Poisonous Plants, Poisonous Leafy Plants, *Castor Beans,* Halifax, Nova Scotia, Canada, 00-03-08.

Pan American Health Organization, Area on Emergency Preparedness and Disaster Relief, the World Health Organization, and the International Committee of the Red Cross. *Management of Dead Bodies After Disasters: A Field Manual for First Responders,* Washington, D.C., 2006.

Pima County Health Department. Communicable Diseases / Bioterrorism, *Pima County Prepares for Smallpox - Frequently Asked Questions,* Tucson, AZ, 2003.

Public Health Agency of Canada, Centre for Infectious Disease Prevention & Control. Influenza, *Avian Influenza - Frequently Asked Questions,* Ottawa, Ontario, Canada, 2005-02-03.

Public Health Agency of Canada, Centre for Infectious Disease Prevention & Control. *Fact Sheet - Clostridium difficile (C. difficile),* Ottawa, Ontario, Canada, 2008-06-20.

Public Health Agency of Canada, Emergency Preparedness. *Anthrax,* Ottawa, Ontario, Canada, 2005-02-18.

Public Health Agency of Canada, Emergency Preparedness. *Botulism,* Ottawa, Ontario, Canada, 2005-02-18.

Public Health Agency of Canada, Emergency Preparedness. *The Plague,* Ottawa, Ontario, Canada, 2005-02-18.

Public Health Agency of Canada, Emergency Preparedness. *Ricin,* Ottawa, Ontario, Canada, 2005-02-18.

Public Health Agency of Canada, Emergency Preparedness. *Smallpox,* Ottawa, Ontario, Canada, 2005-03-01.

Public Health Agency of Canada, Emergency Preparedness. *Viral Haemorrhagic Fevers*, Ottawa, Ontario, Canada, 2005-02-18.

Reader's Digest. *Natural Disasters (The Earth, Its Wonders, Its Secrets)*, London: The Reader's Digest Association, Limited, 1996.

Smithsonian Institution, National Museum of Natural History, Department of Mineral Sciences, Global Volcanism Program. *Frequently Asked Questions, How many active volcanoes are there in the world?*, Washington, DC, 2005.

Spencer, Jack, Senior Policy Analyst for Defense and National Security in the Kathryn and Shelby Cullom Davis Institute for International Studies at The Heritage Foundation. "The Electromagnetic pulse Commission Warns of an Old Threat with a New Face" (Backgrounder # 1784), The Heritage Foundation, Policy Research & Analysis, Defense, National Security, August 3, 2004.

State Farm Insurance. Good Neighbor News, Second Edition, "Generating power", 2008.

State of California Department of Conservation and National Landslide Information Center. U.S. Geological Survey, "Features That May Indicate Catastrophic Landslide Movement", Denver, November 1998.

Stephenson, David, President, Stephenson Strategies. *21st-century disaster prep tips you won't get from officials*, http://stephensonstrategies.com, December 2008.

Survivor Industries, Inc. "The Wallace Guidebook for Emergency Care and Survival", Newbury Park, CA: H. Wallace, 1989.

Swift Aid USA. *SwiftAid to First Aid "What To Do In An Emergency"*, Toledo, OH, 1990.

The Cure, Inc. New CPR Recommendations from the American Heart Association and CPR videos, www.thecuresafety.com, 2008-2009.

Tobin, Rick, President and CEO, TAO Emergency Management Consulting. *Restoring America's Nuclear Civil Defense*, www.ricktobin.com, January 2007.

Tobin, Rick, President and CEO, TAO Emergency Management Consulting. *Surviving Catastrophic Events*, www.ricktobin.com, February 2005.

U.S. Army's Office of the Surgeon General's Medical NBC Online. Medical References Online, "Chemical Agent Terrorism" by Frederick R. Sidell, M.D. of the U.S. Army Medical Research Institute of Chemical Defense, (no date on www.nbc-med.org).

U.S. Department of Health & Human Services. Pandemic Flu.gov, Business & Industry Planning, October 2006.

U.S. Department of Health & Human Services, National Institutes of Health. U.S. National Library of Medicine, Specialized Information Services. Toxicology & Environmental Health, Special Topics, *Biological Warfare*, Bethesda, MD, 02/18/2003.

U.S. Department of Health & Human Services, Office of the Assistant Secretary for Preparedness and Response, National Library of Medicine. Radiation Event Medical Management, *Nuclear Explosions: Weapons, Improvised Nuclear Devices*, 03/10/2007.

U.S. Department of Homeland Security. *National Response Framework*, January 2008.

U.S. Department of Homeland Security, Ready Business. *Influenza Pandemic,* March 2009.

U.S. Department of Homeland Security, Ready Business. *Plan to Stay in Business, (all 8 topics)*, October 2006.

U.S. Department of Homeland Security, Ready Business. *Protect Your Investment, (all 6 topics)*, October 2006.

U.S. Department of Homeland Security, Ready Business. *Talk to Your People, (all 5 topics)*, October 2006.

U.S. Department of the Interior, U.S. Geological Survey, Cascades Volcano Observatory and Washington State Military Department, Emergency Management Division. *What To Do If A Volcano Erupts Volcanic Ashfall - How to be Prepared for an Ashfall*, Vancouver, WA, November 1999.

U.S. Department of the Interior, U.S. Geological Survey and the National Park Service. Yellowstone Volcano Observatory, "Steam Explosions, Earthquakes, and Volcanic Eruptions - What's in Yellowstone's Future?", http://volcanoes.usgs.gov/yvo, 2005.

U.S. Department of the Interior, U.S. Geological Survey Earthquake Hazards Program. For Kids Only, *Cool Earthquake Facts*, Menlo Park, CA, 05-Mar-2003.

U.S. Department of the Interior, U.S. Geological Survey Volcano Hazards Program. *Effects of Lahars*, Menlo Park, CA, 10/15/1998.

U.S. Department of the Interior, U.S. Geological Survey Volcano Hazards Program. *Eruption Warning and Real-Time Notifications*, Menlo Park, CA, 01/30/2001.

U.S. Department of the Interior, U.S. Geological Survey Volcano Hazards Program. *Pilot Project Mount Rainier Volcano Lahar Warning System*, Menlo Park, CA, 09/04/2000.

U.S. Department of the Interior, U.S. Geological Survey Volcano Hazards Program. *Reducing volcanic risk, Photo Glossary of volcano terms*, Menlo Park, CA, 01/30/2001.

U.S. Department of the Interior, U.S. Geological Survey Volcano Hazards Program. *Tephra: Volcanic Rock and Glass Fragments*, Menlo Park, CA, 12/23/1999.

U.S. Department of the Interior, U.S. Geological Survey, Yellowstone National Park and the University of Utah. Yellowstone Volcano Observatory, "Supervolcano Questions", http://volcanoes.usgs.gov/yvo/faqssupervolc.html, April 6, 2006.

U.S. Environmental Protection Agency. Indoor Air Quality, *Molds*, Washington, D.C., 03/03/2003.

U.S. Fire Administration. Carbon Monoxide, *Exposing an Invisible Killer: The Dangers of Carbon Monoxide*, Emmitsburg, MD, March 2006.

U.S. Fire Administration. Carbon Monoxide, *Portable Generator Hazards*, Emmitsburg, MD, March 2006.

U.S.D.A. Forest Service National Avalanche Center. "Avalanche Basics": www.avalanche.org/~nac/ , November 2000.

United Nations Office of Special Envoy for Tsunami Recovery, "The Human Toll", www.tsunamispecialenvoy.org, 2006.

United States Postal Service®, United States Postal Inspection Service. "Notice 71 - Bombs By Mail", Chicago, IL, February 1998.

WebMD, LLC. Health News, "C. diff Epidemic: What You Must Know" by Daniel J. DeNoon, (http://www.webmd.com/news/20080530/c-diff-epidemic-what-you-must-know), 2008.

Wellesley College. Web of Species "Jewelweed, Spotted Touch-Me-Not", Boston, MA, www.wellesley.edu/Activities/homepage/web/Species/ptouchmenot.html , 01/31/2001.

Wikipedia®, the free encyclopedia. "Enhanced Fujita Scale" http://en.wikipedia.org/wiki/Enhanced_Fujita_Scale, 7-April-2007.

WorldNetDaily. "The good news about nuclear destruction" by Shane Connor, www.wnd.com/news/article.asp?ARTICLE_ID=51648, 08/24/2006.

Worldwatch Institute. "Human Actions Worsen Natural Disasters" by Janet N. Abramovitz, Press Release for Worldwatch Paper 159, Washington, DC, www.worldwatch.org, 10/18/2001.

Worldwatch Institute. "Natural disasters – At the hand of God or man?" by Janet N. Abramovitz, Environmental News Network (ENN) Features, 23 June 1999, Copyright 1999.

ADDITIONAL RESOURCES
& WEB SITES

WEB SITES (* = COOL STUFF FOR EDUCATORS, KIDS & PARENTS)

American Avalanche Association www.americanavalancheassociation.org
American Heart Association www.heart.org
American Stroke Association www.strokeassociation.org
* **British Columbia Injury Prevention Centre** www.injuryfreezone.com
Canadian Centre for Emergency Preparedness www.ccep.ca
Central Intelligence Agency www.cia.gov
* **CIA's Homepage for Kids** https://www.cia.gov/kids-page/index.html
DisasterAssistance www.disasterassistance.gov
* **Environment Canada** www.ec.gc.ca
Environmental Protection Agency (EPA) www.epa.gov
* **EPA's Environmental Kids Club** www.epa.gov/kids
Federal Bureau of Investigation www.fbi.gov
* **FBI - For the Family** www.fbi.gov/fbikids.htm
* **FEMA for Kids** www.fema.gov/kids
Health Canada www.hc-sc.gc.ca
Heart and Stroke Foundation of Canada www.heartandstroke.ca
Institute for Business and Home Safety www.disastersafety.org
Insurance Bureau of Canada www.ibc.ca
Munich Re Group's Press Releases www.munichre.com
National Fire Protection Association www.nfpa.org
National Hazards Center (Univ. of Colorado) www.colorado.edu/hazards/
National Safety Council www.nsc.org
NOAA (National Oceanic & Atmospheric Administration) www.noaa.gov
OSHA (Occupational Safety & Health Administration) www.osha.gov
Physicians for Civil Defense www.physiciansforcivildefense.org
* **U.S. Fire Administration** www.usfa.dhs.gov
* **U.S. Nuclear Regulatory Commission** www.nrc.gov
U.S. Small Business Administration www.sba.gov
* **U.S.G.S. Earthquake Hazards Program** www.earthquake.usgs.gov
* **U.S.G.S. Volcano Hazards Program** http://volcanoes.usgs.gov
World Nuclear Association www.world-nuclear.org

More resources available on our "Links" page at www.itsadisaster.net

INDEX

A
activated charcoal, first aid uses for, 17, 163
air pollution, ozone alerts, 51
air quality
  improving with HEPA filter, 27, 230
  mitigation tips, 27
American Red Cross. *See also* Canadian Red Cross
  about, 210
  assistance following disasters, 146
  business continuity information, 233
  FEMA partner, 217
amputation, emergency measures, 170
anthrax (biological agent)
  about, 95
  how spread, 95
  signs and symptoms of exposure, 95
  treatment, 96
asthma attack, first aid treatment, 171
avalanches. *See also* landslides
  basics, 37
  facts and figures, 3
  safety information, 37-39
avian flu (bird flu). *See also* infectious diseases
  about, 197
  pandemic planning, 231-232
  reducing the spread of, 198-199
  symptoms, 197
  where to get more information, 199

B
baking soda
  first aid uses for, 17
  paste for insect bites or stings, 163
  paste for rash, 202
  paste for sea critter sting, 166
  soak for sunburn, 176
  use to put out small grease or oil fire, 53
bedding, items to include in disaster supplies kit, 19-20
biological agents, 78. *See also* terrorism
  about, 94-104
  basic groups of, 94
  how used in an attack, 94
  safety information, 78, 94-104
    after an attack, 103-104

chemical spill. *See* hazardous materials
chlorine (chemical agent), 84
   about, 85
   how spread, 85
   signs and symptoms of exposure, 85
   treatment, 86
choking, first aid treatment, 177-178
   adults or children, 177
   infants, 178
CIA. *See* Central Intelligence Agency
Citizen Corps
   about programs, 222-224
   affiliate programs & organizations, 223-224
   CERT (Community Emergency Response Team), 222, 224
   Fire Corps, 222
   Medical Reserve Corps (MRC), 222
   Neighborhood Watch, 223
   Volunteers in Police Service (VIPS), 223
   where to get more information, 224
civil disturbance (or civil unrest)
   about, 42
   during a riot, 42
clothing
   dressing for evacuation, 48
   dressing for extreme cold, 139
   dressing for extreme heat, 51
   dressing for hazardous materials disaster, 64
   dressing for volcanic eruption, 137
   dressing to avoid ticks, 168
   items to include in disaster supplies kit, 19-20
cold, extreme. *See also* winter storms
   facts and figures, 6, 138
   frostbite, first aid treatment, 179
   hypothermia, first aid treatment, 180
   mitigation tips, 33-34
   safety information, 138-141
   signs of overexposure to, 139-140
computer crimes. *See* cyber threats
convulsions, first aid treatment, 181
cooking, in a disaster situation, 151
CPR (cardio-pulmonary resuscitation), 188-192
   about, 188
   for adults (illustrated), 190
   for children (illustrated), 191
   for heart problems, 188-189
   for infants (illustrated), 192
cyanide (chemical agent), 83

frostbite, first aid information, 139, 179
Fujita scale, now using Enhanced Fujita scale, 129

G
germs
   biological agents and, 94
   infections, first aid treatment, 195
   infectious diseases and, 196-199
   reducing the spread of, 161
Good Samaritan laws, 161

H
H1N1 (swine) flu, 197
hailstorms
   facts and figures, 4
   safety information, 60-61
hazardous materials
   buzzwords, 62
   clean-up, 64
   facts and figures, 4
   household chemical emergency, 65
   Local Emergency Planning Committee (LEPC), about, 62-63
   safe room, 63
   safety information, 62-65
   shelter-in-place, 63
head injuries, first aid treatment, 187
hearing loss from noise, tips to reduce, 184
heart attack, first aid treatment, 188-192
heat, extreme
   facts and figures, 3
   first aid for illnesses caused by, 193-194
   heat cramps, first aid treatment, 193
   safety information, 50-51
heat exhaustion, first aid treatment, 193-194
heat index, 51
heat stroke, first aid treatment, 193-194
Heimlich maneuver, 177
home
   disaster supplies kit, suggested items to include for, 14-23
   escape plan, having a, 9, 52
   household chemical emergency, 65
   mitigation tips to help prevent damage and loss, 26-35
   returning to damaged home, 144-146
   sheltering, things to think about, 24
Homeland Security. *See* Department of Homeland Security
human waste. *See* sanitation
hurricanes

buzzwords, 67-68
different names for, 66
facts and figures, 4, 66
how classed (categories), 67
safety information, 67-71
Saffir-Simpson Hurricane wind scale, 67
storm surge, 66, 67
hypothermia, first aid treatment, 140, 180

I-J
infants
choking, first aid treatment, 178
CPR position for (illustrated), 192
heart problems (CPR), 188-189
special items to include in disaster supplies kit, 20
infections
first aid treatment for, 195
reducing the spread of germs or diseases, 161
infectious diseases
about, 196
how they spread, 198-199
reducing the spread of, 199
types of, 196-199
avian flu (bird flu), 197, 199
C. diff (Clostridium difficile or C. difficile), 197-198, 199
flu (influenza), 196-197, 199
staph (staphyloccus aureus), 198, 199
where to get more information, 199
influenza. *See* flu
insect bites and stings, first aid treatment, 162-165
International Federation Red Cross and Red Crescent
Societies, 210
internet security. *See also* cyber threats
where to get more information, 87
jewelweed, first aid uses for, 202, (illustrated), 204

K-L
Kearny Fallout Meter (KFM kit), detection device, 112
KI. *See* potassium iodide
kits, suggested items to include
for car, 21-22
extra items to add during winter months, 140
for classroom or locker or office, 22-23
for first aid, 15-17
for home (disaster supplies kit), 14-23
reminders about, 23
La Niña, about, 1

landslides
about, 37, 39-40
facts and figures, 3
insurance, 40
safety information, 40-41
warning signs, 40, 41
LEPC. *See* Local Emergency Planning Committee
lightning. *See also* thunderstorms
facts and figures, 5, 127
first aid treatment, 175-176
mitigation tips, 29
safety information, 127-128
livestock, emergency plan checklist, tips for, 11
Local Emergency Planning Committee (LEPC)
about, 62
using LEPC data to help make plan, 62-63
lyme disease. *See* ticks

M
marine animal stings, first aid treatment for, 165-166
Mexican Red Cross, about, 210
mitigation tips (to help prevent damage and loss), 26-35, 149
about mitigation, 26
air quality, learn how to test in home, 27
earthquakes, 27-28
fires, 28, 52-53
floods, 28-29
landslides or mudflows, 40
lightning, 29
power loss (tips on generators), 29-30
wildfires, 30-31
wind, 31-33
winter storms and extreme cold, 33-34
mold
cleaning, tips for, 146
where to get more information, 27
mosquitoes, and West Nile Virus, 164-165
mouth-to-mouth resuscitation (rescue breathing)
about and how to perform, 171-172
for choking, 177-178
with CPR, 188-189
MRSA (methicillin-resistant Staphylococcus aureus), 198-199
mudflows
about, 37, 39-40
facts and figures, 3
flood insurance, 40
safety information, 40-41

mustard gas (chemical agent), 83
    about, 88
    how spread, 88
    signs and symptoms of exposure, 89
    treatment, 89

N
National Incident Management System (NIMS), 217
National Response Framework (NRF), about, 217
National Terrorism Advisory System (NTAS)
    about, 80-81
    alerts
        elevated, 81
        imminent, 80
    sunset provision, 81
    websites, 81
natural disasters. *See* disasters
neck injuries, first aid treatment, 187
nerve gas. *See* chemical agents
9-1-1, tips for calling, 160
NOAA (National Oceanic and Atmospheric Administration)
    Pacific Marine Environmental Laboratory Tropical
    Atmosphere Ocean project
        El Niño and La Niña, about, 1
    Weather Radio
        about, 0
        broadcast warnings for
            flood, 57
            hurricane, 67-68
            thunderstorm, 127
            tornado, 129-130
            tsunami, 133
            winter storm, 138
        disaster kit, including in, 18
        programming, Specific Area Message Encoding (SAME), 0
    web sites, 0, 1, 244
nosebleeds, first aid treatment, 170
NTAS. *See* National Terrorism Advisory System
nuclear blast (detonation), 109-111
nuclear emergency, incident or attack. *See also* radiation
    buzzwords, 74
    community planning for power plant emergencies, 73-74
    electromagnetic pulse (EMP), 110, 119, 124
    facts and figures, 4-5, 72
    fallout
        about, 109-110
        best locations to go during, 116

clean up before entering shelter, 124
filtering water contaminated with, 118
protecting from, 114-117, 122-123
radioactive, 110
reducing exposure to, 114
shelter, about, 115-118
sheltering from, 115-118
potassium iodide (KI), using, 76, 114
power plants, 72-76
radioactive iodine and, 73, 76
safety information
nuclear bomb or device, 109-125
nuclear power plant emergency or incident, 72-76
supplies, storing enough for a, 121
nuclear radiation. *See also* radiation
about, 109
types of, 112
nuclear weapon or bomb
damage estimates, 111
sizes of, 111
surviving an attack, 109-125

O
ozone alerts, 51

P
pain-relief aids (alternative options)
for insect bite or sting, 17, 163
for rash caused by poisonous plant, 202
for sea critter (marine life) sting, 166
for sunburn, 176
pandemic flu
about, 196
avian flu, 197
H1N1 flu, 197
influenza, 196-197
reducing the spread of, 198-199
planning for, 231-232
symptoms of, 196-197
travel updates and restrictions, 232
where to get more information, 199, 232
pee. *See* urine
pets
emergency plan checklist, tips for, 11
emergency shelters and, 11, 150
evacuation, ask about shelters and plans for, 47, 48-49
nuclear emergency or incident and, 76, 124

This Manual is available through the following methods:

- for agencies, companies, and groups to use as customized **giveaways** for employees, customers and communities *(50% to 75% off list ~ provides approximate $4-to-$1 match on grants)*

- for K-12 schools and volunteers to use as a **fundraising** project *(Ad Program, Affiliate Program, Referral Program, and Traditional Fundraiser)*

- for qualified Resellers to offer online and in stores

- for individual purchase from nonprofits, us, and traditional & online bookstores.

Also available as a downloadable **eBook**, customized **CDs**, and customized bulk eBooks. Plus customizable booklets available ~ call for details!

For more information, please call FedHealth at 1-888-999-4325 or visit us online at **www.itsadisaster.net**